Houghton

JOURNEYS
COMMON CORE

Program Authors

James F. Baumann · David J. Chard · Jamal Cooks · J. David Cooper · Russell Gersten · Marjorie Lipson
Lesley Mandel Morrow · John J. Pikulski · Héctor H. Rivera · Mabel Rivera · Shane Templeton · Sheila W. Valencia
Catherine Valentino · MaryEllen Vogt

Consulting Author
Irene Fountas

Cover illustration by Tim Jessell.

Copyright © 2014 by Houghton Mifflin Harcourt Publishing Company

Printed in the U.S.A.

ISBN 978-0-547-88549-0

56789 - 0914 – 21 20 19 18 17 16 15 14 13
4500404929   B C D E F G

Unit 1

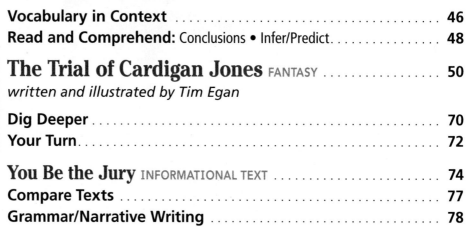

Unit 2

Amos and Boris
FANTASY

written and illustrated by William Steig

Unit 3

Welcome, Reader!

You're about to set out on a reading journey that will take you from the streets of Japan to a fossil field in Canada, bursting with dinosaur bones! On the way, you'll learn amazing things as you become a better reader.

Your reading journey begins with a proud principal who decides five days of learning isn't nearly enough for such a fine school.

Many other reading adventures lie ahead. Just turn the page!

The Authors

unit 1

A FINE, FINE SCHOOL
By Sharon Creech • Pictures by Harry Bliss

One-Room Schoolhouses

✓ TARGET VOCABULARY

principal
soared
strolled
worried
proud
announced
fine
certainly

Vocabulary Reader

SCHOOLS THEN AND NOW

Context Cards

Vocabulary in Context

1 principal
A principal who gets to know the students will be a better leader.

2 soared
Colorful kites soared high in the sky at the school's cultural fair.

3 strolled
Students and their families strolled for miles to raise money for charity.

4 worried
This boy is worried. He is afraid rain will ruin the class field trip.

Go Digital

▶ Study each Context Card.

▶ Use two Vocabulary words to tell about an experience you had.

5 proud

These young actors feel proud of their terrific performance in a school play.

6 announced

Each day, a different student announced school news over a loudspeaker.

7 fine

The sun shines and the air is clear. It is a fine day for the school yard sale.

8 certainly

We certainly should turn off lights when not using them. This surely saves energy.

Read and Comprehend

☑ TARGET SKILL

Story Structure As you read *A Fine, Fine School,* look for the **setting,** or where the story takes place. Look for the main **characters,** or the people in the story. Note the problem that the characters face and how they solve it. That is the **plot** of the story. Use a story map like this one to keep track of the setting, characters, and plot.

Setting	Characters
Plot	
Beginning Middle Ending	

☑ TARGET STRATEGY

Summarize As you read *A Fine, Fine School,* **summarize,** or retell the important parts of the story in your own words. This helps you to keep track of the main events.

 RL.3.2 recount stories and determine their message, lesson, or moral; **RL.3.3** describe characters and explain how their actions contribute to the sequence of events

Education

In the United States, children go to school five days a week for most of the year. On Saturdays and Sundays, children stay home to play, do chores, and spend time with their families. The weekends also can be a time for learning outside of school.

In *A Fine, Fine School*, you'll read about a school that begins to do things differently. You'll find out how the students feel about it. You may even wonder how you would feel if you went to this fine, fine school.

ANCHOR TEXT

A FINE, FINE SCHOOL
By Sharon Creech ● Pictures by Harry Bliss

☑ TARGET SKILL

Story Structure Keep track of the setting, the characters, and the plot. Look for how the characters solve a problem.

☑ GENRE

Humorous fiction has characters and events that are funny. As you read, look for:

▶ mostly realistic characters and events

▶ a setting that is familiar to most readers

▶ funny situations or events

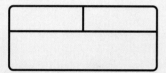 **RL.3.3** describe characters and explain how their actions contribute to the sequence of events; **RL.3.7** explain how illustrations contribute to the words; **RL.3.10** read and comprehend literature

  Go Digital

MEET THE AUTHOR
Sharon Creech

When Sharon Creech is working on a book, she sometimes gets stuck. She doesn't know what to write next. When that happens, she goes for a long walk, does some laundry, or cleans the bathroom. Then she returns to her computer and starts writing again.

MEET THE ILLUSTRATOR
Harry Bliss

Sharon Creech thinks the illustrations Harry Bliss drew for *A Fine, Fine School* are very funny, especially the ones with Tillie's dog in the background. Bliss is a cartoonist whose comic strip appears in daily newspapers. He and his family live in Vermont.

A FINE, FINE SCHOOL

by Sharon Creech 🍎 pictures by Harry Bliss

ESSENTIAL QUESTION

How is learning at school different from learning at home?

15

Mr. Keene was a principal who loved his school. Every morning he strolled down the hallway and saw the children in their classes. He saw them learning shapes and colors and numbers and letters. He saw them reading and writing and drawing and painting. He saw them making dinosaurs and forts and pyramids.

"Oh!" he would say. "Aren't these fine children? Aren't these fine teachers? Isn't this a fine, fine school?"

Near Mr. Keene's school, Tillie lived with her parents and her brother and her dog, Beans, in a small house next to a big tree.

On Mondays and Tuesdays and Wednesdays and Thursdays and Fridays, Tillie went off to school.

At school, Tillie learned her shapes and colors and numbers and letters. Sometimes, when she saw Mr. Keene standing in the hallway, he waved.

"Aren't these fine children?" he said to himself. "Aren't these fine teachers? Isn't this a fine, fine school?"

On the weekends—Saturday and Sunday—
Tillie climbed her favorite tree, and she took
Beans on walks and threw him sticks,

and she pushed her brother on a swing
and tried to teach him how to skip.

But on Mondays and Tuesdays and Wednesdays
and Thursdays and Fridays, Tillie went off to school.
Beans and her brother did not like to see her go.
"Hurry, hurry, hurry home!" her brother called.

One day, Mr. Keene called all the students and teachers together and said, "This is such a fine, fine school! I love this school! Let's have more school! From now on, let's have school on Saturdays, too!"

The teachers and the students did not want to go to school on Saturdays, but no one knew how to tell Mr. Keene that. He was so proud of the children and the teachers, of all the learning they were doing every day.

And so, that Saturday, Tillie set off for school.

"But it's Saturday! What about the swings?" her brother called.

The following month, Mr. Keene announced, "This is such a fine, fine school! I love this school! Let's have more school! From now on, let's have school on Sundays, too!"

The teachers and the students did not want to go to school on Sundays, but no one knew how to tell Mr. Keene that. He was so proud of the children and the teachers, of all the learning they were doing every day.

And so, that Sunday, Tillie set off for school.

"But it's Sunday! What about the skipping?" her brother called.

The following month, Mr. Keene called everyone together again and said, "This is such a fine, fine school! I love this school! Let's have more school! From now on, let's have school in the summer, too, all summer long, every single day!"

"How much we will learn!" he said. "We can learn everything! We will learn all about numbers and letters, colors and shapes, the Romans and the Egyptians and the Greeks. We will learn about dinosaurs and castles and—and—everything! We will learn *everything!*"

The teachers and the students did not want to go to school on Saturdays and Sundays and holidays and all summer long, every single day. But no one knew how to tell Mr. Keene that. He was so proud of the children and the teachers, of all the learning they were doing every day.

And so, on the first day of summer, Tillie set off for school. "But it's summer! What about summer?" her brother called.

ANALYZE THE TEXT

Story Structure What is the main problem in this story? Which story character is responsible for this problem?

And that day, Tillie went to see Mr. Keene. She stood in his office, in front of his desk.

"What a fine, fine school this is!" Mr. Keene said. "What amazing things everyone is learning!"

"Yes," Tillie said, "we certainly are learning some amazing things."

"A fine, fine school!" Mr. Keene said.

"But," Tillie said, "not everyone is learning."

"What?" Mr. Keene said. He looked very worried. "Who? Who isn't learning? Tell me, and I will see that they learn!"

"My dog, Beans, hasn't learned how to sit," Tillie said. "And he hasn't learned how to jump over the creek."

"Oh!" Mr. Keene said.

"And my little brother hasn't learned how to swing or skip."

"Oh!" Mr. Keene said.

"And I—" she said.

"But you go to school!" Mr. Keene said. "To our fine, fine school!"

"True," Tillie said. "But I haven't learned how to climb very high in my tree. And I haven't learned how to sit in my tree for a whole hour."

"Oh!" Mr. Keene said.

That day, Mr. Keene walked up and down the halls,
looking at the children and the teachers. Up and down he
walked. Up and down, up and down.

27

The children and the teachers were very worried.
"And so from now on we will . . . **not** have school on
Saturdays or Sundays or in the summer!"

A huge, enormous, roaring cheer soared up to the ceiling and floated out the windows so that everyone in the town heard the fine, fine children and the fine, fine teachers shout, "Fine! Fine! Fine!"

And the fine, fine children and the fine, fine teachers lifted Mr. Keene up, and they carried him down the hallway and out the doors and through the town, up and down, in and out. And everywhere they went, the people said, "What a fine, fine school with such fine, fine teachers and fine, fine children and a fine, fine principal!"

Dig Deeper

How to Analyze the Text

Use these pages to learn about Story Structure and Analyzing Illustrations. Then read *A Fine, Fine School* again to apply what you learned.

Story Structure

In *A Fine, Fine School*, you read about Tillie and her school. You also read about the school's principal, Mr. Keene, and his plans. Where the story takes place is called the **setting**. The people in the story are the **characters**. Last of all, everything that happens in a story is called the **plot**. The events that make up the plot often happen because of how the characters act and what they say.

Look back at page 20 in *A Fine, Fine School*. In this section of text, you find out what the problem will be. As you keep reading, watch how the problem grows and how it is solved by the characters.

Setting	Characters
Plot	
Beginning, Middle, Ending	

 RL.3.3 describe characters and explain how their actions contribute to the sequence of events; **RL.3.7** explain how illustrations contribute to the words

Analyze Illustrations

Illustrations are drawings or artwork that show the events of a story. Illustrations can also tell you more about the story. For example, they can help you figure out the **mood**, or feeling, of the story.

Turn back to the illustration on pages 16–17. Look at the children's happy faces. Notice that the students are all doing something interesting. The illustration shows a happy mood. No one is gloomy or sad.

Your Turn

RETURN TO THE ESSENTIAL QUESTION

 Review the story with a partner to prepare to discuss this question: *How is learning at school different from learning at home?* As you talk, take turns reviewing and explaining the important ideas in your discussion. Use clues from *A Fine, Fine School,* or text evidence, to support your ideas.

Classroom Conversation

Continue your discussion of *A Fine, Fine School* by explaining your answers to these questions:

1. Why does Mr. Keene start changing the days that school is held?

2. What finally makes Tillie talk to Mr. Keene about going to school all the time?

3. Do you think the author agrees more with Tillie or with Mr. Keene about learning? Use text evidence to explain your answer.

WRITE ABOUT READING

Response Tillie helps Mr. Keene see that some important things are learned outside of school. What are some important things you learn outside of school? Why are they important? List three or more things and write your opinion about why each is important.

Writing Tip

State the things you learn outside of school at the beginning of your response. Then give a reason why each one is important. End your response with a statement that sums up your ideas.

COMMON CORE **RL.3.3** describe characters and explain how their actions contribute to the sequence of events; **W.3.1a** introduce the topic, state an opinion, and create an organizational structure; **W.3.1b** provide reasons that support the opinion; **W.3.1d** provide a concluding statement or section; **W.3.10** write routinely over extended time frames or short time frames; **SL.3.1a** come to discussions prepared/ explicitly draw on preparation and other information about the topic; **SL.3.1d** explain own ideas and understanding in light of the discussion

INFORMATIONAL TEXT

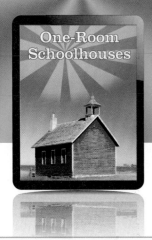

One-Room Schoolhouses

☑ GENRE

Informational text gives factual information about a topic. This is an online encyclopedia article.

☑ TEXT FOCUS

Photographs show true pictures of important text details.

Captions explain a photo or picture. Look at the photos and captions before you read. Discuss what you think the article will be about. After you read, see if your predictions were correct.

COMMON CORE **RI.3.7** use information gained from illustrations and words to demonstrate understanding; **RI.3.10** read and comprehend informational texts

 Go Digital

File   Edit   View   Favorites

Encyclopedia

One-Room Schoolhouses

One-room schoolhouses were once common in America. In the early 1900s, there were more than 250,000. Some children today still attend one-room schoolhouses.

Students of all ages were proud to learn in these small schools. There was usually one teacher and no principal.

search

Search

Daily Life

A ringing bell often announced the start of each day. Students did chores, such as bringing in wood for cooking and heating or raising a flag that soared in the sky above the schoolyard.

The teacher worked with one or two students at a time. They studied subjects like reading, math, history, spelling, and handwriting. Students wrote on small slates, or blackboards, because paper was too expensive.

Mary McLeod Bethune

Famous Students

Some famous Americans learned in one-room schoolhouses. Mary McLeod Bethune went to one in South Carolina in the late 1800s. She became one of America's great teachers. She fought for civil rights.

Former United States President Lyndon Johnson attended a one-room schoolhouse in Texas. Johnson was born near Stonewall, Texas, in 1908. He was President from 1963 until 1969.

Lyndon Johnson

Schoolhouses Today

Some students still study in a one-room schoolhouse. In winter, fewer than one hundred people live on Monhegan Island, in Maine. It is too far to go to the mainland for classes, so students attend the island's little schoolhouse.

In most places, bigger schools opened when one-room schoolhouses became too small. People became worried about losing the fine old buildings. Some became museums. You can tour a school in South Dakota just like one that writer Laura Ingalls Wilder attended.

Other schoolhouses became stores, restaurants, and homes. These little buildings are certainly important pieces of American history.

Laura Ingalls Wilder, writer of *Little House on the Prairie*, strolled several miles to a school like the one shown in the photo below.

Compare Texts

Compare and Contrast Schools Think about the schools in *A Fine, Fine School* and *One-Room Schoolhouses*. Talk with a partner about how Tillie's school is similar to a one-room schoolhouse. Then talk about how the two schools are different. Find text evidence. List at least two ways the schools are the same and two ways they are different.

Talk About It How would you feel about going to school on Saturdays? Discuss with a partner what might be good and what might not be so good about having school on Saturdays.

Connect to Social Studies In some countries, students go to school in summer and on weekends. Work with a group to research more ways in which schools in another country are different from yours. Take notes. Share your results with the class.

COMMON CORE **RI.3.9** compare and contrast important points and details in texts on the same topic; **W.3.8** recall information from experiences or gather information from print and digital sources/take brief notes and sort evidence; **SL.3.1d** explain own ideas and understanding in light of the discussion

Grammar

Simple Sentences A **simple sentence** is a group of words that tells a complete thought. It has a subject and a predicate. The **subject** is the naming part of the sentence. It tells *who* or *what*. The **predicate** is the action part of the sentence. It tells what the subject *does* or *did*.

Subject	Predicate
Our school closes on Saturday.	Our school closes on Saturday.
Marc played soccer that day.	Marc played soccer that day.

 **Copy each sentence. Then circle the subject. Underline the predicate.**

1 My family planned a picnic for Saturday.

2 The rain changed our plans.

3 Jan teaches her dog tricks on Sunday.

4 The dog rolled over three times.

A group of words that does not tell a complete thought is a fragment. A **fragment** is an incomplete sentence. It may be missing a subject or a predicate.

Fragment Missing a Subject	Fragment Missing a Predicate

Rides to school.	My friend Sara.

Complete Simple Sentence

My friend Sara rides to school.

 Connect Grammar to Writing

As you revise your descriptive paragraph, make sure that each sentence has a subject and a predicate. Each sentence must tell a complete thought. Correct any sentence fragments that you find.

43

Narrative Writing

✔ **Word Choice** The author of *A Fine, Fine School* uses exact words. She doesn't just say that children made "things." She says they made "dinosaurs and forts and pyramids." When you write a **descriptive paragraph**, use exact words to describe your thoughts or feelings. They will give your reader a better picture of the experiences or events you are describing.

Sarah wrote a descriptive paragraph about an art room. Later, she replaced unclear words with more exact words.

Writing Traits Checklist

✔ **Ideas**
Did I use details for at least two of the five senses?

✔ **Organization**
Is each detail about my main idea?

✔ **Word Choice**
Did I use exact words?

✔ **Voice**
Did I let my feelings come through?

✔ **Sentence Fluency**
Do my sentences flow smoothly?

✔ **Conventions**
Did I edit for spelling, grammar, and punctuation?

Revised Draft

There's one place I always love to go.

It's the school art room! Even before you
get there, you can smell the ~~art stuff~~ paint and clay. It's

a wonderful smell! Inside the art room,
the walls are covered with ~~things~~ pictures, masks, and puppets that

kids made. Tables and easels are scattered
all around. Jars of red, blue, and yellow paint are stacked up.

44

The Best Place at School

by Sarah Walker

There's one place I always love to go. It's the school art room! Even before you get there, you can smell the paint and clay. It's a wonderful smell! Inside the art room, the walls are covered with pictures, masks, and puppets that kids made. Tables and easels are scattered all around. Jars of red, blue, and yellow paint are stacked up. While we work, Ms. Varga plays music to go with our project. For instance, once she played soft, tinkly music when we made snowflakes. When I'm in the art room, I never want to leave.

Reading as a Writer

Why did Sarah change "art stuff" to "paint and clay"? Where can you add exact words in your descriptive paragraph?

I added some exact words to describe the art room clearly.

trial
jury
convinced
guilty
pointed
honest
murmur
stand

Vocabulary
Reader

Context
Cards

COMMON CORE **L.3.6** acquire and use conversational, general academic, and domain-specific words and phrases

46

Vocabulary in Context

① trial

In a trial, people in a courtroom review what happened to figure out the truth.

② jury

Members of a jury hear the facts of the case and make a decision together.

③ convinced

The lawyer made the jury members believe her. They were convinced.

④ guilty

Jurors tell the judge whether they think the accused person is guilty or innocent.

Go Digital

▶ Study each Context Card.

▶ Make up a new context sentence that uses two Vocabulary words.

5 **pointed**

A witness pointed to a map to show where the crime took place.

6 **honest**

People in court are asked to be honest and tell the truth.

7 **murmur**

The judge asks for silence when he hears a murmur in the courtroom.

8 **stand**

When people take the stand in court, they sit down and answer questions.

Read and Comprehend

 Go Digital

✓ TARGET SKILL

Conclusions As you read *The Trial of Cardigan Jones*, find ways to tie story details together to figure out what really happened. This is called drawing **conclusions**. Use a chart like this one to record your conclusion from text evidence and from your own experience.

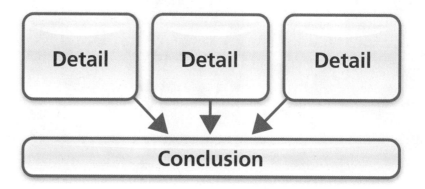

Detail   Detail   Detail

Conclusion

✓ TARGET STRATEGY

Infer/Predict As you read, use the conclusions you draw to **infer,** or figure out, what the characters are like. **Predict** what you think may happen and check whether you were right or not.

COMMON CORE   **RL.3.1** ask and answer questions to demonstrate understanding, referring to the text

Courts play an important part in our cities and towns. Courtroom trials can have a lot of drama. Imagine that a defendant has been accused of breaking a law. The judge sits at the head of the court. Witnesses tell what they know about the crime. The jury, with as many as twelve people, listens to all the evidence. Then the jury draws a conclusion. Is the defendant guilty or not guilty?

In *The Trial of Cardigan Jones*, you'll read about a trial involving a missing pie, a clumsy moose, and a wise judge. Read to find out whether Cardigan Jones is guilty or not guilty.

Tim Egan

Back when Tim Egan was in elementary school, his favorite subject was art. He says he was much better at art than he was at math. Now Egan makes his living as an author and an artist, creating humorous books with serious-looking animal characters, such as *Burnt Toast on Davenport Street* and *Serious Farm.*

Egan lives in California with his wife, two sons, and many pets.

☑ TARGET SKILL

Conclusions Connect story details to figure out what the author does not state directly in the story.

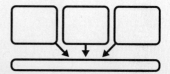

☑ GENRE

A **fantasy** is an imaginative story with characters or events that are not real. As you read, look for:

▶ story events or settings that could not happen in real life

▶ characters that act in an unrealistic way

COMMON CORE   **RL.3.10** read and comprehend literature

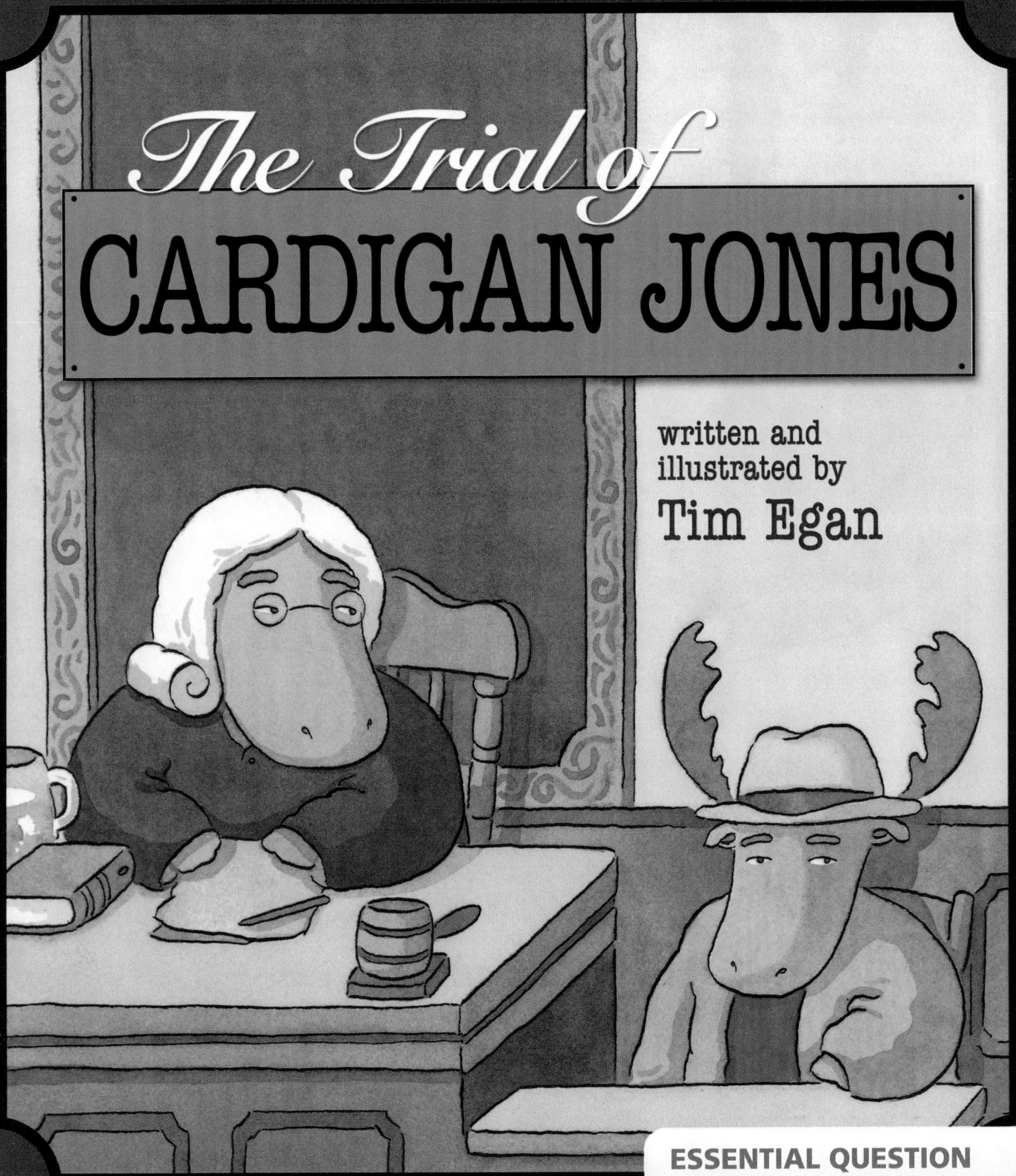

The Trial of CARDIGAN JONES

written and illustrated by **Tim Egan**

ESSENTIAL QUESTION

Why are courts an important part of our government?

Cardigan walked by Mrs. Brown's house just as she was putting a fresh-baked apple pie in her window. Cardigan loved pies.

He walked over and smelled the pie. A neighbor
next door saw him, and a milkman, driving by, saw him
too. Cardigan was new in town, and they weren't sure
what he was up to.

A moment later, Mrs. Brown came back to the window and the pie was gone. She was so upset, she called the police.

She told them that she'd seen a moose just a few minutes before, so they drove around the block and stopped Cardigan.

ANALYZE THE TEXT

Conclusions Why did Mrs. Brown call the police and mention seeing a moose?

Noticing that he had pie crust on his shirt, they arrested him, even though he insisted he hadn't stolen the pie.

A judge and a jury were chosen to decide if he stole the pie or not. The neighbor and the milkman were called as witnesses.

Cardigan's trial started the next day. Mrs. Brown took the stand first. "Is there anyone in this courtroom that you saw the day the pie disappeared?" the judge asked her.

"Yes," she said, "that moose over there." She pointed
to Cardigan.

There was a murmur from the crowd. "He did it.
He's guilty," someone said.

"We don't know that yet," said the judge. The rabbit
then took the stand. "Did you see anyone near the pie?"
the judge asked the rabbit.

"Sure did," said the rabbit. "That moose right there.
He stole it."

"No, I didn't!" shouted Cardigan. "I didn't steal it! I promise!"

"Order!" shouted the judge. Cardigan turned and his antlers bumped a statue and sent it crashing to the floor.

It made a really loud noise, and the jury gave Cardigan dirty looks. "Next witness!" shouted the judge.

The milkman then took the stand. "Who did you see at the time the pie was taken?" the judge asked.

ANALYZE THE TEXT

Author's Word Choice What do the words *dirty looks* tell you about the way the jury felt towards Cardigan?

"The moose," he said, "no question about it. He walked right up to the window. His face was practically touching the pie."

By now, some folks were convinced that Cardigan took the pie, even though the judge kept saying, "We still don't have any proof."

Finally, Cardigan was called to the stand. As he crossed
the courtroom, his antlers got all wrapped up in the flag.
It took him over a minute to get untangled.

"He's a troublemaker," declared a gopher.

Others nodded in agreement as the judge asked, "Well, moose. Did you walk up to the pie?"

"Well, uh, yes, but just to smell it . . ." said Cardigan softly.

"I knew it!" shouted a goat. "Lock him up!"

"Order!" commanded the judge. "Order in the court!"

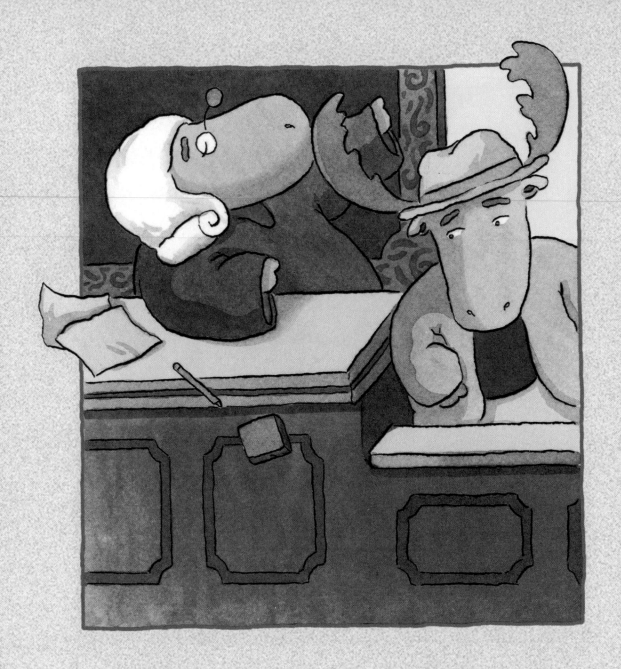

"But I didn't take it!" insisted Cardigan. "Honest!"

He stood up, and his antlers knocked the judge's gavel to the floor.

"Sit down!" shouted the judge. But as Cardigan went to sit, he bumped the judge with his antlers.

The judge fell to the ground.

"He hit the judge!" shouted one of the security guards. They grabbed Cardigan and started taking him away. The jury members had made up their minds.

But the judge stood up and said, "Now just hold on a minute!"

"I'm curious about something," he said. "Follow me."

He walked out of the courtroom, and everyone followed him through the town.

They reached Mrs. Brown's house, and the judge walked around the outside to the window where the pie had been.

Sure enough, there, smushed all over the bushes, was the apple pie. It didn't smell very good anymore.

"You knocked it off the window with those giant antlers of yours, you silly moose," said the judge, laughing. "It was an accident."

Everyone immediately felt terrible for being so rotten to Cardigan, and the jury proclaimed him "not guilty" right then and there.

To make it up to him, they had a party in his honor, and Mrs. Brown baked a pie especially for him, even after he broke her favorite vase.

Dig Deeper

How to Analyze the Text

Use these pages to learn about Conclusions and Author's Word Choice. Then read *The Trial of Cardigan Jones* again to apply what you learned.

Conclusions

Readers can draw conclusions as they read. A **conclusion** is a smart guess about something the author does not say directly. To draw a conclusion, look for text evidence to figure out what really happened. Also use what you already know.

Look back at pages 60 and 61 in *The Trial of Cardigan Jones*. You read that the milkman saw Cardigan at Mrs. Brown's window, smelling the pie. You might use that information to conclude that Cardigan stole the pie. Would you be correct? Why or why not?

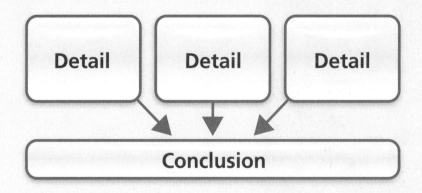

RL.3.1 ask and answer questions to demonstrate understanding, referring to the text; L.3.3a choose words and phrases for effect

70

Author's Word Choice

An author uses words to create a picture in a reader's mind. By carefully choosing **precise words,** an author can help readers see and hear the events and characters of a story.

Look back at page 63 in *The Trial of Cardigan Jones*. The author could have written this:

"Order!" said the judge.

Instead, the author chose the word *commanded*. Using this word helps readers know that the judge has a loud, stern voice.

Your Turn

my WriteSmart

RETURN TO THE ESSENTIAL QUESTION

Turn and Talk

Review the story with a partner to prepare to discuss this question: *Why are courts an important part of our government?* As you discuss, listen carefully to the text evidence your partner gives. Explain your own ideas based on the story.

Classroom Conversation

Continue your discussion of *The Trial of Cardigan Jones* by explaining your answers to these questions:

1. Why are the other characters so ready to believe that Cardigan is guilty?

2. What qualities does the judge have that make him a good judge? What text evidence helps you know?

3. How did the author make the ending believable?

Response Until the end of the story, most of the characters are sure that Cardigan is guilty of taking the pie. Did you agree with them? What lesson can you learn from this story? Write a paragraph that states the message of the story.

Writing Tip

State the message of the story at the beginning of your response. Then explain it with evidence from the story. Include an example from your own experience if you can.

COMMON CORE **RL.3.3** describe characters and explain how their actions contribute to the sequence of events; **W.3.1a** introduce the topic, state an opinion, and create an organizational structure; **W.3.1b** provide reasons that support the opinion; **W.3.10** write routinely over extended time frames or short time frames; **SL.3.1a** come to discussions prepared/explicitly draw on preparation and other information about the topic; **SL.3.1d** explain own ideas and understanding in light of the discussion

☑ GENRE

Informational text gives facts about a topic.

☑ TEXT FOCUS

Headings tell the reader what the sections of text are about.

COMMON CORE
RI.3.10 read and comprehend informational texts

You Be the Jury

by Ruth Masters

Citizens of the United States live in a country where they can take part in their government. Good citizens work together in many ways to serve their government.

lawyer

Being Called to Duty

One way that citizens can help their state government is by serving on a jury. A jury is a group of people that decides whether someone is guilty of breaking a law or not guilty. Members of the jury are called jurors. When people are accused of breaking laws, they have the right to have their case heard by juries. In return, citizens also have a duty to serve as a juror, if asked.

Citizens take turns serving jury duty. A letter tells a person that it is his or her turn. It tells when to go to court.

jury

Sitting at Trial

At court, a juror sits in a room with other jury members. Other people in the courtroom are the judge, the defendant, and lawyers. The defendant is the person who is accused of breaking a law. A lawyer knows the laws. He or she speaks for the defendant. The lawyers tell the facts about what happened. They may put witnesses on the stand. Lawyers on each side try to convince the jury to vote in their favor.

Making a Decision

At the end, it is time for the jury to decide whether a law was broken. Jury members must think about the facts. They must listen to one another. Then they must make a choice.

The jury's decision is called the verdict. The verdict of guilty or not guilty is read out loud. The jury might say, "We find the defendant guilty." After that, the trial is over. The jurors did their duty.

The judge listens carefully during a trial.

lawyer

judge

witness

76

Compare Texts

TEXT TO TEXT

Compare and Contrast Jury Members Think about the jury members in *The Trial of Cardigan Jones* and *You Be the Jury*. How are they the same and different? Discuss your ideas with a partner. Support your ideas with text evidence.

TEXT TO SELF

On Trial How would you feel if you were Cardigan? With a small group, act out the story, taking turns as Cardigan. Afterward, discuss how it might feel to be an innocent person on trial.

TEXT TO WORLD

On the Jury Imagine that you are on the jury at the Cardigan Jones trial. Write several journal entries about the trial. Tell how your opinion about Cardigan's guilt or innocence changes as the trial goes on. Then read them aloud to a partner.

RI.3.9 compare and contrast important points and details in texts on the same topic

Grammar

Go Digital

Kinds of Sentences There are four kinds of sentences. Every sentence begins with a capital letter and ends with an end mark. A **statement** tells something. A **question** asks something. A **command** tells someone to do something. An **exclamation** shows strong feeling, such as excitement, surprise, or fear.

Kind of Sentence	Example
statement	The trial starts today.
question	Who is the judge?
command	Please sit down.
exclamation	Here comes the judge!

Try This! **Work with a partner. Say each sentence aloud. Identify each sentence as a statement, a question, a command, or an exclamation.**

1 The jury listened to the trial.

2 They talked about the case.

3 They cannot decide what to do!

4 What will happen now?

5 Tell the jurors to try again.

You know that sentences can be statements, questions, commands, or exclamations. Make your writing lively by using all four types of sentences.

Paragraph with One Type of Sentence

We all have accidents. We can share those stories with each other. All of us will learn something new. We will be much smarter in the end.

Paragraph with Four Types of Sentences

Don't we all have accidents? Let's share those stories with each other. All of us will learn something new. How much smarter we will be in the end!

 Connect Grammar to Writing

As you revise your story and the dialogue in it, try to use different kinds of sentences to make your writing more lively.

W.3.3a establish a situation and introduce a narrator or characters/organize an event sequence; **W.3.3b** use dialogue and descriptions to develop experiences and events or show characters' responses; **W.3.3d** provide a sense of closure

Narrative Writing

✓ **Ideas** In *The Trial of Cardigan Jones*, the author included dialogue to help the story come to life. **Dialogue** is the exact words that one character says to another. It helps readers imagine the events and the characters.

Travis wrote a first draft of a narrative, or story. In his revised draft, he added more dialogue and details. You can see his revisions in a part of his draft below.

Writing Traits Checklist

✓ **Ideas**
Does my story entertain my audience?

✓ **Organization**
Did I introduce the situation and the characters?

✓ **Word Choice**
Did I include dialogue to help readers hear the characters?

✓ **Voice**
Did I use words that kids would use?

✓ **Sentence Fluency**
Did I use different kinds of sentences?

✓ **Conventions**
Did I use punctuation marks correctly?

Revised Draft

"I mean where is my baseball cap!" Nate exclaimed. "I left it right here.

Someone stole it!"

"No," Jarod said. "It's right there on your head. Don't you remember putting it
The kids laughed.
on before we got in line?"

"No one stole your baseball cap," Jarod said. The other kids at the table smiled.

"Then I've lost it!" Nate shouted.

80

The Mysterious Disappearing Cap

by Travis Payton

Nate and Jarod stood in line in the noisy school cafeteria. Nate chose a cheese sandwich for his lunch. Jarod went for hot soup and a cold green salad. Then the two returned to their table with their trays in hand.

"Where's my brand-new baseball cap?" Nate asked.

"What do you mean?" Jarod replied.

"I mean where is my baseball cap!" Nate exclaimed. "I left it right here. Someone stole it!"

"No one stole your baseball cap," Jarod said. The other kids at the table smiled.

"Then I've lost it!" Nate shouted.

"No," Jarod said. "It's right there on your head. Don't you remember putting it on before we got in line?" The kids laughed.

Nate ate his sandwich quickly. He couldn't wait for lunch to be over.

Reading as a Writer

Travis added dialogue to his story so that his characters can speak for themselves. What dialogue can you add to your narrative?

In my final story, I added dialogue. I also included more details.

afford
customers
contacted
raise
earn
figure
block
spreading

Vocabulary
Reader

Context
Cards

L.3.6 acquire and use conversational, general academic, and domain-specific words and phrases

82

Vocabulary in Context

① afford
Kids collect toys for families who can't afford to buy them.

② customers
Some store owners ask customers to donate a dollar to charity.

③ contacted
This girl contacted neighbors by phone and asked for help with projects.

④ raise
Many groups have bake sales to raise needed money.

COOKIES 50¢

BROWNIES $1.00

Go Digital

▶ Study each Context Card.

▶ Ask a question that uses one of the Vocabulary words.

5 earn

These students are trying to earn enough to help buy new library books.

6 figure

Many schools figure out ways to reuse paper instead of throwing it away.

7 block

Neighbors keep this city block pleasant by having a cleanup day each month.

8 spreading

With floodwaters spreading, people had to pitch in and stack sandbags.

Read and Comprehend

☑ TARGET SKILL

Understanding Characters In *Destiny's Gift*, the main **characters** are Destiny and Mrs. Wade. What they say and do are clues to their feelings, traits, and motivations. **Traits** are qualities that people have, such as kindness. **Motivations** are the reasons for their actions. Use a chart like this one to list text evidence about the feelings, traits, and motivations for each character. Then use those ideas to describe each character.

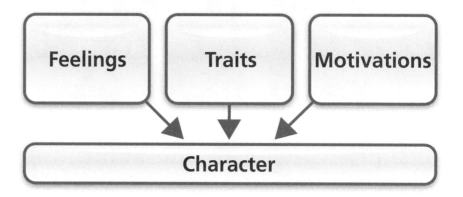

☑ TARGET STRATEGY

Analyze/Evaluate As you read, **analyze,** or think about, what Destiny and Mrs. Wade say and do. This text evidence will help you **evaluate** them or decide what they are like and what their motives are.

Volunteers

A city neighborhood is a busy place. Many people live and work there. They also volunteer their time and money to help one another. Some volunteers organize events such as block parties or street fairs. These events raise money and gather donations for people who can't afford the things they need.

In *Destiny's Gift*, you'll read about a young girl who tries to help her neighborhood bookstore owner keep the store open. Her family organizes other volunteers to help as well. What do you think they do?

ANCHOR TEXT

Destiny's Gift

✓ **TARGET SKILL**

Understanding Characters Look for traits, motivations, and feelings. Use these to understand what the characters are like.

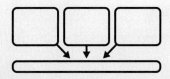

✓ **GENRE**

Realistic fiction has characters and events that are like those in real life. As you read, look for:

▶ a setting that could be real
▶ characters that have feelings that real people have
▶ problems that could be real

COMMON CORE **RL.3.2** recount stories and determine the message, lesson or moral; **RL.3.3** describe characters and explain how their actions contribute to the sequence of events; **RL.3.10** read and comprehend literature

MEET THE AUTHOR

Natasha Anastasia Tarpley

Natasha Tarpley remembers being very shy as a young girl. "Reading for me was a way to escape into whole other worlds," she says. Some of her favorite authors were Judy Blume, Beverly Cleary, and Laura Ingalls Wilder.

MEET THE ILLUSTRATOR

Adjoa J. Burrowes

To make her illustrations look three-dimensional, Adjoa J. Burrowes cuts out each part of a scene separately. Then she pastes the individual pieces of heavy paper on top of each other. "It makes it almost look like it's jumping out from the page," she says.

Go Digital

Destiny's Gift

by
Natasha Anastasia Tarpley

illustrated by
Adjoa J. Burrowes

ESSENTIAL QUESTION

Why is volunteering
good for a community
and its people?

My favorite place in the world was Mrs. Wade's
bookstore, across the street from my house. Mrs. Wade knew
everything there was to know about words, and I loved words!

I went over to Mrs. Wade's every Tuesday and Saturday. As
soon as I walked into the store, the wind chimes above the door
tinkled a special hello.

"Hey there, Destiny!" Mrs. Wade would call out, and stop
whatever she was doing to give me a big hug. She smelled like
flowers and peppermint and had long, silver dreadlocks that fell
to her waist.

"What's the word?" Mrs. Wade would ask.

"Let's go find out," I would say.

We'd rush over to the big, thick dictionary Mrs. Wade kept on a pedestal in the store. I'd close my eyes, open the dictionary, and point.

Whatever word my finger landed on was our word for the day. Mrs. Wade always helped me with words I didn't understand. We sounded out each word and picked it apart like a puzzle, until I knew all there was to know about the word.

I wrote down everything in my notebook, which I carried everywhere I went.

When I wasn't writing words, I was reading them—
gobbling them up from the pages of books as if they were
candy. Mrs. Wade always gave me new books to read. She even
introduced me to real authors who came to read their books at
her store. I liked to talk to them because they loved words just
like I did.

That's how I decided I wanted to become a writer when
I grew up.

On Saturdays Mama and Daddy let me stay at Mrs. Wade's until closing. I helped Mrs. Wade around the store. I watered the plants and fluffed the big, comfy pillows where people could curl up and read on the floor.

Then Mrs. Wade and I would put the new books on the shelves. Sometimes I'd open a book, stick my nose in between the pages, and take a big whiff. It smelled like ink and grass and the old clothes in my granny's closet. The crisp paper felt like autumn leaves between my fingers.

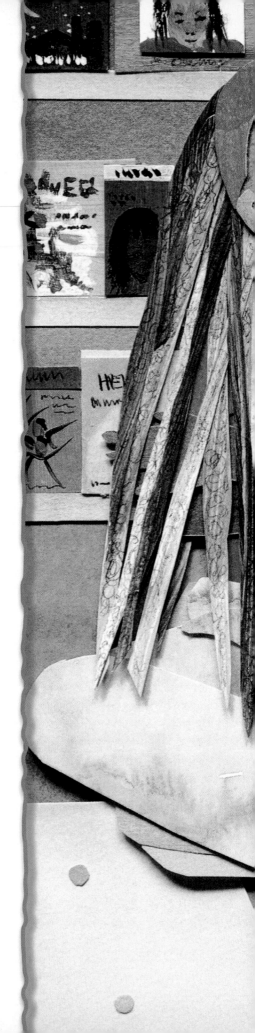

The part I liked best about these Saturdays was the end of the day, after all the customers had gone. Mrs. Wade would set up a tray with peppermint tea and butter cookies, the kind with a hole in the middle. We would drink our tea and pretend the butter cookies were diamond rings around our fingers.

Then I would read to Mrs. Wade from my notebook. She'd listen to my stories and poems with her eyes closed. I'd imagine I was a famous author, reading to a room full of people. Sometimes, after I finished reading, Mrs. Wade would open her eyes and say, "Words are a very powerful gift."

I wasn't sure what she meant, but I felt very important indeed!

ANALYZE THE TEXT

Understanding Characters
Why is the bookstore so special to Destiny? Use details from the story to explain your answer.

Then one Saturday everything was different when I got to Mrs. Wade's store. Instead of talking to her customers or unpacking new books as usual, Mrs. Wade was reading a letter and looking very sad. She put away the letter and smiled when she saw me, but I could tell she wasn't her usual cheerful self.

Later, while we had our tea, Mrs. Wade told me what was wrong. She took my hands in hers, and we sat with our knees touching.

"Have you ever had a really tough assignment in school, but no matter how hard you try you just can't seem to figure it out?" she asked.

I nodded. Math problems were always like that for me.

"Well, I've been trying for a long time to figure out a way to keep the bookstore open, but I haven't had much luck," Mrs. Wade said, sighing. "My landlord is raising my rent, and I can't afford to pay the new amount. I may have to close the store." Mrs. Wade sighed again, and I thought I saw a small tear in the corner of her eye.

My heart froze midbeat. Close? No! I couldn't believe it.

"Why? Why do you have to close the store?" I asked, my voice shaking.

"I need to earn more money in order to pay the higher rent, and there just aren't enough customers for that," Mrs. Wade said.

"We can get more!" I shouted.

"We'll see." Mrs. Wade smiled a sad smile. "We'll see."

When I got home, I told Mama and Daddy about
Mrs. Wade's store. I cried so hard, I didn't think I'd ever stop.
   Mama and Daddy wrapped me in their arms.
   "I know how much the store means to you," Mama said,
stroking my hair.
   "Maybe there's something we can do to help," said Daddy.
   Mama and Daddy got on the telephone and called all
our neighbors. The next day everybody on our block came
to our house to talk about what we could do to save
Mrs. Wade's store.

The following Saturday, all the kids in the neighborhood passed out fliers to get folks to come to Mrs. Wade's bookstore. The grown-ups contacted the local TV news stations and newspapers and called Mrs. Wade's landlord to ask him to lower her rent so the store could stay open.

On Sunday we made signs that said "Save Our Store" and then marched around the neighborhood. It felt like being in a parade.

The next Saturday we had a huge block party to raise money. There was singing and dancing and tables full of good food. I helped Mrs. Wade at her table, and we sold boxes and boxes of books.

ANALYZE THE TEXT

Story Message What message is the author giving to readers?

I had so much fun, I almost forgot to feel sad. Almost.

I closed my eyes and followed Mama's suggestion. Suddenly I had an idea! I jumped up, got out a new notebook, and started to write.

I wrote down everything I loved about Mrs. Wade's store, from the sound of the wind chimes hanging on the door to the smell of the brand-new books and Mrs. Wade's peppermint tea.

I wrote all afternoon and all evening long. Mama and Daddy even let me write during dinner.

The next morning I finished writing and ran over to
Mrs. Wade's store at its usual opening time. But when I got
there, the store was closed!

My heart pounded with fear as I peeked through the front
window. Could Mrs. Wade have closed the store without
telling me?

I was about to go home to tell Mama and Daddy when I heard Mrs. Wade's voice.

"Destiny, here I am!" Mrs. Wade called from her stoop next door.

"Why isn't the store open?" I asked.

"I just needed some time to think," Mrs. Wade said.

"Will you have to close the store forever?" I whispered.

"I hope not, but I'm just not sure, Destiny," Mrs. Wade said sadly. "It's hard to know if customers will keep coming back."

I didn't know what to say. Then I remembered my notebook.

"I have a present for you," I said and handed the notebook to Mrs. Wade. Her eyes lit up with surprise when she opened it and saw: "Mrs. Wade's Bookstore, by Destiny Crawford."

"Why don't you read it to me?" Mrs. Wade asked, a big smile spreading across her face.

I read every word as Mrs. Wade listened with her eyes closed.

When I finished, Mrs. Wade gave me a big, long hug.

"Destiny, this is the best present anyone has ever given me," she said, beaming. "Words are a powerful gift, indeed."

That time I knew exactly what she meant.

Mrs. Wade and I don't know if the store will close, but until then we are going to keep reading and writing and gobbling up all the words we can!

Dig Deeper

How to Analyze the Text

Use these pages to learn about Understanding Characters and Story Message. Then read *Destiny's Gift* again to apply what you learned.

Understanding Characters

Realistic fiction like *Destiny's Gift* has characters that are like real people. Like real people, the characters have **feelings.** The characters also have **traits,** or qualities that describe them. Characters also have reasons for the way they act, just as real people do. These reasons are called **motivations.**

By using text evidence, you can figure out characters' feelings, traits, and motivations. Look back at pages 88 and 89 in *Destiny's Gift*. On these pages, you can learn about Mrs. Wade's feelings, traits, and motivations by what she says and does.

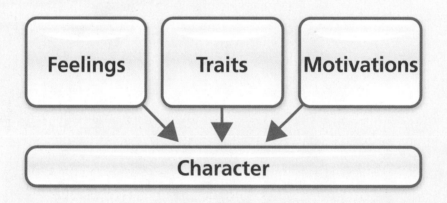

```
┌──────────┐   ┌──────────┐   ┌──────────────┐
│ Feelings │   │  Traits  │   │ Motivations  │
└────┬─────┘   └────┬─────┘   └──────┬───────┘
     └──────────────┼────────────────┘
              ┌──────────────┐
              │  Character   │
              └──────────────┘
```

RL.3.2 recount stories and determine the message, lesson or moral; **RL.3.3** describe characters and explain how their actions contribute to the sequence of events

  Go Digital

Story Message

Authors write because they want to tell readers something. They may have a **message** or lesson to deliver, but they tell it through a story. Readers must think, "What is the author saying about real life in this story? What is the story's message?"

For example, a story may be about a boy who finds a lost and frightened dog. He cleans, feeds, and cares for the dog. The dog becomes his best friend. The story message is "Be kind and caring."

Your Turn

RETURN TO THE ESSENTIAL QUESTION

 **Review the story with a partner to prepare to discuss** this question: *Why is volunteering a good thing for a community and its people?* Take turns talking about your ideas using text evidence to explain.

Classroom Conversation

Continue your discussion of *Destiny's Gift* by explaining your answers to these questions:

1 Why do Mrs. Wade and Destiny become such good friends?

2 Do you think the people of the neighborhood are being helpful? Why or why not?

3 Why doesn't the author tell you what happens to the bookstore? Are you satisfied with the ending? Explain.

WRITE ABOUT READING

Response In the story, Mrs. Wade says twice, "Words are a powerful gift." What do you think this statement means? Why do you think the author has Mrs. Wade say it twice? Write a paragraph that answers these questions. Find text evidence to support your opinion.

Words are a powerful gift.

Writing Tip

State your opinion. Then give reasons to support it. Include examples to help explain your opinion. Then end with a statement that wraps up your ideas.

COMMON CORE **RL.3.1** ask and answer questions to demonstrate understanding, referring to the text; **RL.3.3** describe characters and explain how their actions contribute to the sequence of events; **W.3.1a** introduce the topic, state an opinion, and create an organizational structure; **W.3.1b** provide reasons that support the opinion; **W.3.1d** provide a concluding statement or section; **W.3.10** write routinely over extended time frames or short time frames; **SL.3.1a** come to discussions prepared/explicitly draw on preparation and other information about the topic; **SL.3.1d** explain own ideas and understanding in light of the discussion

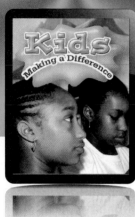

☑ GENRE

Informational text gives factual information about a topic.

☑ TEXT FOCUS

A **map** is a drawing of an area such as a neighborhood, a town, or a state.

COMMON CORE

RI.3.7 use information gained from illustrations and words to demonstrate understanding; **RI.3.10** read and comprehend informational texts

Kids
Making a Difference

by Jeremy Stone

National and Global Youth Services Day began in 1988. Celebration of this day is spreading around the world.

Go Digital

A Day to Help

Would you like the chance to figure out fun ways to improve your school, block, or town? Put your ideas into action in April on National and Global Youth Services Day!

On this day, kids across the country work to make their communities safer and cleaner, or to help others. Some collect food for people who can't afford it. Others raise money for local charities. They earn this money by holding fundraisers or getting customers at local shops to make donations.

Texas Kids Help Out

On Youth Service Day in Arlington, Texas, more than 800 kids help their community. Some visit nursing homes. Others plant flowers. In historic Arlington Cemetery, youth baseball teams pick up trash. The cemetery is next to the teams' ball fields.

After a busy day, it's party time in Vandergriff Park! The hardworking kids gather there to celebrate.

30 80 30
303
Arlington
Arlington
Cemetery
180
Division St.
Collins St.
820
Pioneer Pkwy 303
Lake
Arlington
Vandergriff
Park
360
20
Arlington
Matlock Road
Arlington
Municipal
Airport
20
Texas
496

Helping with Art

One group of artists in San Francisco is helping children make their city beautiful all year round. Adult artists from a group called Kids Serve go to schools around the city. The artists help students plan special murals. The murals are usually about topics the children are studying in class.

Once the mural is planned, the children work together to create the mural in a public area. When it is done, neighbors are contacted and invited to celebrate and enjoy the mural.

This mural celebrates California's Civil Rights leaders.

Compare Texts

Compare Ways to Help Think about the ways people help others in *Destiny's Gift* and *Kids Making a Difference*. Do children and adults help in different ways? What reasons do people have for helping? Discuss your ideas with a partner. Use important details and other text evidence to explain your answers.

Talk About Making a Difference Kids help out in *Destiny's Gift* and *Kids Making a Difference*. Tell the class about a time you helped your community. Listen carefully and ask questions as other students talk about what they have done.

Apply Character Traits Do you think Destiny would have liked Mr. Keene's decision to have school on Saturdays in the story *A Fine, Fine School* from Lesson 1? Why or why not? Write your thoughts in your notebook.

COMMON CORE **RL.3.3** describe characters and explain how their actions contribute to the sequence of events; **RI.3.9** compare and contrast important points and details in texts on the same topic; **SL.3.1c** ask questions to check understanding, stay on topic, and link comments to others' remarks

117

Grammar

Compound Sentences A **compound sentence** is made of two simple sentences joined by the word *and, but, or,* or *so.* These joining words are called **conjunctions**. A comma comes before the conjunction.

Simple Sentences	Compound Sentence
I love books. I want to be a writer.	I love books, and I want to be a writer.
Dad bought a book. He lost it.	Dad bought a book, but he lost it.
We can read this. We can read that.	We can read this, or we can read that.
Ty reads a lot. He buys many books.	Ty reads a lot, so he buys many books.

 **Copy each sentence. Then write *simple* or *compound* to tell which kind of sentence it is.**

❶ This book is good, but that book is better.

❷ We can go to the library this morning.

Write a compound sentence for each pair of simple sentences. Use the conjunction in parentheses and a comma.

❸ I wanted a book. The bookstore was closed. (but)

❹ The library has that book. I will go there today. (so)

Sometimes a writer puts two simple sentences together with no comma and conjunction. This kind of mistake is called a **run-on.** Run-ons are confusing because readers don't know where one idea stops and another begins. One way to fix a run-on is to write a compound sentence.

Run-on Sentence

We lined up at the bookstore the author signed our books.

Compound Sentence

We lined up at the bookstore, and the author signed our books.

 Connect Grammar to Writing

As you revise your personal narrative, make sure you have no run-ons. To join simple sentences, use a comma and a conjunction between them.

W.3.3a establish a situation and introduce a narrator or characters/organize an event sequence; **W.3.3b** use dialogue/descriptions to develop experiences and events or show characters' responses; **W.3.3c** use temporal words and phrases to signal event order; **W.3.3d** provide a sense of closure; **W.3.8** recall information from experiences or gather information from print and digital sources/take brief notes and sort evidence

Narrative Writing

✔ **Voice** In *Destiny's Gift*, when Mrs. Wade says that words are powerful, Destiny tells us her thoughts and feelings. She says, "I wasn't sure what she meant, but I felt very important indeed!" In your **personal narrative**, you can share your thoughts and feelings just as Destiny did.

Callie wrote about the time she helped a neighbor. Later, she added some of her thoughts and feelings. She also used time-order words and ended with a strong conclusion.

Writing Traits Checklist

✔ **Ideas**
Did I use details that help readers picture the events?

✔ **Organization**
Did I tell the events in order?

✔ **Word Choice**
Did I use clear, vivid words?

✔ **Voice**
Did I share what I thought and felt?

✔ **Sentence Fluency**
Did I write complete sentences?

✔ **Conventions**
Did I leave space between each word in my sentences?

Revised Draft

One day I asked my neighbor Mr. Mazur where his cat was. He said, "I had an operation. Chester has to stay at a shelter until I can take care of him again." Then I had an idea. I asked Mom if I could take care of Chester so Mr. Mazur could keep him at home.

I felt so sad for Mr. Mazur and for myself, too, because I love Chester!

120

Mr. Mazur, Chester, and Me
by Callie Perakis

One day I asked my neighbor Mr. Mazur where his cat was. He said, "I had an operation. Chester has to stay at a shelter until I can take care of him again." I felt so sad for Mr. Mazur and for myself, too, because I love Chester! Then I had an idea. I asked Mom if I could take care of Chester so Mr. Mazur could keep him at home. When she said yes, I yelled, "Yippee!"

So, all summer I went over to Mr. Mazur's every day. I gave Chester his food and water. Then I talked with Mr. Mazur and played with Chester. When I went home, I felt good inside because I knew Mr. Mazur would not be lonely.

Reading as a Writer

Which sentences tell you how Callie felt? Where can you add your thoughts and feelings in your own paper?

I added my thoughts and feelings. I also made sure to write complete sentences.

Vocabulary in Context

crew
tide
cling
balancing
foggy
disappears
stretch
excitement

Vocabulary Reader

Context Cards

 L.3.6 acquire and use conversational, general academic, and domain-specific words and phrases

① crew

A crew, or group of workers, has just started to build a new bridge.

② tide

When the sea falls at low tide, it's a good time to make repairs.

③ cling

Painters cling to the bridge when the wind blows. They hold on tightly!

④ balancing

Workers must be good at balancing on high, thin beams without falling.

 Go Digital

▶ Study each Context Card.

▶ Discuss one picture. Use a different Vocabulary word from the one on the card.

5 foggy

On foggy days, thick mist makes it hard to see. Drivers must go slowly.

6 disappears

Half of the bridge disappears in this photo. It seems to vanish in the fog.

7 stretch

Bridges may stretch over land or run across large bodies of water.

8 excitement

Marathon runners feel excitement as they cross this bridge. It is a thrill!

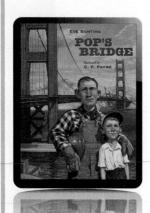

Read and Comprehend

Go Digital

✓ TARGET SKILL

Compare and Contrast In *Pop's Bridge*, the main characters are alike in some ways but different in others. As you read, **compare** and **contrast** the characters, or think of how they are alike and different. Look at their words and actions as well as their traits, motivations, and feelings. How do these differences contribute to the sequence of events in the story?

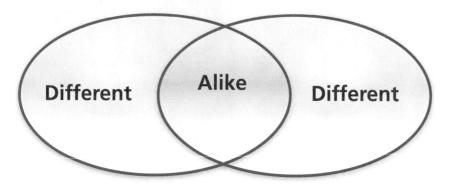

Different | Alike | Different

✓ TARGET STRATEGY

Infer/Predict As you read *Pop's Bridge*, use text evidence to **infer**, or figure out, more about what it takes to build a bridge. Also use the evidence to **predict** what will happen next in the story. Check to see if your predictions are correct.

Engineering

Engineering is the branch of science that deals with designing and building structures. Work crews follow engineering plans to construct bridges, machines, and buildings. For example, on a suspension bridge, engineers design the giant steel cables and high towers that hold up the road.

In *Pop's Bridge,* you'll read about the brave workers who built the Golden Gate Bridge in San Francisco. You'll also learn about the pride and fear their families felt every day as those workers did one of the most dangerous jobs in the world.

ANCHOR TEXT

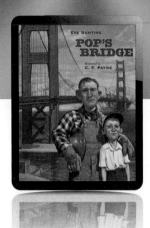

☑ TARGET SKILL

Compare and Contrast
Tell how characters are alike and different.

☑ GENRE

Historical fiction is a story that is set in the past.
As you read, look for:
▶ a setting that is a real time and place in the past
▶ realistic characters and events
▶ some made-up events and and details

COMMON CORE **RL.3.3** describe characters and explain how their actions contribute to the sequence of events; **RL.3.10** read and comprehend literature

Go Digital

MEET THE AUTHOR
Eve Bunting

The first time Eve Bunting ever saw the Golden Gate Bridge was in 1958. On that day, she had moved to California from Ireland, where she had been born. "I thought it the most beautiful bridge I had ever seen," she recalls.

MEET THE ILLUSTRATOR
C. F. Payne

C. F. Payne, whose initials stand for Chris Fox, is famous for drawing people with very large heads, noses, and ears. Sometimes Payne uses friends as models for his drawings, as he did in *Pop's Bridge*.

POP'S BRIDGE

by Eve Bunting • illustrated by C. F. Payne

My pop is building the Golden Gate Bridge.

Almost every day after school, Charlie Shu and I go to Fort Point and watch. The bridge will stretch across the bay, from San Francisco to Marin. People said this bridge couldn't be built. Some call it the impossible bridge. They say the bay is too deep, the currents too strong, the winds blowing in from the ocean too fierce.

But I know my pop can do it. Whenever I say he's building the bridge, Mom laughs. "There's a crew of more than a thousand men working on that bridge, Robert. Including Charlie's dad," she reminds me. I know that, but I just shrug.

To me, it's Pop's bridge.

129

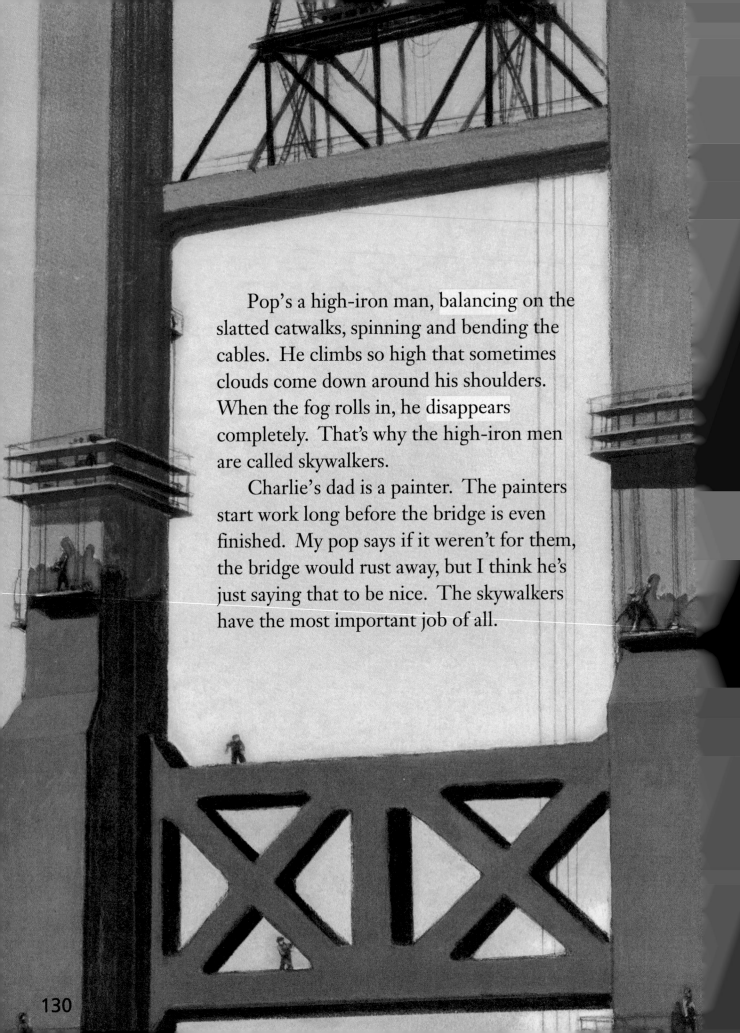

Pop's a high-iron man, balancing on the slatted catwalks, spinning and bending the cables. He climbs so high that sometimes clouds come down around his shoulders. When the fog rolls in, he disappears completely. That's why the high-iron men are called skywalkers.

Charlie's dad is a painter. The painters start work long before the bridge is even finished. My pop says if it weren't for them, the bridge would rust away, but I think he's just saying that to be nice. The skywalkers have the most important job of all.

At Fort Point I look for Pop through the binoculars Mom lends me. The workers look alike in their overalls and swabbie hats, but I can always find my pop because of the red kerchief he ties at his throat. It's our own scarlet signal.

I don't worry much about him on days when the sun sparkles on the water, when sailboats skim below. It's so beautiful I can forget that it's dangerous, too. But when the wind blows through the Golden Gate, the men cling to the girders like caterpillars on a branch. On foggy days my hands sweat on the binoculars. *Where is he?* When I find him, I try not to look away, as though the force of my eyes can keep him from falling.

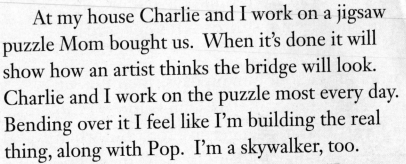

At my house Charlie and I work on a jigsaw puzzle Mom bought us. When it's done it will show how an artist thinks the bridge will look. Charlie and I work on the puzzle most every day. Bending over it I feel like I'm building the real thing, along with Pop. I'm a skywalker, too.

"We're almost done," Charlie says. "I wonder which of us will put in the last piece?"

I shrug. But what he says makes me think. My pop built that bridge. He should set the last puzzle piece in place. That's only fair, even though Charlie might think his dad should do it. When Charlie isn't looking, I slip one of the pieces into my pocket. Later I hide it in my room. I'm saving it for Pop.

ANALYZE THE TEXT

Compare and Contrast What does Robert think about the last piece of the puzzle? How would Charlie's ideas be different? How would they be the same?

The "impossible bridge" is nearly finished. One evening Mom and Pop and I walk down to Fort Point. The bridge hangs between stars and sea.

"It's like a giant harp," my pop says. "A harp for the angels to play." I look up at him, and I can tell this wasn't just a job to my pop. He loves the bridge.

In San Francisco there is great excitement. Everyone is waiting for opening day.

Charlie and I have watched nearly every bit of the bridge go up. We saw the two spans come together from opposite directions. We saw them meet. We saw the roadway go in. And my pop did it. No one can be as proud as I am. Not even Charlie. After all, my dad is a skywalker.

And then one day, something terrible happens. Charlie and I are watching as the scaffolding pulls away from the bridge. There's a noise like a train wreck as the scaffolding crashes down into the safety net. The net tears loose, and men go with it into the swirling tide.

I can't breathe. I can't think.

But then I look hard through the binoculars and see Pop still on the bridge, his red kerchief whipping. "Pop!" I whisper in relief. Beside me Charlie is screaming, "Where's my dad? Where's my dad?"

We had seen him working close to that scaffolding. I can't see him now.

"We'll find him," I promise. "We have to." I sweep the binoculars up and down the bridge cables, looking at every painter hanging high on his Jacob's ladder or swinging in a bosun's chair, like a knot on a rope.

"Be there, Mr. Shu," I plead, and then spot him. "Over by that cross girder!" I yell. Charlie fumbles for the binoculars. I help him. He looks where I point.

"He's there! He's safe!" Charlie gasps.

The next day we find out that only two of the twelve men in the water were saved.

I think and think about that day. At night, half asleep, I see the bridge shake. I hear the crash. One of those men in the water could have been Pop. Or Charlie's dad.

I finally understand, and I feel ashamed. Equal work, equal danger, for skywalkers *and* for painters.

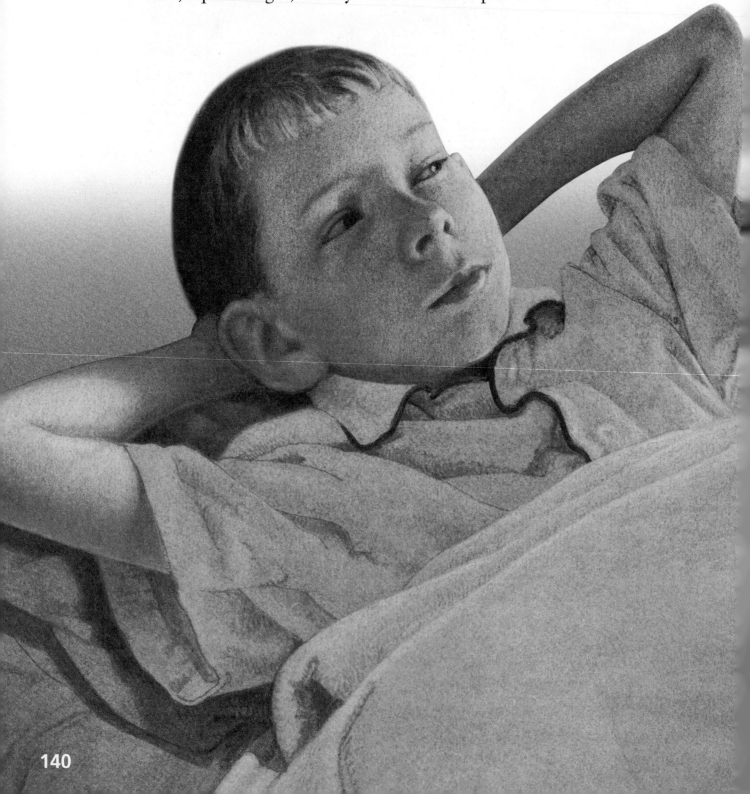

The work goes on. A new safety net is put in place.
Pop says there's less talking and joking now among the men.
There's a remembering.

But the bridge must be finished. And at last it is.
We watch through Mom's binoculars as the golden spike
is drilled in at the center of the main span. Now the
celebration can begin.

On opening day no cars are allowed. Thousands of people walk and dance and roller-skate across the bridge, including us. I wear Pop's kerchief around my neck. There's a man riding a unicycle. There's another on stilts. Navy biplanes fly above the great steel towers. Battleships and cruisers sail below the bridge and into San Francisco Bay. Wind strums its music through the stretch of the cables, and I think of my pop's harp.

That night our family has our own party with Charlie and his dad. There's stewed chicken and a Chinese noodle dish Charlie's dad made and a snickerdoodle pie.

The jigsaw puzzle sits on the coffee table with a gap in the middle. "I've searched and searched for that missing piece," my mother says.

"A good thing we didn't leave our bridge with a space like that," Mr. Shu says.

Pop chuckles. "We'd be working still."

It's time.

I slip upstairs to get the hidden puzzle piece, then find the scissors and cut the piece carefully in half. I go back down and put a half piece in Mr. Shu's hand and the other in my pop's. "Finish it," I say. "It's your bridge. It belongs to both of you."

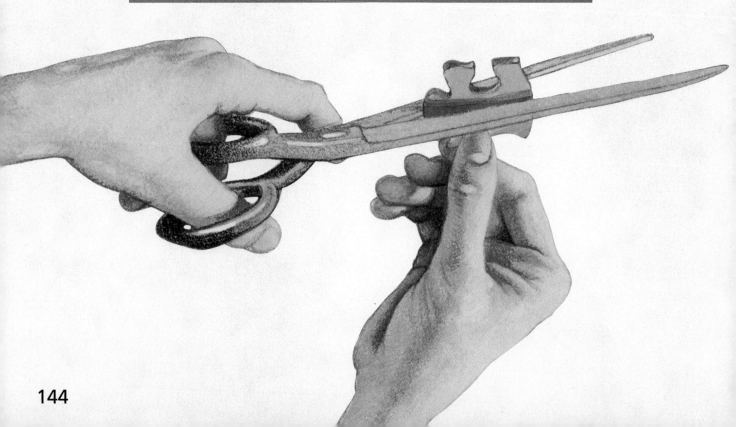

ANALYZE THE TEXT

Story Structure Robert hides a piece of the puzzle. How does this action affect the sequence of events?

145

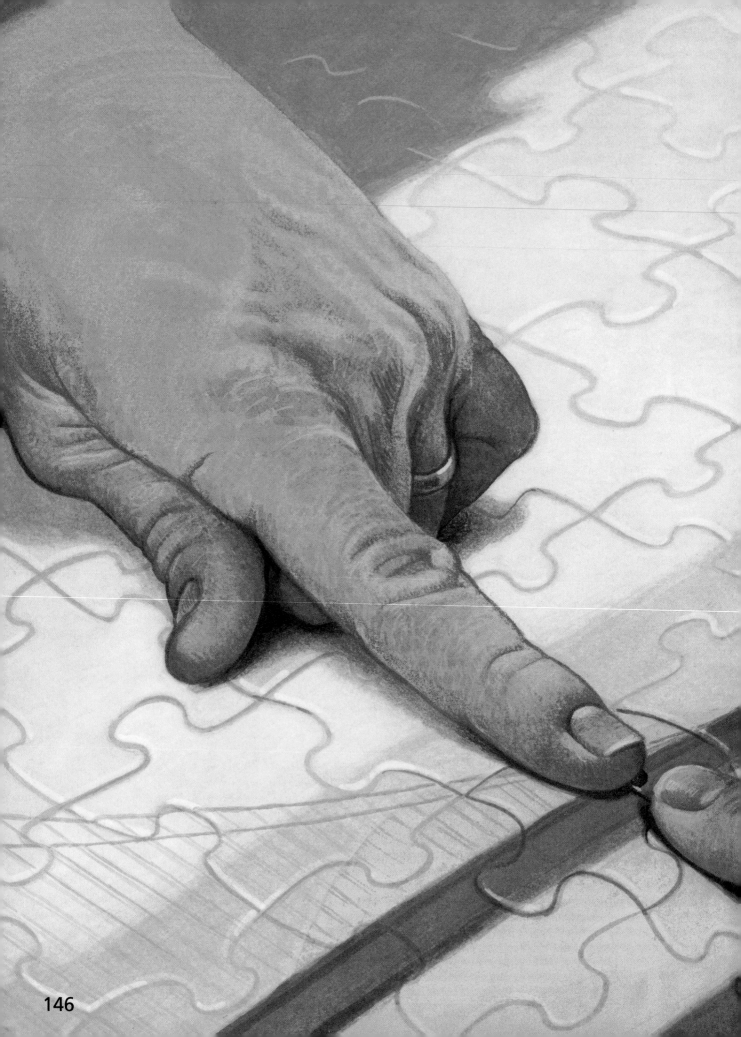

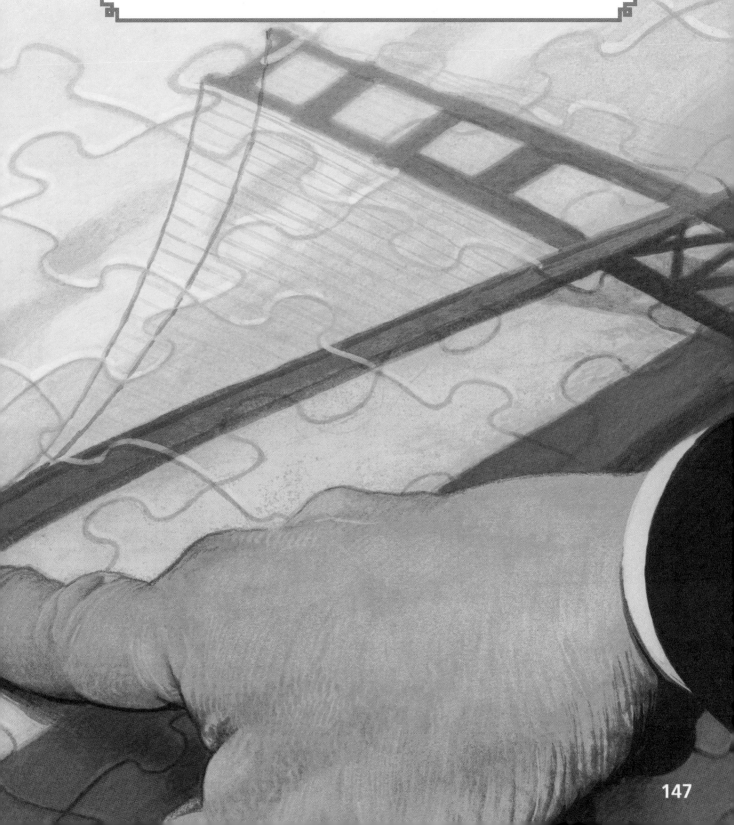

My mother raises her eyebrows and Charlie says, "Hey, where . . . ?" But I just watch as the two pieces fit in, so perfectly, so smoothly.

"Team effort," my pop says.

We raise our glasses of sarsaparilla to celebrate the laborers and riveters, the carpenters and the painters and the skywalkers. All the men who worked together to build the most beautiful bridge in the world.

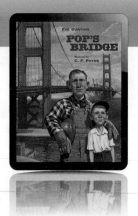

Dig Deeper

How to Analyze the Text

Use these pages to learn about Comparing and Contrasting and Story Structure. Then read *Pop's Bridge* again to apply what you learned.

Compare and Contrast

The characters in *Pop's Bridge* have things about them that are the same and things about them that are different. You can **compare** and **contrast** the characters in a story to explain what they are like.

Robert and Charlie's dads have similar and different traits, motivations, and feelings. You can describe how the two dads are alike and different by looking for text evidence. Explain their actions and look for what Robert and Charlie say about them.

Look at page 130 in *Pop's Bridge* again. In this section, you first read about the two dads. As you read on, keep looking for ways to compare and contrast the two men.

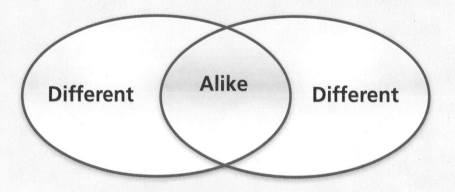

Different   Alike   Different

RL.3.3 describe characters and explain how their actions contribute to the sequence of events

Story Structure

A story's **setting** is where and when the story happens. The **characters** are the people, and sometimes animals, that appear in the story.

The **plot** is made up of the important events, or the things that happen in a story. A character's actions play a part in what happens next. Think about what Robert does. Ask yourself how his actions affect the **sequence of events.** How do his actions lead to what happens at the end of the story?

Your Turn

 Review the story with a partner to prepare to discuss this question: *Why is everyone's role on a project important?* As you discuss, ask questions to make sure you understand your partner's ideas. Use text evidence from the story.

Classroom Conversation

Continue your discussion of *Pop's Bridge* by explaining your answers to these questions:

1. Why does Robert think that skywalkers have the most important job?

2. If Robert's dad were a bridge painter, would Robert have a different opinion? Why or why not?

3. Do you think that Charlie realized what Robert thought about painters through most of the story? Explain your answer.

WRITE ABOUT READING

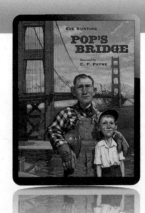

Response Think about the illustrations in *Pop's Bridge*. What do they tell you about the story? Notice the story details that the illustrations show. Then take note of what the illustrations show that is not described in the story. Write a paragraph that explains how certain illustrations help you understand what happened in the story. State the reasons for your opinions.

Writing Tip

Begin your paragraph by giving your opinion. Then give reasons and examples to support and explain your opinion. End with a statement that wraps up your ideas.

COMMON CORE **RL.3.1** ask and answer questions to demonstrate understanding, referring to the text; **RL.3.3** describe characters and explain how their actions contribute to the sequence of events; **RL.3.7** explain how illustrations contribute to the words; **W.3.1a** introduce the topic, state an opinion, and create an organizational structure; **W.3.1b** provide reasons that support the opinion; **W.3.1d** provide a concluding statement or section; **SL.3.1a** come to discussions prepared/explicitly draw on preparation and other information about the topic

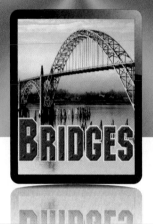

COMMON CORE **RI.3.7** use information gained from illustrations and words to demonstrate understanding; **RI.3.10** read and comprehend informational texts

Go Digital

BRIDGES

by Matthew Danzeris

Bridges help people get from place to place. They join communities. They stretch across waterways and the swirling tide. They take us over roadways and landforms.

People have been building bridges for thousands of years. They think about how long the bridge must be. They think about what the bridge will cost. Then they decide what kind of bridge to build.

The arch bridge shown here is the Bayonne Bridge, which goes from New Jersey to New York. Workers finished building it in 1931.

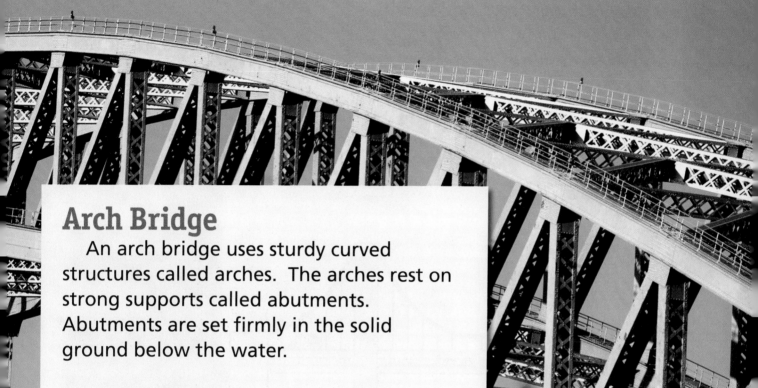

Arch Bridge

An arch bridge uses sturdy curved structures called arches. The arches rest on strong supports called abutments. Abutments are set firmly in the solid ground below the water.

Beam Bridge

The beam bridge is the simplest kind of bridge for a crew to build. It costs the least, too!

A beam bridge has a beam. It lies across supports called piers. The piers must be close enough together to give the beam strength. That way, the roadway won't bend or sag too much when traffic crosses it. Each span of a beam bridge is usually less than 250 feet long.

Florida's Rickenbacker Causeway Bridge is a beam bridge. It connects the city of Miami to the island of Key Biscayne.

155

Suspension Bridge

A suspension bridge can stretch as far as 7,000 feet. That's more than a mile! On a suspension bridge, the roadway hangs from cables. The cables rest on top of towers. At each end of the bridge, an anchorage holds the cables in place.

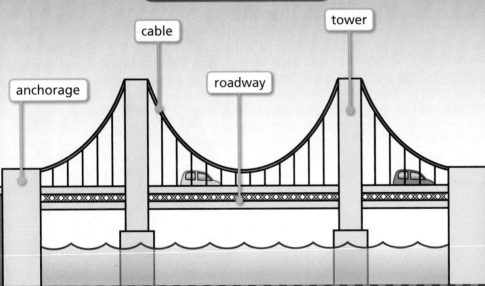

Suspension Bridge

cable

tower

anchorage

roadway

Building Bridges

A large crew of workers builds most bridges. The work is dangerous. Workers wear harnesses to stay safe when they are balancing up high. Strong winds and foggy weather make the work even more dangerous. Builders cling to the bridge. When at last the work is done, excitement grips everyone. A ceremony may be held to celebrate.

St. John's Bridge, in Portland, Oregon, is a suspension bridge. When the fog is heavy, the bridge practically disappears!

Compare Texts

Compare Bridges Compare and contrast the suspension bridge, like the one in *Pop's Bridge*, with the beam bridge that you read about in *Bridges*. List three differences between the kinds of bridges. Then list three similarities. Discuss your ideas with a partner. Use text evidence to explain your ideas.

Write About Work In *Pop's Bridge*, Robert writes about being both proud of and worried about his father's job. Write a paragraph about a job that you find interesting and how you feel about it.

Connect to Math Use the Internet or another source to find the lengths of the Golden Gate, Verrazano-Narrows, and Akashi Kaikyo bridges. Then make a bar graph to compare the lengths of these suspension bridges.

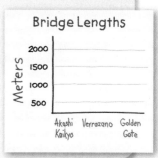

Bridge Lengths

Meters

2000
1500
1000
500

Akashi   Verrazano   Golden
Kaikyo   Gate

COMMON CORE **RI.3.9** compare and contrast important points and details in texts on the same topic; **SL.3.1a** come to discussions prepared/explicitly draw on preparation and other information about the topic; **SL.3.1d** explain own ideas and understanding in light of the discussion

Grammar

Common and Proper Nouns   A **noun** names a person, a place, or a thing. A noun that names any person, place, or thing is called a **common noun**. A noun that names a particular person, place, or thing is called a **proper noun**.

Common Nouns	Proper Nouns
The bridge is long.	The Golden Gate Bridge is long.
My uncle likes to paint.	Uncle Bob likes to paint.

In book and story titles, the first word is always capitalized. Also capitalize most words even if they are not proper nouns.

When writing about an adult, use his or her title. Titles, such as Ms., Mrs., Mr., and Dr., are always capitalized.

Titles of Stories	Titles of People
The Wolf and the Three Pigs	Dr. Carla West
One Day on a Ship	Mr. Martinez

Try This!   **Work with a partner. Read each item aloud. Identify each as a common noun, a proper noun, a story title, or a personal title.**

1. Ash Road
2. country
3. Mexico
4. Mrs. Kim Robson
5. teacher
6. On the Way to School

Use exact nouns to make your writing clearer and more interesting. Exact nouns help your readers picture what you are writing about.

Noun	Exact Noun
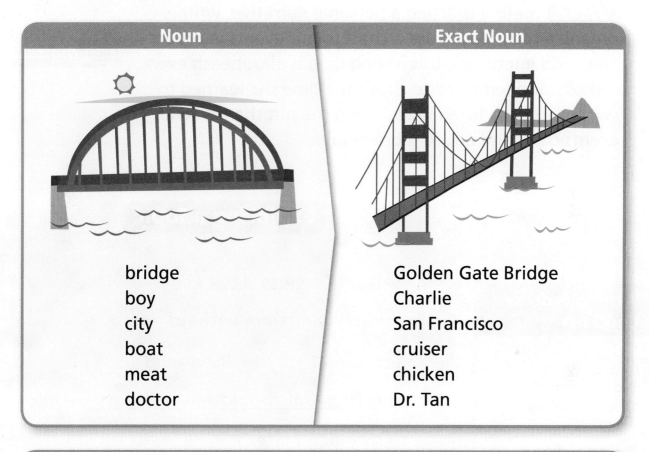	
bridge	Golden Gate Bridge
boy	Charlie
city	San Francisco
boat	cruiser
meat	chicken
doctor	Dr. Tan

Less Exact Noun: The bridge is painted the color of rust, not gold.

More Exact Noun: The Golden Gate Bridge is painted the color of rust, not gold.

 Connect Grammar to Writing

As you revise your personal narrative next week, think of exact nouns you can use. Exact nouns will help make your writing easy to understand.

W.3.3a establish a situation and introduce a narrator or characters/organize an event sequence; **W.3.5** develop and strengthen writing by planning, revising, and editing; **W.3.8** recall information from experiences or gather information from print and digital sources/take brief notes and sort evidence

Narrative Writing

Reading-Writing Workshop: Prewrite

✅ **Ideas** Before drafting a **personal narrative**, writers organize their ideas. Use a chart to put events in order. Then add important, interesting details about each event.

Kelly decided to write about the time she learned to swim. First, she listed ideas. Then she put them into an events chart and added more details.

Writing Process Checklist

▶ **Prewrite**

- ✅ Did I pick a topic I'll enjoy writing about?
- ✅ Will my audience like my topic?
- ✅ Did I write down all the main events?
- ✅ Did I add details to make the events more interesting?
- ✅ Did I put the events in order?

Draft

Revise

Edit

Publish and Share

Exploring a Topic

<u>afraid to go in deep end</u>

-everyone swam without me

-couldn't play water games

<u>brother Cal taught me to swim</u>

-treading water

-floating on back

-~~bandage fell off knee~~

<u>first time in deep end</u>

-scared — stayed near side

-wouldn't let go of Cal

-started floating on my own

Events Chart

Event: I was afraid to go in the deep end of the swimming pool.

Details: had to sit out when my friends played games
missed a lot of fun

Event: My brother Cal gave me lessons.

Details: helped me practice strokes
learned to float on back
tread water

Event: I finally swam in the deep end.

Details: scared at first
wouldn't let go of Cal
floated on my own
love deep end now

Reading as a Writer

Which of Kelly's details did you find most interesting? Where can you add details to your own chart?

When I organized my personal narrative, I added important, interesting details.

Vocabulary in Context

✓ **TARGET VOCABULARY**

stands
fans
score
league
slammed
polish
style
pronounced

Vocabulary Reader

Context Cards

COMMON CORE **L.3.6** acquire and use conversational, general academic, and domain-specific words and phrases

1 stands
Peanut vendors walk up and down through the stands at a baseball game.

2 fans
Happy fans cheer when players on their favorite teams play well.

3 score
Soccer players must work together to score a goal and earn one point.

4 league
These volleyball players are in a league, or group of teams.

 Go Digital

▶ Study each Context Card.

▶ Tell a story about two or more pictures, using their Vocabulary words.

5 **slammed**

This player slammed the puck so hard that it went straight into the net.

6 **polish**

Before bowlers play a game, they may polish the ball to remove any dust.

7 **style**

This fan has her own special style. It's a clever way to show team spirit.

8 **pronounced**

The announcer pronounced, or said, each player's name loudly and clearly.

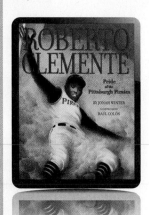

Read and Comprehend

Cause and Effect As you read *Roberto Clemente*, look for examples of cause and effect. An **effect** is what happened. A **cause** is why something happened. Look for words such as *so, if, then, because*, and *since* to help you identify causes and effects. A graphic organizer like the one below will help you to list what you find.

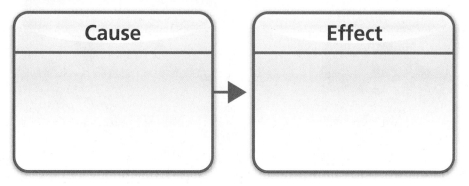

Cause	Effect

☑ **TARGET STRATEGY**

Visualize As you read *Roberto Clemente*, think about how details in the biography help you **visualize**, or see, events. Note the words that help you create pictures in your mind.

RI.3.3 describe the relationship between a series of historical events/scientific ideas/steps in technical procedures; **RI.3.8** describe the connection between sentences and paragraphs in a text

COMMON CORE

164

Sports

Many people enjoy playing different sports like basketball and football. Many more like to watch sports and cheer for their favorite teams and players. Baseball is one of those sports. It's a game that many Americans love to play, watch, and talk about.

Some great players in the history of baseball stand out as heroes. In *Roberto Clemente,* you'll learn about one of those players. You will read about the things he did that made him a hero.

ANCHOR TEXT

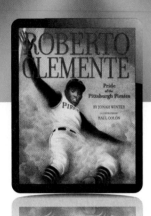

Cause and Effect Think about how the author uses words to connect events with their causes or effects.

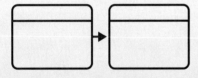

☑ GENRE

In a **biography,** an author tells about a person's life. As you read, look for:

▶ information about why the person is important

▶ opinions and personal judgments based on facts

▶ events in time order

MEET THE AUTHOR

JONAH WINTER

Although Jonah Winter was raised in Texas, as a kid he rooted for the Pittsburgh Pirates and Roberto Clemente. "Growing up, he was my hero," Winter says. Today Winter lives in Pittsburgh, where he plays the clarinet, writes poetry, and watches baseball.

MEET THE ILLUSTRATOR

RAÚL COLÓN

Like Roberto Clemente, Raúl Colón is from Puerto Rico. While Colón is known mainly as a book illustrator, his artwork is also familiar to people who ride the New York City subway. An enormous mural he created called *Primavera* (Springtime) fills a whole wall of a subway station.

ROBERTO CLEMENTE

PRIDE OF THE PITTSBURGH PIRATES

by
JONAH WINTER

illustrated by
RAÚL COLÓN

ESSENTIAL QUESTION

What are the traits
of a hero?

On an island called Puerto Rico, where baseball players are as plentiful as tropical flowers in a rain forest, there was a boy who had very little but a fever to play and win at baseball.

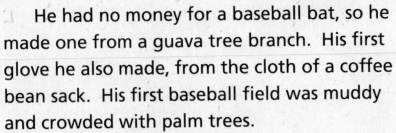

He had no money for a baseball bat, so he made one from a guava tree branch. His first glove he also made, from the cloth of a coffee bean sack. His first baseball field was muddy and crowded with palm trees.

For batting practice he used empty soup cans and hit them farther than anyone else. Soup cans turned into softballs. Softballs turned into baseballs. Little League turned into minor league turned into winter league: professional baseball in Puerto Rico.

ANALYZE THE TEXT

Literal and Nonliteral Meanings What does the author mean when he writes that soup cans turned into softballs? Is that a literal or a nonliteral meaning?

He played so well he received an invitation to play in . . . the major leagues in America! What an honor!

But the young man was sent to a steel-mill town called Pittsburgh, Pennsylvania, where his new team, the Pittsburgh Pirates, was in *last place*. Now this was something very strange, being on a losing team.

For the young Puerto Rican, everything was strange. Instead of palm trees, he saw smokestacks. Instead of Spanish, he heard English. Instead of being *somebody*, he was nobody.

His first time at bat, he heard the announcer stumble through his Spanish name: "ROB, uh, ROE . . . BURRT, um, let's see, TOE CLUH-MAINT?" It echoed in the near-empty stands.

Roberto Clemente was his name, and this is pronounced "Roe-BEAR-toe Cleh-MEN-tay." As if to introduce himself, Roberto *smacked* the very first pitch.

But it went right up the infield . . . and into
the second baseman's glove. Still, Roberto ran
like lightning—and beat the throw to first base.
   The Pittsburgh fans checked their scorecards.
Who was this guy, "Roberto Clemente"?

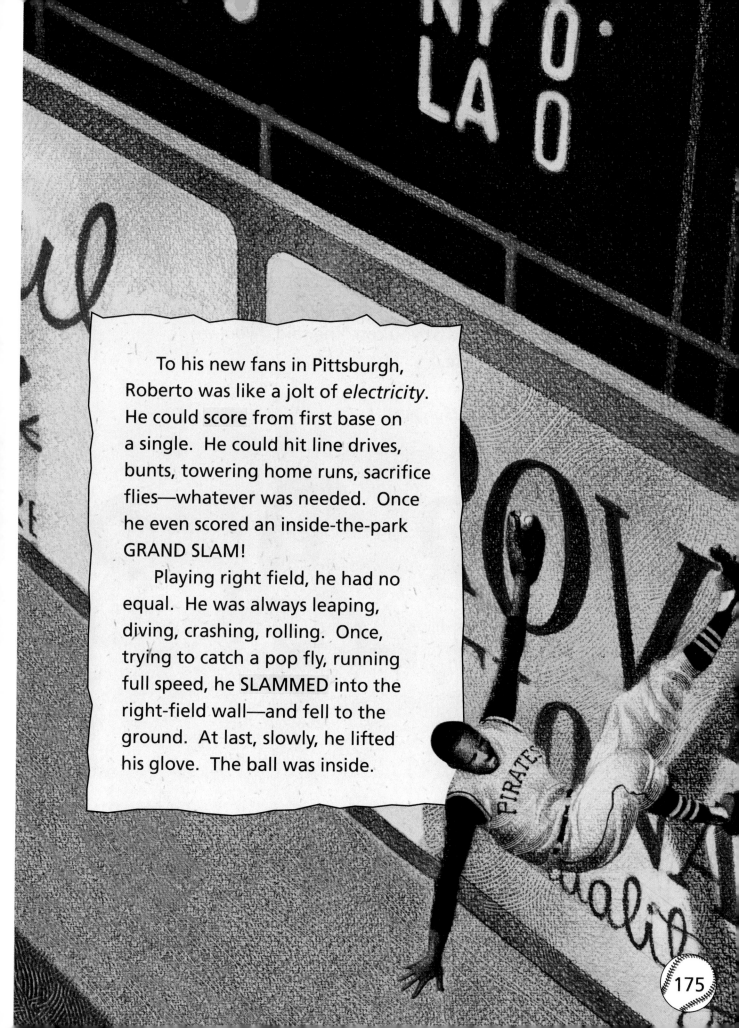

To his new fans in Pittsburgh, Roberto was like a jolt of *electricity*. He could score from first base on a single. He could hit line drives, bunts, towering home runs, sacrifice flies—whatever was needed. Once he even scored an inside-the-park GRAND SLAM!

Playing right field, he had no equal. He was always leaping, diving, crashing, rolling. Once, trying to catch a pop fly, running full speed, he SLAMMED into the right-field wall—and fell to the ground. At last, slowly, he lifted his glove. The ball was inside.

But it wasn't just how he played. He had *style*. He was *cool*.

He had this move he did with his neck before each at bat, creaking it one way, then the other. Soon kids who wanted to be just like Roberto were doing it too, twisting their necks this way and that.

Roberto did it to ease the pain he felt from playing his heart out in every game. "If you don't try as hard as you can," he said, "you are wasting your life."

Roberto tried so hard, he helped the last-place Pirates make it all the way to the World Series where they beat the mighty NEW YORK YANKEES!

After the series, down in the streets of Pittsburgh, Roberto walked alone among his fans, who were so busy celebrating, they didn't even notice him. That didn't bother Roberto. He was happy to feel lost in the crowd of a party he had helped create.

ANALYZE THE TEXT

Cause and Effect What happens as a result of Clemente's hard work?

But there was something that would have made Roberto's joy a little sweeter. As much as fans loved him, the newspaper writers did not. When Roberto was in such pain he couldn't play, they called him "lazy." They mocked his Spanish accent, and when Roberto got angry, the mainly white newsmen called him a Latino "hothead."

Roberto swore he would be so good, he would *have* to get the respect he deserved. He would become the greatest all-around baseball player there ever was.

At home that Christmas, Roberto went back to the same muddy field he'd played on as a boy. In his pocket was a bag full of bottle caps that he emptied into the hands of some kids. They threw him the caps, and he hit each one again and again.

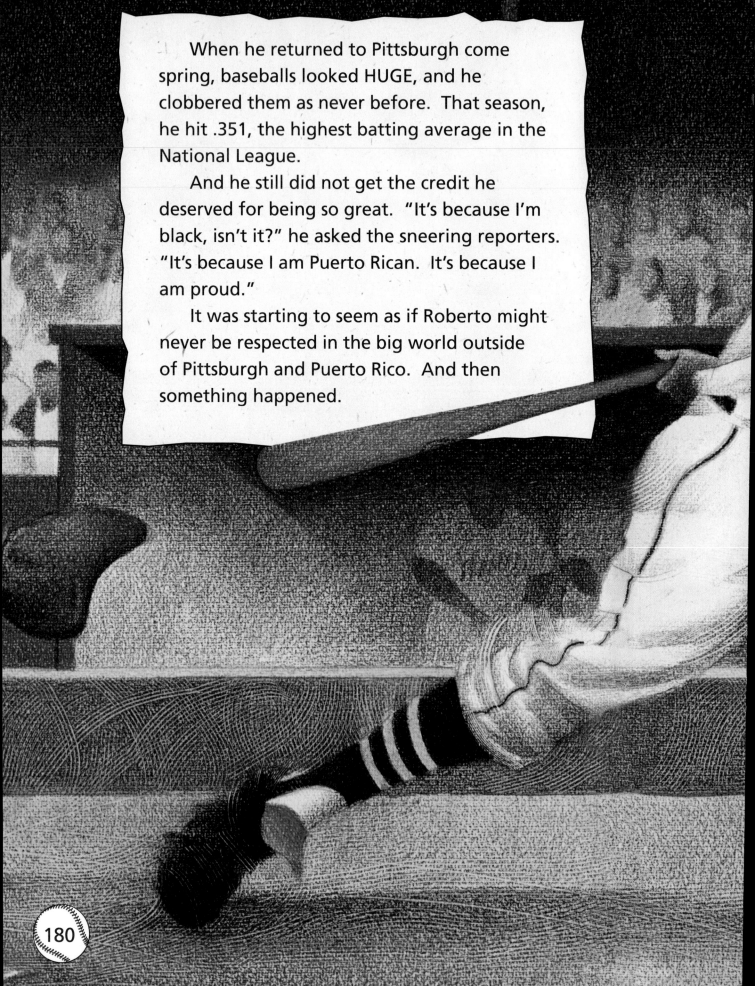

When he returned to Pittsburgh come spring, baseballs looked HUGE, and he clobbered them as never before. That season, he hit .351, the highest batting average in the National League.

And he still did not get the credit he deserved for being so great. "It's because I'm black, isn't it?" he asked the sneering reporters. "It's because I am Puerto Rican. It's because I am proud."

It was starting to seem as if Roberto might never be respected in the big world outside of Pittsburgh and Puerto Rico. And then something happened.

181

The year was 1971. The Pirates were in the World Series again, playing against the Baltimore Orioles, who were favored to win.

All around America and Puerto Rico, people sat watching on TV . . . as Roberto put on a one-man show. Stealing bases, hitting home runs, playing right field with a *fire* most fans had never seen before.

Finally, *finally*, it could not be denied: Roberto was the greatest all-around baseball player of his time, maybe of all time.

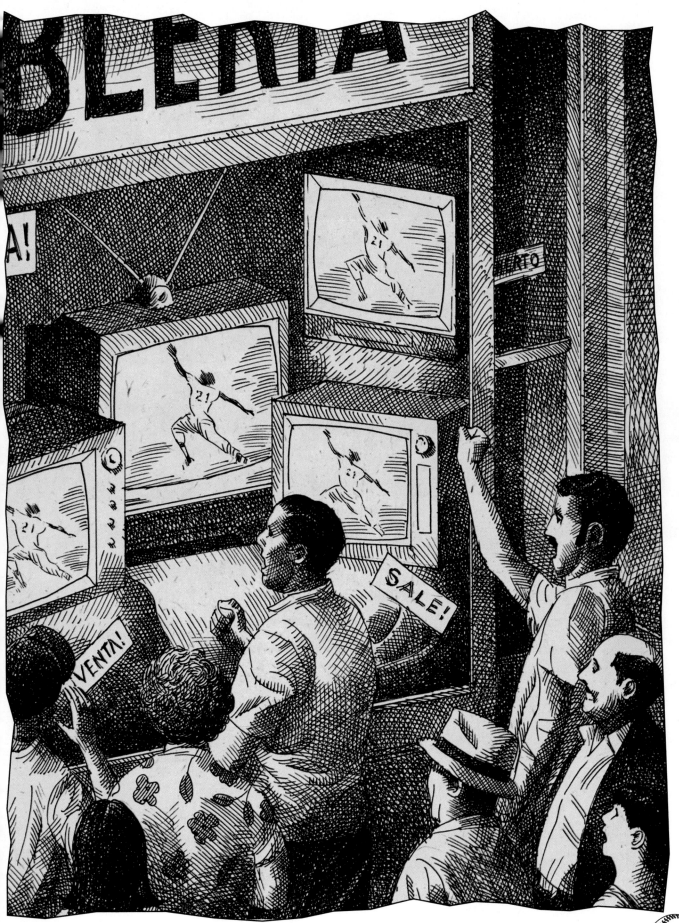

The very next year, he did something few have ever done: During the last game of the season, Roberto walked to the plate, creaked his neck, dug in his stance, stuck his chin toward the pitcher, and walloped a line drive off the center-field wall—his *three thousandth* hit!

The crowd cheered, and they wouldn't stop cheering. For many minutes the players stopped playing and Roberto stood on second base, amazed. How far he had come.

Roberto is now one of 11 players in major league history to get 3000 or more hits!

And yet, when the season was over, the hero returned to the place where his story began, to the land of muddy fields and soup cans and bottle caps, to his homeland of Puerto Rico, where he was worshipped.

But did he sit around and polish his trophies? No. That rainy New Year's Eve, Roberto sat in the San Juan airport and waited for mechanics to fix the tired old airplane that would take him to Central America. There had been a terrible earthquake, and he wanted to help the victims. The plane would carry food and supplies that Roberto paid for.

Right before midnight, he boarded. The rain was really coming down. One of the propellers buzzed loudly. As the plane took off, the engines failed and the plane fell into the ocean.

Just like that, it was over. Roberto was gone. How could his story end this way, so suddenly, and with such sadness?

The story doesn't end here. When someone like Roberto dies, his spirit lives on in the hearts of all he touched.

187

And Roberto's spirit is still growing. It grows in the bats and gloves and arms and legs of all the Latino baseball players who have flooded into the major leagues. His spirit grows in the charities he started for poor people in Puerto Rico. And his spirit is still growing in Pittsburgh, where people who saw him play tell their children and grandchildren of how he used to sparkle—running, diving, firing game-saving throws from deep right field all the way to home plate—SMACK—right into the catcher's glove.

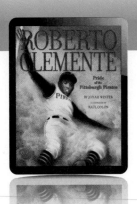

Dig Deeper

How to Analyze the Text

Use these pages to learn about Cause and Effect and Literal and Nonliteral Meanings. Then read *Roberto Clemente* again to apply what you learned.

Cause and Effect

In Roberto Clemente's life, many events caused other events to happen. A **cause** is why an event happened. An **effect** is something that happened as a result of a cause. Sometimes **signal words** will help you find a cause and an effect. Some common signal words are *so, if, then, because,* and *since.*

Look back at page 170 in *Roberto Clemente*. On this page, the author tells one fact about Roberto Clemente's life and the effects that it has on his childhood. As you read, notice how the author groups sentences into paragraphs.

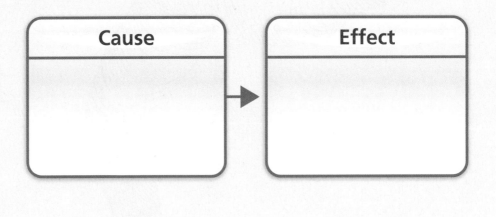

Cause		Effect

RI.3.3 describe the relationship between a series of historical events/scientific ideas/steps in technical procedures; **RI.3.8** describe the connection between sentences and paragraphs in a text; **L.3.4a** use sentence-level context as a clue to the meaning of a word or phrase; **L.3.5a** distinguish the literal and nonliteral meanings of words and phrases in context

Literal and Nonliteral Meanings

Every word has an exact or a **literal meaning**. For example, the literal meaning of *fever* is "a high body temperature."

A word can also have a **nonliteral meaning**. As a boy, Roberto Clemente had a fever to play and win at baseball. The sentences around the word show that, in this sentence, *fever* has a nonliteral meaning. In this **context**, *fever* means "passion or great excitement."

Your Turn

Turn and Talk Review the biography with a partner to prepare to discuss this question: *What are the traits of a hero?* While you discuss the question, use text evidence from *Roberto Clemente* to support your ideas. Listen carefully to your partner's ideas and add your own thoughts.

Classroom Conversation

Continue your discussion of *Roberto Clemente* by explaining your answers to these questions. Give text evidence for your responses:

1. What qualities made Roberto Clemente a hero as a baseball player?

2. What qualities made Roberto Clemente a hero as a person?

3. Which do you think was more important to Clemente— being a great baseball player or earning a lot of money? Explain your answer.

WRITE ABOUT READING

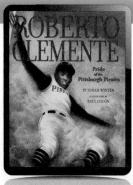

Response If Roberto Clemente were here today, what would he tell a young person who wants to become a great athlete? Write a letter that Clemente might write to give advice. Include details that he might suggest for reaching such a goal. Use facts from the selection to support those details.

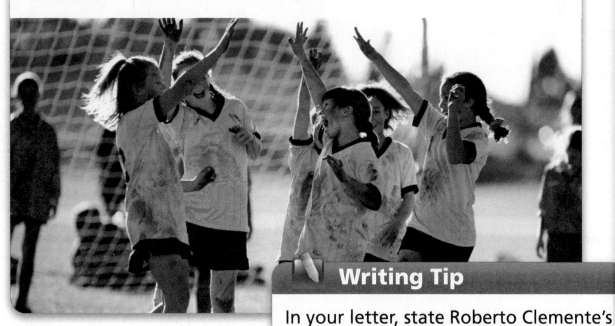

Writing Tip

In your letter, state Roberto Clemente's opinions and give reasons for them. Include examples from his life. Also, make sure that the first letter of each proper noun is capitalized.

COMMON CORE **RI.3.1** ask and answer questions to demonstrate understanding, referring to the text; **W.3.1b** provide reasons that support the opinion; **SL.3.1a** come to discussions prepared/explicitly draw on preparation and other information about the topic; **SL.3.1d** explain own ideas and understanding in light of the discussion

POETRY

Poetry uses the sound and rhythm of words to show images and express feelings.

Rhyme is often found in poems. It happens when words end with the same sound.

COMMON CORE **RL.3.5** refer to parts of stories, dramas, and poems/describe how each part builds on earlier sections; **RL.3.10** read and comprehend literature

BASEBALL POEMS

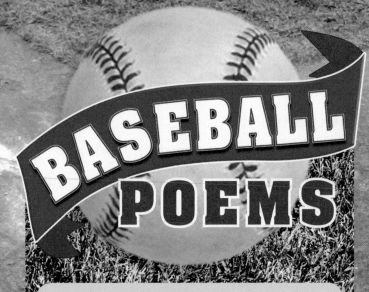

What did most kids do for fun before television, computers, and video games were invented? They played baseball! For years, it was the most widely played sport in the United States. That's how baseball came to be called "America's Pastime."

The ball game is over,
And here is the score —
They got ninety-seven,
We got ninety-four.
Baseball is fun,
But it gives me the blues
To score ninety-four
And still manage to lose.

by Jack Prelutsky

HOMER

Summer words, like *raspberry ice*,
beach, and *barbecue*, are all gone now.
But I find another warm word,
shaped like a bat. HOMER.
I wrap my fingers tightly round it
and swing.

by Nikki Grimes

Radio Days

When kids weren't playing baseball, they were listening to it. Major League Baseball games were heard on the radio starting in 1921. Announcers described the action in detail. They pronounced each word clearly so that fans didn't miss a thing.

Sounds gave clues about the action. The crack of a bat meant someone had slammed the ball out of the park. Boos from the stands meant the umpire had made a bad call. Cheering meant someone had been able to score.

If you used your imagination, listening to a game on the radio was almost as good as being in the ballpark!

Write a Baseball Poem

Write a baseball poem of your own. You might want to write about a game you have watched or about a favorite player.

Compare Texts

TEXT TO TEXT

Compare Baseball Illustrations Study the illustrations and photos in *Roberto Clemente* and *Baseball Poems*. How do the illustrations help you understand who Clemente was? How do the photos create the mood or feeling of the poems? Discuss your ideas with a partner. Use details from the art and text to support your answers to the questions.

TEXT TO SELF

Sports Senses Imagine being at a baseball game or other sports game. What might you see, hear, smell, touch, and taste? Write about how you would experience the game through your senses.

TEXT TO WORLD

Connect to Social Studies Roberto Clemente was born and raised in Puerto Rico. He moved to Pittsburgh, Pennsylvania, to play baseball. Find both places on a map. Find out how many miles apart they are. Then draw your own map, showing both places.

COMMON CORE **RL.3.7** explain how illustrations contribute to the words; **W.3.3b** use dialogue and descriptions to develop experiences and events or show characters' responses

Grammar

Plural Nouns with -s and -es A noun that names only one person, place, or thing is a **singular noun.** A noun that names more than one person, place, or thing is a **plural noun.** Add -s to form the plural of most singular nouns. Add -es to form the plural of a singular noun that ends with s, sh, ch, or x.

Singular Nouns	Plural Nouns
Julie has a baseball bat.	Julie has two baseball bats.
She is faster than her brother.	She is faster than her brothers.
They play after class.	They play between classes.
She is an inch taller than Joe.	She is four inches taller than Joe.

 **Write the plural of each underlined noun.**

1. A <u>boy</u> walked to the park.

2. He met his <u>friend</u>.

3. They opened a <u>box</u> with a new baseball inside.

4. Their <u>game</u> lasted all afternoon.

5. They missed the <u>bus</u> home.

When you edit your writing, it is important to always check your spelling. Using the correct spelling of plural nouns will make your writing clearer and easier to understand.

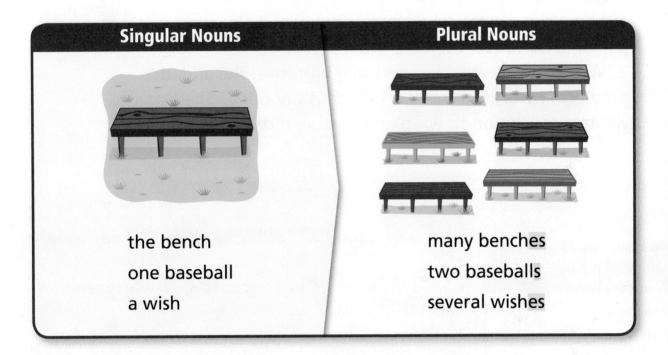

Singular Nouns	Plural Nouns
the bench	many benches
one baseball	two baseballs
a wish	several wishes

Singular: He swung the bat at the very first pitch.

Plural: He did not swing the bat at the first two pitches.

 Connect Grammar to Writing

As you edit your personal narrative, be sure to write the correct form of each plural noun.

W.3.3a establish a situation and introduce a narrator or characters/organize an event sequence; **W.3.3b** use dialogue/descriptions to develop experiences and events or show characters' responses; **W.3.3c** use temporal words and phrases to signal event order; **W.3.3d** provide a sense of closure; **W.3.8** recall information from experiences or gather information from print and digital sources/take brief notes and sort evidence

Narrative Writing

Reading-Writing Workshop: Revise

✔ **Sentence Fluency**   In *Roberto Clemente*, the author uses time-order words such as *first* and *then*. These are time clues to tell when events happened. In your **personal narrative**, use time-order words.

When Kelly revised her personal narrative, she added time-order words to connect her ideas smoothly. She also wrote a conclusion to wrap up the story nicely.

Writing Process Checklist

Prewrite

Draft

▶ **Revise**

✔ Is my beginning interesting?

✔ Did I include important events and details?

✔ Are the events in order?

✔ Did I include time-order words?

✔ Did I share my thoughts and feelings?

Edit

Publish and Share

Revised Draft

I begged my older brother Cal for help.

"I'm tired of being scared," I whispered.

"Can you give me some lessons?"

He took me to the pool when there

weren't many other people around.

First,
∧We practiced a few strokes. Then ∧He taught

me how to tread water and float on my

back.

200

Summer Splash!

by Kelly Belson

I used to hide whenever anyone said, "We're going to the deep end!" That was before everything changed.

Last summer, I was at the city pool when my friends played volleyball in the deep end. Of course, I sat out for the millionth time. I could hear them laughing and cheering. I was so jealous!

I begged my older brother Cal for help. "I'm tired of being scared," I whispered. "Can you give me some lessons?" He took me to the pool when there weren't many other people around. First, we practiced a few strokes. Then he taught me how to tread water and float on my back.

By the end of the summer, I was swimming and playing with my friends. It took a lot of hard work, but it was worth it!

Reading as a Writer

What words did Kelly use to show when events happened? Where could you add time clues in your own personal narrative?

In my final paper, I used time clues to connect ideas. I also made sure to use commas correctly.

Read the story "Dinner at Binh's House." As you read, stop and answer each question using text evidence.

Dinner at Binh's House

"Good-bye Mom," I called before I shut our front door. I walked to the house next door. My best friend, Binh, lives there. I was going to have dinner with Binh and his family.

Binh and I are the same age. He and his family are from Vietnam. Vietnam is a country in Asia. It is far away from the United States, on the other side of the world.

> **1** What do you see in the picture that helps you understand more about the story? Explain what the picture tells you.

Binh's family came to the United States to start a new life. They have lived next door to me for three years. Last month they became United States citizens. Binh's mom and dad had to study hard and learn a lot about our country. They are proud to be citizens of the United States. Binh is proud of them, too.

 COMMON CORE **RL.3.1** ask and answer questions to demonstrate understanding, referring to the text; **RL.3.2** recount stories and determine the message, lesson or moral; **RL.3.3** describe characters and explain how their actions contribute to the sequence of events; **RL.3.7** explain how illustrations contribute to the words

I like eating meals with Binh's family. Sometimes we eat American foods, such as pizza or barbecue. These foods were new to Binh's family when they came here, but they found out they like them.

Other times, Binh's mother and father make foods that people in Vietnam usually eat. When they became citizens of the United States, they had a big party. People brought all kinds of food. Some brought American food, and others brought Vietnamese food. It was a great party!

That night, Binh's mom said we were having Vietnamese food for dinner. I was happy to hear that. Eating new foods is an adventure.

My favorite dish at dinner was a beef and noodle soup called Bun Bo Hue. I have had beef many times before, and have had noodles in my soup, too. Some of the other ingredients were strange to me, though. I didn't think I would like the soup, but it was delicious!

The food was spicy, too. That's one way Vietnamese food is like some American foods. Binh taught me how to use chopsticks when eating Vietnamese food. Using chopsticks can be a challenge when you are used to eating with a spoon or fork.

---

 2 How does the narrator of this story feel about trying new things?

During dinner, we talked about school and work. We talked about our weekend plans, too. Sometimes Binh's family spoke to each other in Vietnamese, the language spoken by people from Vietnam. Mostly, though, they spoke in English, because I was there. They understand that English is the only language I know.

I remembered the very first time that I went to Binh's house. I wondered why Binh's father was very quiet. Later, Binh explained that his family usually speaks Vietnamese at home. His father understood English, but it was hard for him to speak it. Now Binh's father knows a lot more English, and he speaks often when I visit.

Binh told me that the English and Vietnamese languages are very different. For example, the Vietnamese word *ma* has six meanings. The meaning changes with the tone of voice you use to say the word.

One meaning for *ma* is mother. If you use a different tone, *ma* can mean horse. If you say *ma* another way, it means rice seedling. Imagine how confusing that can be!

 3 What does the narrator learn about the Vietnamese language?

I'm amazed that Binh has learned how to speak English so quickly. I'm trying to learn some Vietnamese, but it's going slowly for me. All the different tones are perplexing. I do not want to call my mother a horse or a rice seedling by mistake!

After dinner, I thanked Binh's family for the delicious meal. Then I invited Binh to come to my house for dinner the following night. We're having spicy barbecued shrimp. I know Binh will like it.

 4 What message does the author of this story give readers? Use examples from the story to support your answer.

Unit 2

Vocabulary in Context

☑ **TARGET VOCABULARY**

twitch
swoops
squeak
echoes
detail
slithers
snuggles
dozes

Vocabulary Reader

Context Cards

Nighttime Animals

COMMON CORE **L.3.6** acquire and use conversational, general academic, and domain-specific words and phrases

1 twitch
Rabbits twitch their noses, or move them quickly, to improve their sense of smell.

2 swoops
A bat quickly swoops down to catch insects.

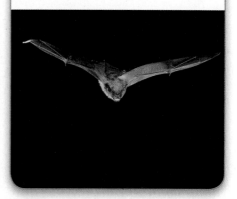

3 squeak
Hamsters and mice sometimes make a squeak, or high sound.

4 echoes
Hikers may hear echoes as sounds bounce off the walls of large caves.

Go Digital

▶ Study each Context Card.

▶ Make up a new sentence that uses two Vocabulary words.

5 detail

You can describe a moth by telling about each detail of its appearance.

6 slithers

This snake slithers, or slides, through the leaves looking for its dinner.

7 snuggles

An animal often snuggles with others for warmth and comfort.

8 dozes

The bat dozes lightly before falling asleep.

Read and Comprehend

✓ TARGET SKILL

Sequence of Events As you read *Bat Loves the Night,* note the **sequence of events** as Bat wakes up and goes out to hunt in the night. Look for signal words such as *now, then*, and *soon* to help you understand the connection between sentences and paragraphs. Use an organizer like the one below to record important events and keep track of the sequence.

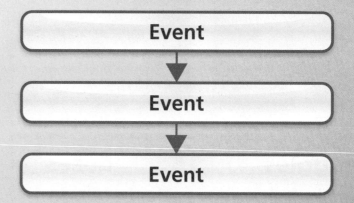

Event

↓

Event

↓

Event

✓ TARGET STRATEGY

Question Ask yourself **questions** about the selection as you read. Look for text evidence to help you answer the questions.

COMMON CORE **RI.3.1** ask and answer questions to demonstrate understanding, referring to the text; **RI.3.8** describe the connection between sentences and paragraphs in a text

208

Mammals

The many kinds of animals called mammals are different sizes and colors, and they live all over the world. They are all alike in a few important ways. All mammals

- are warm blooded. This means that their bodies stay the same temperature in hot and cold climates;

- have fur or hair;

- are vertebrates, which means they have a spine or backbone;

- drink milk from their mothers. Mothers care for their babies for a while before they can live on their own.

In *Bat Loves the Night*, you'll read about a mammal that flies, hunts at night, and uses its ears to find its way in the dark.

ANCHOR TEXT

BAT
LOVES
THE
NIGHT

✓ TARGET SKILL

Sequence of Events
Follow the sequence of events. Look for time-order words to help you.

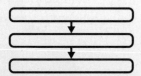

✓ GENRE

Narrative nonfiction
gives information about a topic but is told as a story. As you read, look for:

▶ factual information that tells a story
▶ features such as captions and realistic illustrations
▶ events that are told in time order

COMMON CORE **RI.3.4** determine the meaning of general academic and domain-specific words and phrases; **RI.3.8** describe the connection between sentences and paragraphs in a text; **RI.3.10** read and comprehend informational texts

  Go Digital

MEET THE AUTHOR

Nicola Davies

Nicola Davies has always been interested in animals. As a child, she spent much of her time in the garden, looking at ants and bird nests. After college, Nicola Davies worked as a zoologist. She studied bats, geese, and whales. Now Nicola Davies combines her love of animals and her writing. She has written books about sharks, turtles, and polar bears.

MEET THE ILLUSTRATOR

Sarah Fox-Davies

While Sarah Fox-Davies was making the illustrations for *Bat Loves the Night*, a bat flew into her studio. It landed right on her desk! Fox-Davies likes to draw animals in their natural environments. Her drawings of bats, beavers, bears, and other animals have appeared in many different magazines and children's books. Fox-Davies used pencils and watercolors to create the realistic illustrations for this book.

BAT
LOVES
THE
NIGHT

by Nicola Davies

illustrated by Sarah Fox-Davies

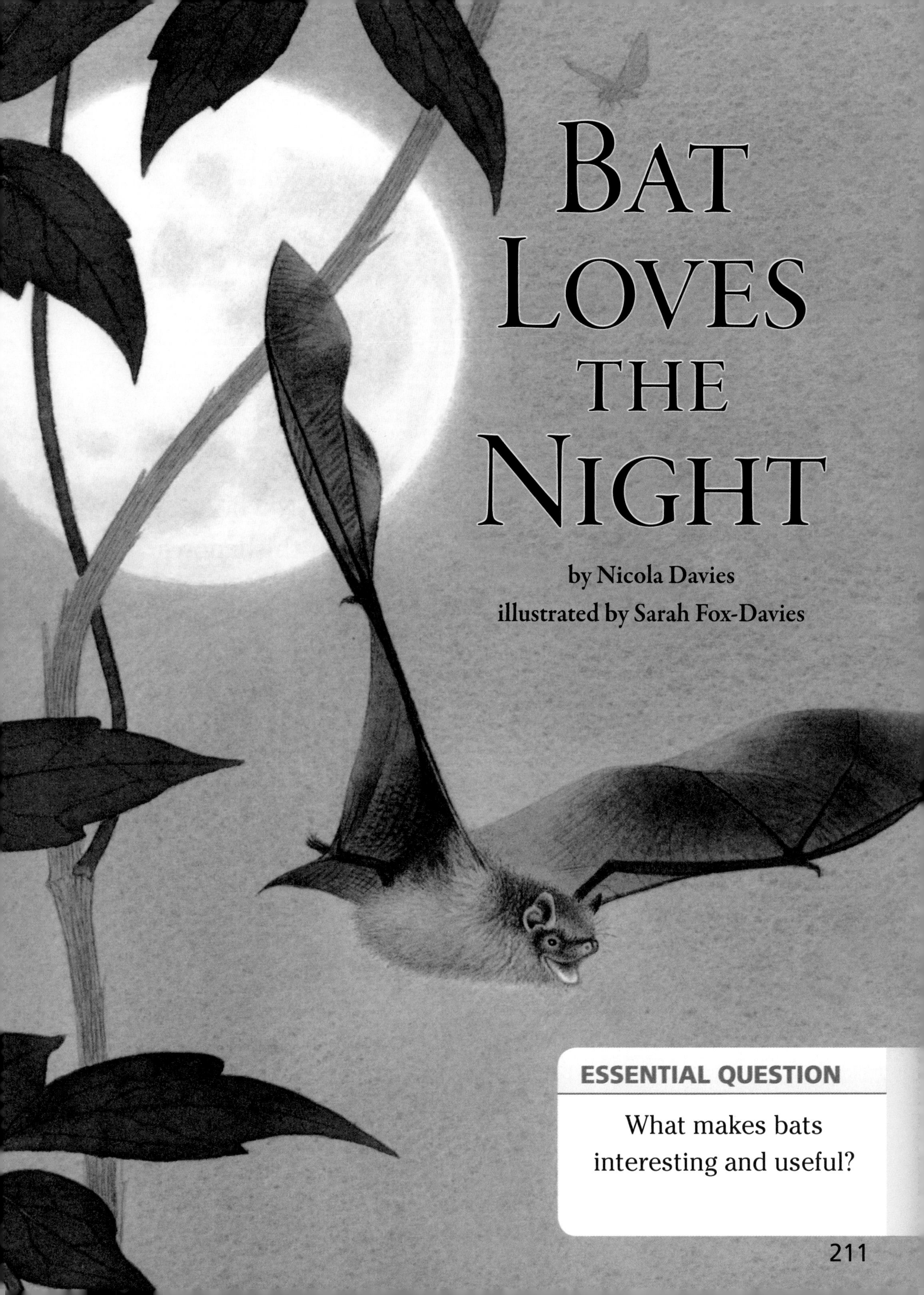

ESSENTIAL QUESTION

What makes bats interesting and useful?

Bat is waking, upside
down as usual, hanging
by her toenails.

Her beady eyes open.
Her pixie ears twitch.
She shakes her thistledown
fur.

She unfurls her wings,
made of skin so fine the
finger bones inside show
through.

The pipistrelle bat's body is no bigger than your thumb.

Now she unhooks her toes and
drops into black space. With a sound
like a tiny umbrella opening, she
flaps her wings.
    Bat is flying.

A bat's wing is its arm and hand. Four extra-long
fingers support the skin of the wing.

Out!

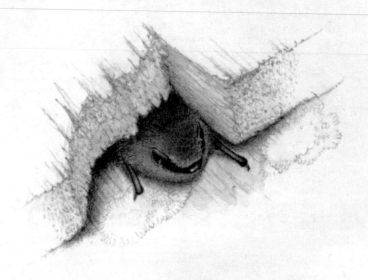

Out under the broken tile
into the nighttime garden.

Bats can see. But in the dark, good ears
are more useful than eyes.

Over bushes, under trees, between fence posts, through the tangled hedge she **swoops** untouched. Bat is at home in the darkness as a fish is in the water. She doesn't need to see—she can hear where she is going.

Bat shouts as she flies, louder than
a hammer blow, higher than a squeak.
She beams her voice around her like a
flashlight, and the echoes come singing
back. They carry a sound picture of all
her voice has touched. Listening hard,
Bat can hear every detail, the smallest
twigs, the shape of leaves.

Using sound to find your way like this is called
echolocation. The noise bats make when they
shout is too high for humans to hear.

Gliding and fluttering back and forth, she shouts her torch of sound among the trees, listening for her supper.

All is still. . . .

ANALYZE THE TEXT

Domain-Specific Vocabulary
What word on page 216 are you likely to find only in science-related texts? What does it mean?

Then a fat moth takes flight below her.

A bat can eat dozens of big moths in a single night—
or thousands of tiny flies, gnats, and mosquitoes.

Bat plunges, fast as blinking,
and grabs it in her open mouth.
But the moth's pearly scales are
moon-dust slippery. It slithers
from between her teeth.

Bat dives, nets it with a wing tip,
scoops it to her mouth.
This time she bites hard. Its
wings fall away, like the wrapper
from a candy.

In a moment the
moth is eaten. Bat
sneezes. The dusty
scales got up her
nose.

Most species of bats eat insects, but there are
some that eat fruit, fish, frogs, even blood!

219

Hunting time has run out. The dark will soon be gone. In the east, the sky is getting light. It's past Bat's bedtime.

Bats are nocturnal. That means they rest by day and come out at night to search for food.

She flies to the roof in the last shadows
and swoops in under the broken tile.

ANALYZE THE TEXT

Sequence of Events What sequence of events does this selection tell about?

The place where bats sleep in the day is called a roost.
It can be in a building, a cave, or a tree,
so long as it's dry and safe.

221

Inside, there are squeakings. Fifty
hungry batlings hang in a huddle,
hooked to a rafter by oversized feet.
Bat lands and pushes in among them,
toes first, upside down again.

Baby bats can't fly. Sometimes mother bats carry their babies
when they go out, but mostly the babies stay behind in the roost
and crowd together to keep warm.

Bat knows her baby's voice, and calls
to it. The velvet scrap batling climbs aboard
and clings to Bat's fur by its coat-hanger feet.
Wrapped in her leathery wings, the baby
snuggles to sleep.

Baby bats drink mother's milk until they learn to fly at a few
weeks old. Then they can leave the roost at night to find
their own food.

Outside, the birds are singing. The flowers turn their faces to the sun. But inside the roof hole, the darkness stays. Bat dozes with her batling, waiting.

When the tide of night rises again, Bat will wake and plunge into the blackness, shouting.

Bat loves the night.

Dig Deeper

How to Analyze the Text

Use these pages to learn about Sequence of Events and Domain-Specific Vocabulary. Then read *Bat Loves the Night* again to apply what you learned.

Sequence of Events

In narrative nonfiction like *Bat Loves the Night,* an author may choose to arrange events and details in the **sequence,** or order, in which they happen. Look back at page 212. Note the action sequence in which Bat wakes up.

Time-order words also are included to help readers connect the order of events as they read from sentence to sentence and paragraph to paragraph. Look at pages 218 and 219, where Bat catches a moth. The words *then, this time*, and *in a moment* show the sequence of what happens.

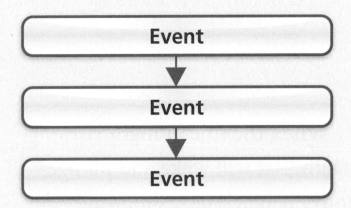

Event

↓

Event

↓

Event

RI.3.4 determine the meaning of general academic and domain-specific words and phrases; **RI.3.8** describe the connection between sentences and paragraphs in a text; **L.3.4.a** use sentence-level context as a clue to the meaning of a word or phrase

Domain-Specific Vocabulary

In *Bat Loves the Night*, you read a lot of scientific information about bats. Some words are related to the topic, or **domain,** of science. A science word may be explained in the text, or you can use context clues to figure out the meaning.

The word *species* is on page 219. The text does not define the word, but it talks about what some bats eat. From this context, you can figure out that *species* means "a kind of." On page 220, you read the word *nocturnal*. How does the text define that word?

Your Turn

Turn and Talk Review the selection with a partner to prepare to discuss this question: *What makes bats interesting and useful?* As you discuss, take turns listening carefully and adding your own ideas to those of your partner. Point to text evidence to support your answer.

Classroom Conversation

Continue your discussion of *Bat Loves the Night* by explaining your answers to these questions:

1 How does Bat see in the dark?

2 How does the author use words to help you picture Bat's hunt?

3 Do you think you could find your way in the dark by listening? What would you listen for?

Response In *Bat Loves the Night* you read about what bats eat. Why do bats hunt for moths and insects at night? Write a paragraph that explains what you learned. Use evidence from the text to support your answer.

Writing Tip

Use a variety of simple and compound sentences in your writing. Make sure that you use a conjunction and correct punctuation in each compound sentence.

COMMON CORE **RI.3.2** determine the main idea/recount details and explain how they support the main idea; **RI.3.7** use information gained from illustrations and words to demonstrate understanding; **W.3.10** write routinely over extended time frames or short time frames; **SL.3.1a** come to discussions prepared/explicitly draw on preparation and other information about the topic; **L.3.1h** use coordinating and subordinating conjunctions; **L.3.1i** produce simple, compound, and complex sentences

POETRY

☑ GENRE

Poetry uses the sound and rhythm of words to show images and to express feelings.

☑ TEXT FOCUS

Imagery is the use of vivid descriptions that help readers form an image, or picture, in their minds.

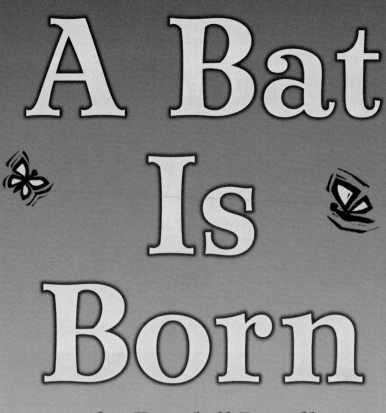

A Bat Is Born

by Randall Jarrell

illustrated by

Sue Todd

 COMMON CORE **RL.3.5** refer to parts of stories, dramas, and poems/describe how each part builds on earlier sections; **RL.3.10** read and comprehend literature

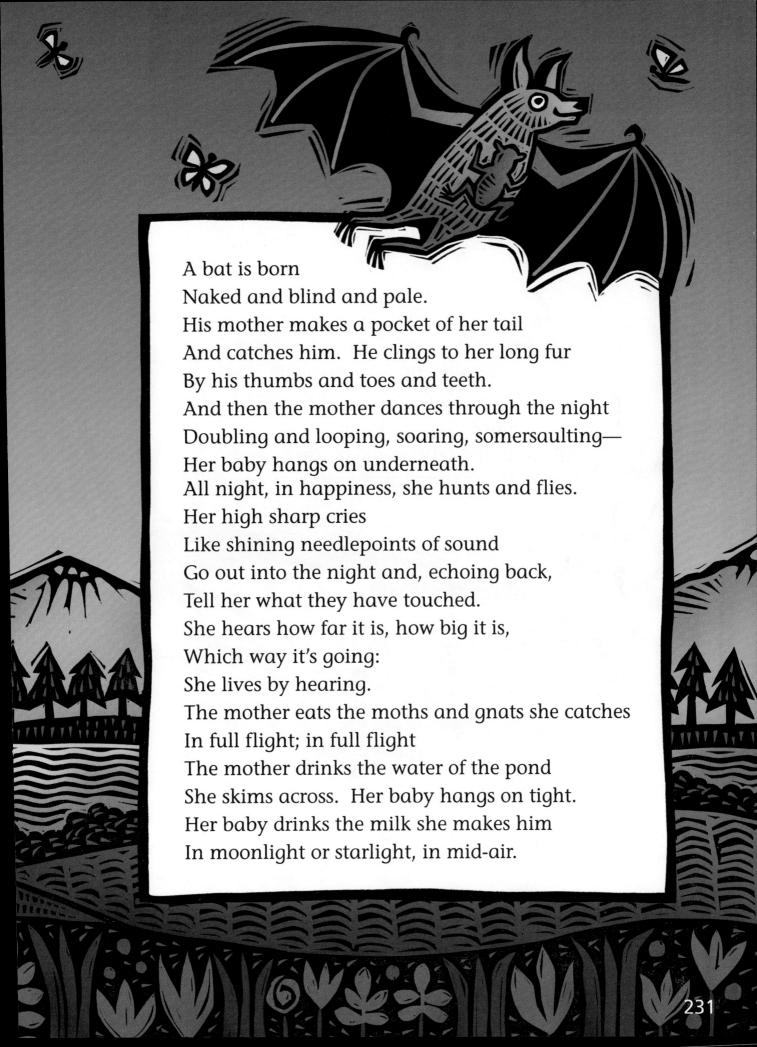

A bat is born
Naked and blind and pale.
His mother makes a pocket of her tail
And catches him. He clings to her long fur
By his thumbs and toes and teeth.
And then the mother dances through the night
Doubling and looping, soaring, somersaulting—
Her baby hangs on underneath.
All night, in happiness, she hunts and flies.
Her high sharp cries
Like shining needlepoints of sound
Go out into the night and, echoing back,
Tell her what they have touched.
She hears how far it is, how big it is,
Which way it's going:
She lives by hearing.
The mother eats the moths and gnats she catches
In full flight; in full flight
The mother drinks the water of the pond
She skims across. Her baby hangs on tight.
Her baby drinks the milk she makes him
In moonlight or starlight, in mid-air.

Their single shadow, printed on the moon
Or fluttering across the stars,
Whirls on all night; at daybreak
The tired mother flaps home to her rafter.
The others all are there.
They hang themselves up by their toes,
They wrap themselves in their brown wings.
Bunched upside down, they sleep in air.
Their sharp ears, their sharp teeth, their
    quick sharp faces
Are dull and slow and mild.
All the bright day, as the mother sleeps,
She folds her wings about her sleeping child.

Compare Texts

TEXT TO TEXT

Write an Explanation Use information from *Bat Loves the Night* and "A Bat Is Born" to write an explanatory paragraph about bats. Use scientific words such as *echolocation* to tell about bats' special abilities. Include an illustration of a bat with your paragraph. Share your paragraph with the class.

TEXT TO SELF

Share Information What new information did you learn about mother bats and their babies in *Bat Loves the Night* and "A Bat Is Born"? Make a list and share it with a partner.

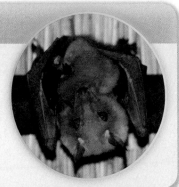

TEXT TO WORLD

Defend Bats Using the information you have learned about bats, what would you say if your town wanted to get rid of bats? Discuss your ideas with a small group.

COMMON CORE **RL.3.1** ask and answer questions to demonstrate understanding, referring to the text; **RI.3.1** ask and answer questions to demonstrate understanding, referring to the text; **W.3.2a** introduce a topic and group related information/include illustrations; **SL.3.1a** come to discussions prepared/explicitly draw on preparation and other information about the topic; **L.3.6** acquire and use conversational, general academic, and domain-specific words and phrases

Grammar

What Is a Verb? The **verb** is the main word in the predicate. An **action verb** is a word that tells what people or things do.

Action Verb	
The bats roost in an old attic.	At sunset, they leave the attic.
They sleep during the day.	They search for food.

Forms of the verb *be* do not show action. They tell what something is or was.

> The bat is a mammal that can fly.
> That fact was surprising to me.

Try This! **Work with a partner. Read each sentence aloud. Identify the verb in each sentence. Explain whether the verb is an action verb or a form of *be*.**

1. Mother bats snuggle with their babies.

2. Each mother hears her baby's voice.

3. At night they swoop through the air.

4. Bats catch moths and mosquitoes.

5. The night is full of sounds.

Combining sentences can make your writing clearer. When two sentences have the same subject, you can put the sentences together. Join the predicates and put the word *and* between them to form a compound predicate.

Short, Choppy Sentences

Eli builds a bat house.

Eli puts it in his garden.

Longer, Smoother Sentence

Eli builds a bat house and puts it in his garden.

 Connect Grammar to Writing

As you revise your response paragraph, try to use compound predicates to join short sentences. Join the predicates with the conjunction *and*.

W.3.1a introduce the topic, state an opinion, and create an organizational structure; **W.3.1b** provide reasons that support the opinion; **W.3.1c** use linking words and phrases to connect opinion and reasons; **W.3.1d** provide a concluding statement or section

Opinion Writing

☑ **Ideas** When you write a **response paragraph** to give your opinion about a text, start by introducing the topic. Write your sentence so that your opinion is clear. Then support your opinion by giving examples or details from the text. End your paragraph with a concluding statement that wraps up your ideas.

Kareem wrote a response to this question, *In* Bat Loves the Night, *why is sound so important to Bat?* As Kareem revised his answer, he added examples from the selection.

Writing Traits Checklist

☑ **Ideas**
Did I use examples from the selection?

☑ **Organization**
Did I use words from the question?

☑ **Word Choice**
Did I use linking words to connect my opinions and reasons?

☑ **Voice**
Did I use formal language to address my audience?

☑ **Sentence Fluency**
Did I combine short, choppy sentences?

☑ **Conventions**
Did I use a computer to check my spelling?

Revised Draft

In <u>Bat Loves the Night</u>, sound is important to Bat because she uses it to find her way and to hunt in the dark. She calls out as she flies. The sound bounces off objects, and ~~The sound bounces~~ back to Bat's ears.

This call is a sound that is too high for humans to hear.

236

Bats Listen

by Kareem Mahmood

In <u>Bat Loves the Night</u>, sound is important to Bat because she uses it to find her way and to hunt in the dark. She calls out as she flies. This call is a sound that is too high for humans to hear. The sound bounces off objects and back to Bat's ears. Bat's hearing is so good she can "hear" the smallest details, such as a small twig. Bat also uses sound to find food. When Bat's call bounces off a moth, Bat hears where the insect is. Then she can catch and eat the insect. Sound helps Bat locate her baby in her roost as well. She knows her baby's squeak, and the baby knows its mother's call. Without sound, Bat would bump into things while flying, and she could not find food or her baby.

Reading as a Writer

Which examples did Kareem use to explain his answer? Where can you add selection details or examples in your paragraph?

I added more examples from the selection. I also combined sentences that had the same subject.

Vocabulary in Context

☑ TARGET VOCABULARY

imagine
tools
illustrate
scribbles
sketches
tracing
research
textures

Vocabulary Reader

Context Cards

COMMON CORE

L.3.6 acquire and use conversational, general academic, and domain-specific words and phrases

238

1 imagine
Some artists paint real things. Other artists paint things that they imagine.

2 tools
Artists use tools such as brushes, pencils, and markers to make art.

3 illustrate
This artist has started to illustrate, or draw, pictures for a storybook.

4 scribbles
Most children make messy scribbles before they learn to draw well.

Go Digital

▶ Study each Context Card.

▶ Discuss one picture. Use a different Vocabulary word from the one on the card.

5 sketches

Painters often make sketches, or rough drawings, before they begin to paint.

6 tracing

Using see-through tracing paper lets you make an exact copy of something.

7 research

Sometimes artists need to do research to find out what things look like.

8 textures

Paper can have different textures. It can look and feel smooth or rough.

Read and Comprehend

 Go Digital

☑ TARGET SKILL

Text and Graphic Features Authors use **text features,** such as headings, and **graphic features,** such as drawings, to help them organize and explain their ideas. As you read *What Do Illustrators Do?*, look for text and graphic features the author uses to make her ideas clearer. A chart like the one below will help you list special features and tell why the author used them.

Text or Graphic Feature	Purpose

☑ TARGET STRATEGY

Analyze/Evaluate As you read *What Do Illustrators Do?*, **analyze,** or think about, the information. Then **evaluate,** or judge, how well the author explained her ideas with examples and text evidence.

Visual Arts

Art is found in many places. Visual art is something you can see and examine. You'll find visual art in museums, on buildings, and maybe on the walls of your own home. You can also see art in many books.

In *What Do Illustrators Do?*, you will learn how illustrators create the pictures that help tell a story. You will also see how the author, who is also an illustrator, wrote and illustrated her own book.

ANCHOR TEXT

What Do Illustrators Do?

Written and Illustrated by
Eileen Christelow

☑ TARGET SKILL

Text and Graphic Features Think about how words and art work together to explain ideas.

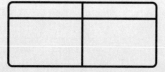

☑ GENRE

Informational text gives you facts about a topic. As you read, look for:

▶ details that support facts
▶ the way the information is organized
▶ illustrations that help explain the topic

 COMMON CORE **RI.3.3** describe the relationship between a series of historical events/scientific ideas/steps in technical procedures; **RI.3.7** use information gained from illustrations and words to demonstrate understanding; **RI.3.8** describe the connection between sentences and paragraphs in a text; **RI.3.10** read and comprehend informational texts

242 Go Digital

MEET THE AUTHOR AND ILLUSTRATOR

Eileen Christelow

Whenever Eileen Christelow speaks to students, they always ask, "What do you do?" To explain her job as both a writer and an illustrator, she created the books *What Do Authors Do?* and *What Do Illustrators Do?*

The funny cat in *What Do Illustrators Do?* is based on her daughter's cat, Leonard. Actually, the cat in the book is orange because Christelow wanted a more colorful cat. The real Leonard is mostly gray and tan.

What Do Illustrators Do?

written and illustrated by
Eileen Christelow

ESSENTIAL QUESTION

How do pictures help to tell a story?

What do illustrators do? They tell stories with pictures. This picture shows where two illustrators live and work.

Suppose those two illustrators each decided to illustrate *Jack and the Beanstalk*. Would they tell the story the same way? Would they draw the same kind of pictures?

I'm going to retell and illustrate JACK AND THE BEANSTALK. Go lie down, Scooter! I'll take you for a walk later.

I've been asked to illustrate JACK AND THE BEANSTALK. Go away, Leonard!

First, illustrators decide which scenes in the story they want to illustrate . . .

There are so many scenes I want to illustrate! But I need to fit all of JACK AND THE BEANSTALK into 32 pages. That's a tight fit!

Are all books 32 pages?

Most picture books are.

A *plan* shows which pictures go on which pages.

After illustrators make a plan for their book, they need to make a *dummy*. (A dummy is a model of the book.) First they decide what shape and size the book will be.

Would you choose a square, vertical, or horizontal dummy?

Dummy? I'm not a dummy!

Then they make sketches of the pictures that will go on each page of the dummy. The first sketches are often rough scribbles on tracing paper.

As they are sketching, illustrators need to decide how things will look: the characters, their clothes, the setting. Illustrators can use their imaginations or they may have to do some research.

ANALYZE THE TEXT

Text and Graphic Features
How do the graphic features on this page help you understand the text?

Some illustrators are also authors. They can change their story as they work on the sketches.

Each illustration has a different problem. For instance: From what *point of view* do you draw the magic bean being planted?

How do you draw a beanstalk so it looks like it's growing?

Raised eyebrows? Eyes wide open? Mouth open?

Jacqueline tiptoed across the table. "Hurry up!" whispered the hen. "She never sleeps for long!"

How would it feel to run across a table right under the nose of a sleeping GIANT?

Illustrators need to draw how their characters feel. Sometimes they make faces in a mirror to see how an expression would look. Other times illustrators need someone else to model for them.

Each illustrator has a different *style* of drawing, just as every person has a different style of handwriting.

Different styles for drawing Jack and Jacqueline

We're trying a new style.

When illustrators have finished their dummies, they show them to the editor and the designer at the publishing company.

The editor decides whether the pictures tell the story. The designer makes suggestions about the design of the book. She chooses the typeface for the words and the cover.

I love your illustrations! But Jack looks too old at the end of the book. And on page 21 the giant doesn't look mean enough.

Okay, those things should be easy to fix.

If she loves his book, why does she want him to change it?

She's just suggesting ways to make it better!

ANALYZE THE TEXT

Sequence of Events How does the author show the steps in time order? Remember to look at the text in the illustrations, too.

253

Illustrators need to decide how they want to do the finished illustrations.

They can draw different kinds of lines and textures with different kinds of tools.

pencil

brush

pen with flexible point

felt tip pen

They can color their illustrations with paint,
pastels, pencils, or crayons. They can do an illustration
without any black line at all!

watercolors

watercolor crayons

colored pencils

no black line

Sometimes illustrators throw away their pictures and start again. Sometimes they change the colors. Or they may change the composition. It can take months to finish all the illustrations for a picture book.

Before they are sent to the publisher, they need to be checked to make sure nothing is left out.

Illustrators often do the cover of the book last. The cover tells a lot about a story: What is it about? Does it look interesting?

The cover is a clue to how the illustrator will tell the story. Would these covers make you want to read the books?

This illustration tells how the two illustrators celebrated when they finally finished all that work!

Dig Deeper

How to Analyze the Text

Use these pages to learn about Text and Graphic Features and Sequence of Events. Then read *What Do Illustrators Do?* again to apply what you learned.

Text and Graphic Features

In an informational text like *What Do Illustrators Do?*, words and art work together to tell about a topic. **Text features** help readers find information. For example, bold or dark type shows important words. Labels tell you more about pictures.

Graphic features can be pictures and charts. They give more information about the text. For example, text can tell about a dog. A picture can show you exactly what the dog looks like.

Look back at page 244 in *What Do Illustrators Do?* Notice how the author uses speech balloons to tell two stories. As you read, watch for other features.

Text or Graphic Feature	Purpose

COMMON CORE **RI.3.3** describe the relationship between a series of historical events/scientific ideas/steps in technical procedures; **RI.3.7** use information gained from illustrations and words to demonstrate understanding; **RI.3.8** describe the connection between sentences and paragraphs in a text

Sequence of Events

The informational text *What Do Illustrators Do?* tells about the steps an illustrator takes to illustrate a book. The author wrote about the steps in the **sequence,** or order, they happen. Turn to pages 245 and 246 to read about the first steps. If you made a list, it would look something like this:

1. Decides which scenes to illustrate

2. Makes a plan

3. Makes a dummy

Your Turn

 Turn and Talk Review the selection with a partner to prepare to discuss this question: *How do pictures help to tell a story?* During your discussion, ask questions if you do not understand something your partner said.

 Classroom Conversation

Continue your discussion of *What Do Illustrators Do?* by explaining your answers to these questions:

1. What are some decisions an illustrator must make when illustrating a book?

2. How does an illustrator work with others to produce a book?

3. Do you think the author did a good job illustrating this selection? What evidence from the text supports your opinion?

264

WRITE ABOUT READING

Response Which is more important in a book—the words or the pictures? Write a paragraph that states your opinion. Support your opinion with evidence from *What Do Illustrators Do?* and other books you have read.

Writing Tip

State your opinion clearly at the beginning of your paragraph. Then give reasons to support it. Use linking words such as *because* and *for example*. End with a concluding statement that wraps up your ideas.

COMMON CORE **RI.3.7** use information gained from illustrations and words to demonstrate understanding; **W.3.1a** introduce the topic, state an opinion, and create an organizational structure; **W.3.1b** provide reasons that support the opinion; **W.3.1d** provide a concluding statement or section; **SL.3.1a** come to discussions prepared/explicitly draw on preparation and other information about the topic; **SL.3.1c** ask questions to check understanding, stay on topic, and link comments to others' remarks

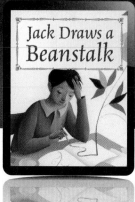

Jack Draws a Beanstalk

by Anne O'Brien

Jack loved to make up stories and illustrate them. He did research to find out what things looked like. He sketched his ideas over and over on tracing paper. He colored the pictures with different textures. When his pictures were just right, he could imagine that his stories were real.

One night, Jack drew a bean vine. "I wish I had a magic bean vine, just like in the fairy tale," Jack said. He worked on the sketches until he fell asleep.

When he woke up, there was the bean vine, growing out of his sketchbook. His scribbles were coming to life!

Go Digital

Jack grabbed his sketchbook and pencil and began to climb the beanstalk. He came to a huge castle in the clouds, just like the one in the fairy tale. And there was the giant's wife, who happily served Jack tea.

"But you must leave before my husband comes home," the giant's wife said. "He might try to eat you for dinner!"

Just then they heard a rumble like loud thunder. "He's home early!" cried the wife. She popped Jack into her apron pocket.

Jack heard the giant's voice yelling, "FEE FI FO FUM!"

"Oh, no," Jack said to himself. "This is too much like the fairy tale! The only tools I've got to help me escape are my sketchbook and pencil!"

Jack was shaking when he began to draw. He drew a magic
hen. The hen came to life and laid a golden egg, just like in the
fairy tale.

"Cluck, cluck!"

The wife reached into her pocket and pulled out the hen and
the golden egg. While the two giants exclaimed over the hen,
Jack escaped out of the castle and climbed down the vine.

When Jack got home, he opened his sketchbook.
He erased the bean vine as fast as he could. "From now
on, I'll be careful about what I wish for!" said Jack.

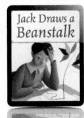

Compare Texts

TEXT TO TEXT

Compare Stories Find a copy of the traditional tale "Jack and the Beanstalk" in your library or online. *Jack Draws a Beanstalk* is based on this story. In a small group, talk about how the two stories are alike and different. Give details about characters, setting, and plot. Share what you like about each story.

TEXT TO SELF

Illustrate a Scene Choose a scene from *Jack Draws a Beanstalk*. Use what you learned in *What Do Illustrators Do?* to illustrate that part of the story.

TEXT TO WORLD

Compare Characters Think about Jack in *Jack Draws a Beanstalk* and the illustrators in *What Do Illustrators Do?* How are these characters the same and different? Which illustrator's job seems the most exciting? Discuss your ideas with a partner. Provide evidence from both texts to support your ideas.

COMMON CORE **RL3.1** ask and answer questions to demonstrate understanding, referring to the text; **RL.3.3** describe characters and explain how their actions contribute to the sequence of events; **SL.3.1a** come to discussions prepared/explicitly draw on preparation and other information about the topic

Grammar

Verb Tenses A verb tells when something happens. The **tense** of a verb lets you know whether something happens in the **present**, in the **past**, or in the **future**. In the chart below, notice how the verb form of *stay* and *illustrate* changes to explain when something happens.

Present Tense	Past Tense	Future Tense
Now, the dog stays inside.	Yesterday, the dog stayed inside.	Tomorrow, the dog will stay inside.
The artist illustrates a book.	The artist illustrated a book.	The artist will illustrate a book.

Try This! **Work with a partner. Tell whether the underlined verb is in the present tense, the past tense, or the future tense.**

1 Andy <u>works</u> as an illustrator.

2 He <u>painted</u> pictures in art class.

3 The teachers <u>showed</u> him other paintings.

4 A company <u>will publish</u> his new book next year.

5 His friends <u>will get</u> a copy then.

When you write, make sure your verbs all tell about actions that happen in the same time. This will help make your writing clear.

Incorrect Paragraph

Yesterday, Mary looked at a book. Then she will paint an elephant. Last, she colors a shady tree.

Correct Paragraph

Yesterday, Mary looked at a book. Then she painted an elephant. Last, she colored a shady tree.

 Connect Grammar to Writing

As you revise your opinion piece, make sure all the verbs are in the same tense.

W.3.1a introduce the topic, state an opinion, and create an organizational structure; **W.3.1b** provide reasons that support the opinion; **W.3.1c** use linking words and phrases to connect opinion and reasons; **W.3.1d** provide a concluding statement or section

Opinion Writing

✔️ **Organization** In an **opinion piece,** a good writer first states an opinion. The opinion tells readers what the writer believes or thinks about a topic. Then the writer gives reasons that support the opinion. **Linking words and phrases,** such as *since* and *for example,* connect the opinion and reasons. Finally, the writer ends with a **conclusion** that sums up all the ideas.

Emma wrote a first draft of her opinion piece about the illustrations in *Jack Draws a Beanstalk*. Then she revised her draft. She added a reason to make her writing stronger. She also added a linking phrase to help connect the ideas.

Writing Traits Checklist

✔️ **Ideas**
Did I give reasons to support my opinion?

✔️ **Organization**
Did I tell my opinion in the introduction?

✔️ **Word Choice**
Did I use linking words and phrases?

✔️ **Voice**
Did I let my feelings come through?

✔️ **Sentence Fluency**
Do my sentences flow smoothly?

✔️ **Conventions**
Did I indent each paragraph?

Revised Draft

First, the pictures are big, bright, and
I love the blues and greens that the
illustrator chose.

colorful. The pictures are clever, too.
  ∧
For example,

The illustrator draws the beanstalk
∧

growing right off the page.

272

Good Story, Great Pictures

by Emma Corcoran

Pictures are important in a storybook. The pictures in <u>Jack Draws a Beanstalk</u> were a big reason I enjoyed reading the story. In fact, it is one of the best illustrated stories I have seen.

First, the pictures are big, bright, and colorful. I love the blues and greens that the illustrator chose. The pictures are clever, too. For example, the illustrator draws the beanstalk growing right off the page.

Second, the illustrations really help tell the story. They show me that the giant's wife looks kind and that the castle is grand. I would not know these things if the illustrations weren't there.

The illustrator did a wonderful job drawing pictures for <u>Jack Draws a Beanstalk</u>. I just wish the story was longer so there would be more illustrations to see.

Reading as a Writer

Emma added a phrase to help you see how her ideas are connected. What linking words or phrases can you add to your opinion piece?

In my final paper, I added another reason I thought the illustrations were good. It helps support my opinion. I added a linking phrase, too.

Vocabulary in Context

✓ **TARGET VOCABULARY**

harvest
separate
ashamed
borders
advice
borrow
patch
serious

Vocabulary Reader

All About Grass

Context Cards

COMMON CORE

L.3.6 acquire and use conversational, general academic, and domain-specific words and phrases

274

---

1 harvest

When there is a lot of corn to pick, it makes a good harvest.

2 separate

Separate, or divide, different kinds of seeds before planting them.

3 ashamed

Don't feel ashamed, or guilty, if you forget to water a plant!

4 borders

This farm has a fence along its borders to keep the animals inside.

Go Digital

▶ Study each Context Card.

▶ Make up a new context sentence using two Vocabulary words.

5 advice

Adults often give good advice. They have ideas about solving problems.

6 borrow

If you do not have gardening tools, you could borrow some from a friend.

7 patch

You can use a fairly small patch, or area, of land to grow vegetables.

8 serious

If you are serious about something, you are not joking or fooling around.

Read and Comprehend

✓ TARGET SKILL

Conclusions As you read *The Harvest Birds*, look for details about events and characters in the story. Use these details to draw **conclusions**, or figure out what the author means but does not directly state. Use a chart like this one to record text evidence. Describe your conclusions and list the details that helped you draw them.

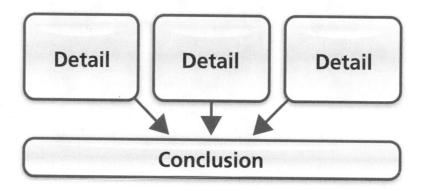

| Detail | Detail | Detail |

Conclusion

✓ TARGET STRATEGY

Infer/Predict Use your conclusions to **infer,** or figure out, the message of this story. **Predict** what the author wants to teach readers through the story.

 COMMON CORE

RL.3.1 ask and answer questions to demonstrate understanding, referring to the text; **RL.3.2** recount stories and determine the message, lesson, or moral

276

Traditions

Our world is made up of many cultures. Groups of people who share a way of life have their own culture. It includes language, music, art, and food. Each culture also has traditions. These are beliefs and actions that have been followed and passed down from one generation to the next.

Folktales are part of a culture's traditions. These stories explain the world in some way or teach people how to behave. *The Harvest Birds* is a Mexican folktale. In this story, the main character learns lessons about nature, farming, and even about himself.

ANCHOR TEXT

THE
HARVEST
BIRDS

✓ TARGET SKILL

Conclusions Use details to figure out ideas about story events and characters that the author doesn't state.

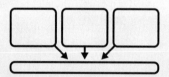

✓ GENRE

Folktales are stories that were first told orally. They reflect a culture's customs. As you read, look for:

▶ a plot that may also teach a lesson
▶ a main character who shows the values of a culture
▶ information about the customs of a culture

COMMON CORE **RL.3.1** ask and answer questions to demonstrate understanding, referring to the text; **RL.3.10** read and comprehend literature

 Go Digital

MEET THE AUTHOR

Blanca López de Mariscal

Blanca López de Mariscal teaches at a university in Mexico. She writes and gives speeches about Mexican art, history, and literature. *The Harvest Birds* is her first children's book. She says she wrote this story because it was important to her to introduce children to Mexican storytelling.

MEET THE ILLUSTRATOR

Linda Cane

Linda Cane lives in the country. She has two dogs, a horse, a cat, and two peacocks! Cane loves outdoor activities, such as hiking, skiing, and horseback riding. She has traveled to many places in the United States and all over the world.

THE HARVEST BIRDS

by Blanca López de Mariscal

illustrated by Linda Cane

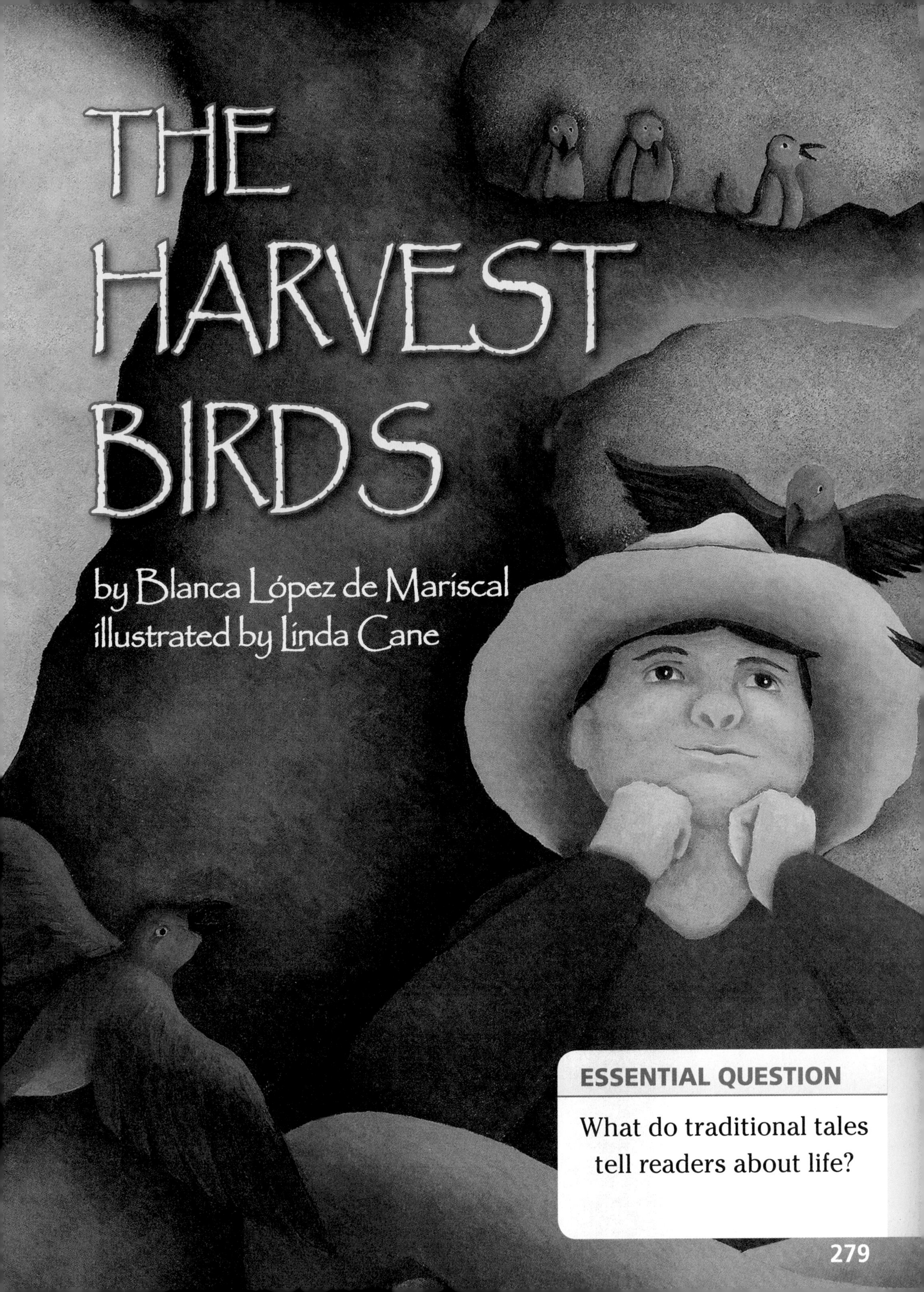

ESSENTIAL QUESTION

What do traditional tales tell readers about life?

In a little town where everyone knew everyone, there lived a young man called Juan Zanate (sah NAH tay). He was given this name because he was always seen with one or two zanate birds.

Juan used to sit under his favorite tree, dreaming and planning his life. He had wanted to have his own land, as his father and grandfather had. However, when his father died and the land was divided, there was enough for only his two older brothers. Because of this, Juan had to go to work in the shops of the town.

"If only I had my own land, my life would be different," Juan thought. He went to see Don Tobias, the richest man in town, and asked to borrow a little piece of his land.

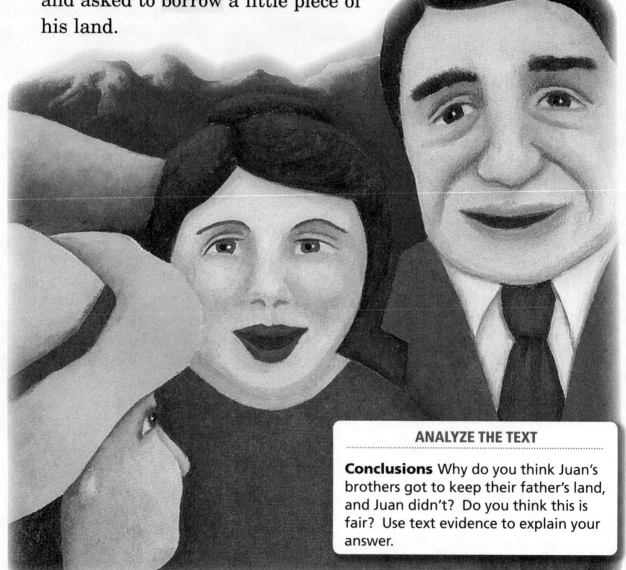

ANALYZE THE TEXT

Conclusions Why do you think Juan's brothers got to keep their father's land, and Juan didn't? Do you think this is fair? Use text evidence to explain your answer.

280

Don Tobias burst out laughing, and his wife laughed with him. "Why should I let you use my land?" he asked. "You don't know anything about making things grow."

Sad and ashamed, Juan returned to sit under his tree. It was the only place where he felt really happy. In its huge branches lived a flock of zanate birds who were so used to him that they thought of him as their friend.

There was one bird who cared very much for Juan and wanted him to find his way in life. This bird was always around Juan, resting on his shoulder or riding on his hat. Juan named him Grajo (GRAH hoh), or Crow, because zanates have black feathers.

After sitting and thinking for a long time, Juan decided to visit the oldest man of the town. "Old people know many things because they've lived longer," Juan thought. "He'll give me some advice, and maybe he'll even help me."

Juan greeted the old man, whom everyone called Grandpa Chon, with respect. The old man seemed to be in a good mood, so Juan dared to ask him for a piece of land. "Let me prove to you that I can be a good farmer and make things grow," he begged.

Grandpa Chon became serious. "I will help you," he said. "I will let you use some land. If you fail, however, you must work for me for free for as many days as you have used my land."

Juan ran into the town, shouting the good news. Instead of being happy for him, though, people laughed at him.

"Better you should straighten up my shop. Where you plant, not even weeds will grow," shouted the carpenter.

"Don't waste your time Juan. Come and work on this wheel," called the blacksmith.

"Help me with these sacks of flour and stop dreaming," added the baker.

Juan decided that nothing anyone said would stop him. "It's time to get to work," he told himself. He began to prepare his land for planting. It was a very tiny patch of land and didn't offer much promise of a big harvest. Still, Juan kept working, watched over by his good friends, the zanates.

"My head is small, like my garden patch, but it is big enough to hold many dreams," thought Juan.

He needed seeds to plant, but didn't have money to buy them, so he went to the shop and asked for some.

"Juan, sweep up the corn, bean, and squash seeds from my floor and take them to my pigs," the shop owner said. "Then if you wish, you can take some seeds for yourself."

Juan was happy, because now he had
seeds to plant. He didn't scare away
the zanates the way the other farmers
did. Instead, he gave them some of his
leftover seeds to eat so they wouldn't
be hungry. After all, the zanates were
his friends and he cared for them very
much. Grajo was always with him,
giving him advice as he worked.

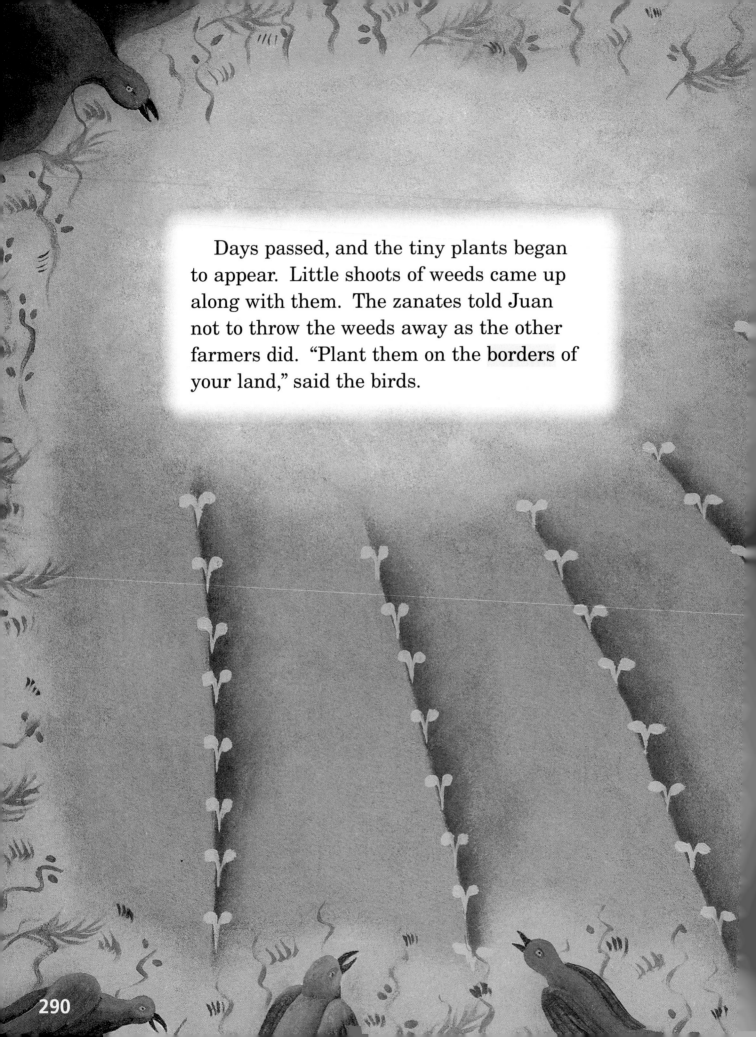

Days passed, and the tiny plants began to appear. Little shoots of weeds came up along with them. The zanates told Juan not to throw the weeds away as the other farmers did. "Plant them on the borders of your land," said the birds.

When the other farmers heard what Juan was doing, they laughed at him. "Imagine keeping weeds in your field!"

At harvest time, everyone was waiting to make fun of Juan once again. They were sure he would fail. When Juan arrived in town, everyone was amazed. He brought a wonderful harvest—huge ears of corn, brightly colored squashes, and tasty-looking beans.

"How did you do it?" they all wanted to know. Juan smiled and answered, "I did it with the help of my friends the zanates, the harvest birds. I learned to listen to the voice of nature!"

"Work for me, Juan!" everyone shouted. "Teach me your secrets!"

"No," answered the old man. "Juan works for no one now, because I am going to give him the land that he harvested."

ANALYZE THE TEXT

Literal and Nonliteral Meanings
Where does the author use words that make nature seem like a person? What do these words really mean?

After selling the crop at an excellent price, Juan Zanate and Grandpa Chon returned to the little patch of land that was now Juan's. The old man asked Juan to tell him his secret.

"The zanates taught me that all plants are like brothers and sisters," replied Juan. "If you separate them, they become sad and won't grow. If you respect them and leave them together, they will grow happily and be content."

Dig Deeper

How to Analyze the Text

Use these pages to learn about Conclusions and Literal and Nonliteral Meanings. Then read *The Harvest Birds* again to apply what you learned.

Conclusions

Folktales like *The Harvest Birds* often have a lesson about life to teach readers. The lesson is not always stated, so readers must draw a conclusion about what it is. A **conclusion** is a smart guess that can be made by thinking about story details.

You can draw conclusions about characters and events. Look back at page 286 in *The Harvest Birds*. The townspeople have a lot to say about Juan's news. As you read the details on the page, you can draw a conclusion about what they really think. Look for text evidence, including what the townspeople say and how they act, to help you.

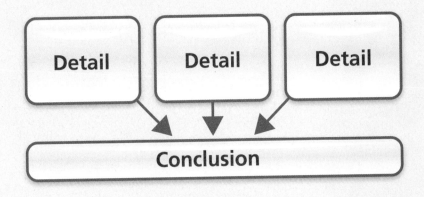

COMMON CORE **RL3.1** ask and answer questions to demonstrate understanding, referring to the text; **RL.3.4** determine the meaning of words and phrases, distinguishing literal from nonliteral language; **L.3.5a** distinguish the literal and nonliteral meanings of words and phrases in context

298

Literal and Nonliteral Meanings

The exact meaning of a word is its **literal meaning.** Look back at page 286. When you read the phrase "Juan ran into the town," you know that the author means exactly what the words say. Words and phrases can also have **nonliteral meanings.** If you read the phrase "Juan ran like the wind," would you think the author means exactly what the words say? What does this phrase really mean?

Your Turn

Turn and Talk

Review the selection with a partner to discuss this question: *What do traditional tales tell readers about life?* As you discuss, listen to your partner's ideas. Then explain your own ideas. Use evidence from *The Harvest Birds* to support your thoughts.

Classroom Conversation

Continue your discussion of *The Harvest Birds* by using text evidence to explain your answers to these questions:

1. What does *The Harvest Birds* tell you about life?

2. What do the townspeople learn about Juan?

3. How does Juan teach readers about the importance of following a dream? Do you agree with Juan's point of view? Explain.

WRITE ABOUT READING

Response With a partner, make up a song or a poem about harvest time. You may want to use details from the story or use words that the characters say. Perform your song or poem for the class.

COMMON CORE **RL.3.1** ask and answer questions to demonstrate understanding, referring to the text; **RL.3.2** recount stories and determine the message, lesson, or moral; **RL.3.6** distinguish own point of view from the narrator or characters' point of view; **W.3.10** write routinely over extended time frames or short time frames; **SL.3.1a** come to discussions prepared/explicitly draw on preparation and other information about the topic; **SL.3.1d** explain own ideas and understanding in light of the discussion

FOLKTALE

☑ GENRE

A **folktale** is a story that has been told for many years.

☑ TEXT FOCUS

A **lesson,** or **moral,** is often part of a folktale. The lesson is usually taught through something that happens to a main character or through what the character learns.

COMMON CORE **RL.3.2** recount stories and determine the message, lesson, or moral; **RL.3.10** read and comprehend literature

The Treasure

written and
illustrated by

Uri Shulevitz

Go Digital

There once was a man and his name was Isaac.

He lived in such poverty that again and again he went to bed hungry.

One night, he had a dream.

In his dream, a voice told him to go to the capital city and look for a treasure under the bridge by the Royal Palace.

"It is only a dream," he thought when he woke up, and he paid no attention to it.

The dream came back a second time. And Isaac still paid no attention to it.

When the dream came back a third time, he said, "Maybe it's true," and so he set out on his journey.

Now and then, someone gave him a ride, but most of the way he walked.

He walked through forests.

He crossed over mountains.

Finally he reached the capital city.

But when he came to the bridge by the Royal Palace, he found that it was guarded day and night.

He did not dare to search for the treasure. Yet he
returned to the bridge every morning and wandered
around it until dark.

One day, the captain of the guards asked him,
"Why are you here?"

Isaac told him the dream. The captain laughed.

"You poor fellow," he said, "what a pity you wore
your shoes out for a dream! Listen, if I believed a dream
I once had, I would go right now to the city you came
from, and I'd look for a treasure under the stove in the
house of a fellow named Isaac." And he laughed again.

Isaac bowed to the captain and started on his long
way home.

He crossed over mountains.

He walked through forests.

Now and then, someone gave him a ride, but most of the way he walked.

At last, he reached his own town.

When he got home, he dug under his stove, and there he found the treasure.

In thanksgiving, he built a house of prayer, and in one of its corners he put an inscription: *Sometimes one must travel far to discover what is near.*

Isaac sent the captain of the guards a priceless ruby. And for the rest of his days he lived in contentment and he never was poor again.

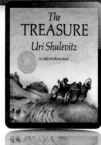

Compare Texts

TEXT TO TEXT

Compare Folktales How are *The Harvest Birds* and *The Treasure* alike? How are they different? Write a paragraph that compares and contrasts the messages in the two stories. Give details about the characters, the settings, and the plots to support your ideas.

TEXT TO SELF

Give a Speech Imagine you are Juan at the end of the story. What would you say to Don Tobias about the way he treated you? Give a speech to a partner. Explain your feelings.

TEXT TO WORLD

Connect to Science Storytellers once told stories while people sat and listened. How have inventions changed the way stories are told? What new inventions might change how stories are told in the future? Explain your ideas in a short paragraph.

Go Digital

COMMON CORE **RL.3.1** ask and answer questions to demonstrate understanding, referring to the text; **RL.3.2** recount stories and determine the message, lesson, or moral; **RL.3.3** describe characters and explain how their actions contribute to the sequence of events; **W.3.10** write routinely over extended time frames or short time frames; **SL.3.4** report on a topic or text, tell a story, or recount an experience/speak clearly at an understandable pace

Grammar

Using Commas A **comma** tells a reader where to pause. A comma also helps make the meaning of a sentence clear. When you list three or more words together in a sentence, the list is called a **series**. Use commas to separate the words in a series.

Another place that commas are needed is in writing a street address. Always use a comma between the name of a town and the state. If you are writing an address in a sentence, use a comma at the end of the street name as well.

Nouns in a Series
Mark saw gulls, pelicans, and terns near his home.

Verbs in a Series
They dove, swooped, and soared through the sky.

Street Address in a Sentence
The school is located at 146 Oak Street, Atlanta, Georgia.

 **Write each sentence. Put commas where they are needed.**

1. Mike Jen and John worked at the school garden.

2. The garden had tomatoes cucumbers and lettuce.

3. The kids picked washed and ate the vegetables.

4. Mary is moving to 818 Ladybug Lane Dallas Texas.

Good writers combine short, choppy sentences into longer, smoother sentences. One way of combining short, choppy sentences is to join single words in a series. Remember to add *and* after the last comma.

Short, Choppy Sentences

Carlos harvested beans.

Carlos harvested corn.

Carlos harvested squash.

Longer, Smoother Sentence

Carlos harvested beans, corn, and squash.

Connect Grammar to Writing

As you revise your response paragraphs, look for ways to combine choppy sentences. You may be able to join single nouns or verbs in a series.

W.3.1a introduce the topic, state an opinion, and create an organizational structure; **W.3.1b** provide reasons that support the opinion; **W.3.1c** use linking words and phrases to connect opinion and reasons; **W.3.1d** provide a concluding statement or section

Opinion Writing

☑ **Word Choice** In a **response paragraph**, you respond to a reading selection by giving your opinion. Begin by introducing the selection and stating your opinion. Then explain your opinion with reasons and text evidence. Use linking words to connect your reasons to your opinions.

Ben wrote a few paragraphs to answer this question: *In* The Harvest Birds, *does Juan make a good decision by visiting Grandpa Chon?* Later, he added linking words to connect his opinion to his reasons.

Writing Traits Checklist

☑ **Ideas**
Did I include important events and a concluding statement?

☑ **Organization**
Did I state my opinion and then support it with reasons?

☑ **Word Choice**
Did I use linking words?

☑ **Voice**
Did I show how I feel?

☑ **Sentence Fluency**
Did I write complete sentences?

☑ **Conventions**
Did I use a dictionary to check my spelling?

Revised Draft

At first, it seems that Grandpa Chon expects Juan to fail. He says that if Juan does not grow a good crop, he will have to work for free. ∧However, By the end of the story, Juan proves that he is a good farmer, and Grandpa Chon gives him the plot of land.

This shows that Juan was smart to ask because the old man is both wise and kind Grandpa Chon for help. ∧

Juan Proves He Is Smart

by Ben Novak

In <u>The Harvest Birds</u>, Juan Zanate's decision to visit Grandpa Chon is a very smart one. Juan thinks that because Grandpa Chon is the oldest person in the town, he will have helpful advice. The old man does not give Juan advice, but he does allow him to use a plot of land.

At first, it seems that Grandpa Chon expects Juan to fail. He says that if Juan does not grow a good crop, he will have to work for free. However, by the end of the story, Juan proves that he is a good farmer, and Grandpa Chon gives him the plot of land. This shows that Juan was smart to ask Grandpa Chon for help because the old man is both wise and kind.

Another reason that Juan made a good decision is that none of the other people in town believed in him. If he had listened to them, he would never have learned how to be a farmer. Instead, he believed in himself and proved them wrong.

Reading as a Writer

What linking words did Ben use in his paragraphs? How do they make his opinion stronger?

I used linking words to connect my opinion to details from the story.

Vocabulary in Context

KAMISHIBAI MAN
ALLEN SAY

The True Story of Kamishibai

familiar
applause
vacant
rickety
blurry
blasted
jerky
rude

Vocabulary Reader

Puppets, Puppets, Puppets

Context Cards

COMMON CORE **L.3.6** acquire and use conversational, general academic, and domain-specific words and phrases

1 familiar
This illustration is from a familiar, or well-known, story. It is from Cinderella.

2 applause
At first, the applause was soft. Then the clapping grew louder.

3 vacant
This old movie theater is vacant. Nobody comes here anymore.

4 rickety
Some puppet theaters are rickety and can easily collapse.

 Go Digital

▶ Study each Context Card.

▶ Use two Vocabulary words to tell about an experience you had.

---

5 blurry

When a sad movie makes you cry, everything looks blurry, or fuzzy.

---

6 blasted

Horns blasted loudly during this school concert.

---

7 jerky

This dance uses quick, jerky motions that stop and start back up again.

---

8 rude

It is very rude, or impolite, to talk during a movie or a play.

KAMISHIBAI MAN
ALLEN SAY

Read and Comprehend

Go Digital

☑ **TARGET SKILL**

Cause and Effect In a story like *Kamishibai Man*, some events make other events happen. An event that makes something else happen is a **cause.** The event that happens as a result is an **effect.**

As you read *Kamishibai Man*, look for events that are connected. Think about which events are causes and which are effects. Use a graphic organizer like this one to keep track of causes and their effects.

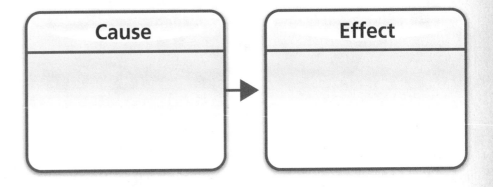

Cause	Effect

☑ **TARGET STRATEGY**

Monitor/Clarify As you read, be sure to **monitor,** or pay attention to, the parts you don't understand. If you do not understand something, **clarify** it by rereading or looking for text evidence to make sense of the text.

COMMON CORE

RL.3.1 ask and answer questions to demonstrate understanding, referring to the text; **RL.3.5** refer to parts of stories, dramas, and poems/ describe how each part builds on earlier sections

Performance Arts

People around the world love stories and storytellers. Some storytellers tell their tales with words alone. Some use puppets. In Japan, kamishibai is the old art of telling stories with beautiful large picture cards and a small stage. The word *kamishibai* means "paper drama." The storyteller claps together two wooden blocks to announce his arrival.

In *Kamishibai Man*, you'll read about such a storyteller. You'll find out that storytelling may change through the years, but people will always love to hear stories.

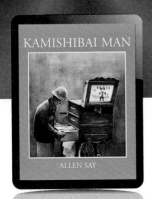

KAMISHIBAI MAN

ALLEN SAY

**MEET THE AUTHOR
AND ILLUSTRATOR**

Allen Say

If you were to drop in on Allen Say in his art studio, you might find him lying on the floor. That's how he does his best thinking. He doesn't own a TV and never listens to music when he works because he likes to work in complete silence.

When he's creating a book, Say first paints all the pictures in order. Then he writes the words. His book *Grandfather's Journey* was awarded the Caldecott Medal for best illustrations.

☑ TARGET SKILL

Cause and Effect Tell how one event makes another happen and why.

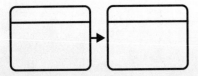

☑ GENRE

Realistic fiction is a story that could happen in real life. As you read, look for:

▶ a setting that could be a real place

▶ realistic characters and events

▶ a plot with a beginning, middle, and ending

COMMON CORE **RL.3.1** ask and answer questions to demonstrate understanding, referring to the text; **RL.3.5** refer to parts of stories, dramas, and poems/describe how each part builds on earlier sections; **RL.3.7** explain how illustrations contribute to the words; **RL.3.10** read and comprehend literature

KAMISHIBAI MAN

by Allen Say

ESSENTIAL QUESTION

How is a live performance different from other kinds of entertainment?

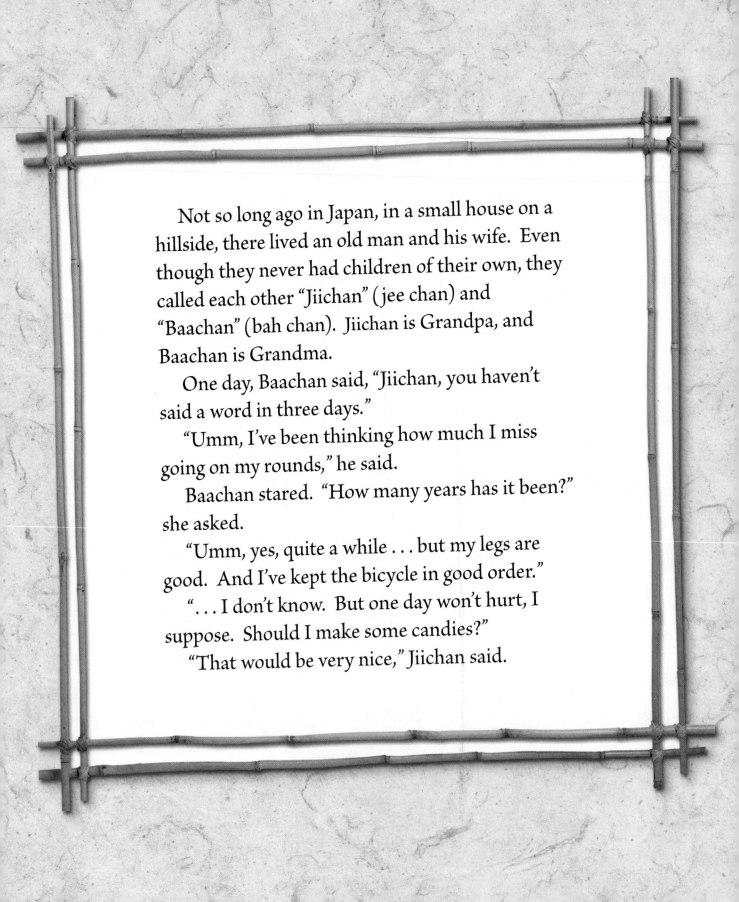

Not so long ago in Japan, in a small house on a hillside, there lived an old man and his wife. Even though they never had children of their own, they called each other "Jiichan" (jee chan) and "Baachan" (bah chan). Jiichan is Grandpa, and Baachan is Grandma.

One day, Baachan said, "Jiichan, you haven't said a word in three days."

"Umm, I've been thinking how much I miss going on my rounds," he said.

Baachan stared. "How many years has it been?" she asked.

"Umm, yes, quite a while . . . but my legs are good. And I've kept the bicycle in good order."

". . . I don't know. But one day won't hurt, I suppose. Should I make some candies?"

"That would be very nice," Jiichan said.

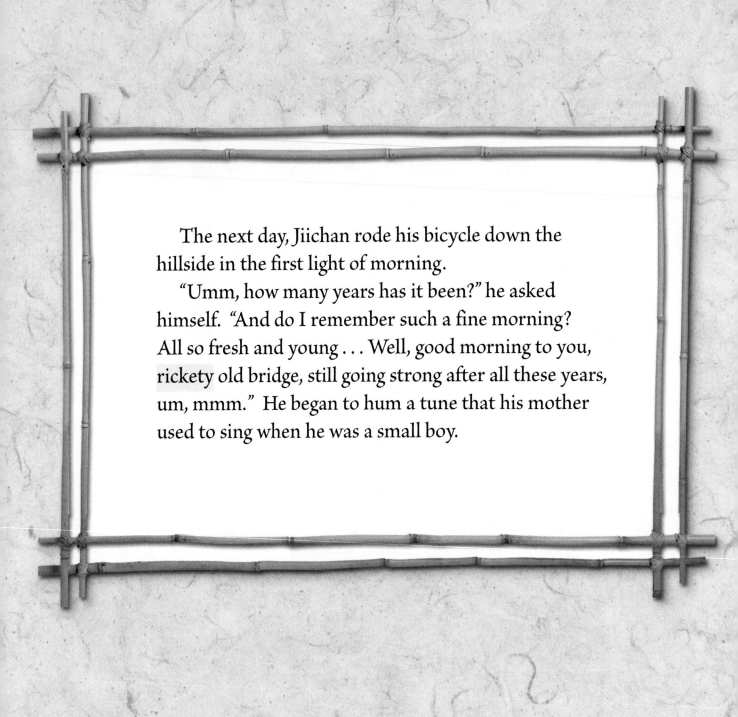

The next day, Jiichan rode his bicycle down the hillside in the first light of morning.

"Umm, how many years has it been?" he asked himself. "And do I remember such a fine morning? All so fresh and young . . . Well, good morning to you, rickety old bridge, still going strong after all these years, um, mmm." He began to hum a tune that his mother used to sing when he was a small boy.

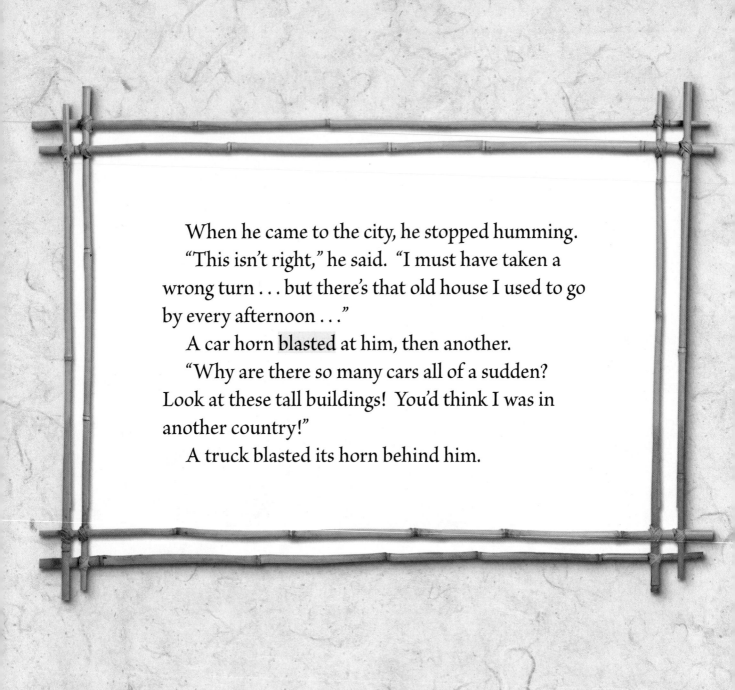

When he came to the city, he stopped humming.

"This isn't right," he said. "I must have taken a wrong turn . . . but there's that old house I used to go by every afternoon . . ."

A car horn blasted at him, then another.

"Why are there so many cars all of a sudden? Look at these tall buildings! You'd think I was in another country!"

A truck blasted its horn behind him.

He pulled into a vacant lot and panted. "Can't a man ride his bicycle in peace? Don't remember such rude drivers." Catching his breath, he looked across the street and gaped.

"Can this be? There's that old noodle shop . . . used to be the only building here—that and a nice park all around. Now look at all these shops and restaurants. They chopped down all those beautiful trees for them. Who needs to buy so many things and eat so many different foods?"

ANALYZE THE TEXT

Cause and Effect The city has grown, causing more traffic. What is another result, or effect, of the city growing larger and busier?

"So, which story will it be today? The mighty 'Peach Boy'! Born from a giant peach! But wait, let's start at the beginning, umm . . . Long, long ago, there once lived an old man and his wife who had no children . . ."

"After 'The Peach Boy,' 'The Bamboo Princess' was a nice change, a gentle story. Then my favorite, 'The Old Man Who Made Cherry Trees Bloom.' And when I was finished, you all went home happy, except for that poor boy. 'Would you like a candy?' I asked once. He said, 'I don't like candies!' and ran away.

"Then one night I was going home and saw a crowd of people gathered in front of a shop. They were staring at something called television. I was curious too, but not for long. It showed moving pictures; they were all jerky and blurry and had no colors at all.

"It wasn't long after that when television antennas started to sprout from the rooftops like weeds in the springtime. And the more they grew, the fewer boys and girls came out to listen to my stories.

"How can they like those blurry pictures better than my beautiful paintings? I asked. But there was nothing to be done. As I went around the familiar neighborhoods, the children started to act as though they didn't know me anymore.

"Even so, I went on clacking my clappers, and one day a little girl poked her head out the window and shushed me. Imagine, a little girl shushing me. The kamishibai man was making too much noise!

"I sat on a park bench and ate a candy for lunch. How could the world change so quickly? Was I a bad storyteller? Then that boy came, the boy who didn't like candies. 'Why aren't you watching television?' I asked. 'I don't like television!' he said. 'But you like my stories,' I said, and he nodded his little head.

"I got up and set the stage. 'What's your favorite story?' I asked. 'Little One Inch,' he answered. So I told him the story of a brave little boy who was only one inch tall. And as I told the story, the boy never looked at the picture cards in the stage. He was looking at me the whole time, with his mouth wide open. He even smiled now and then.

"When I finished the story, I started to take out some sweets to give him, but he was already running away. 'Wait!' I shouted, but he kept running and never turned his head. That was the last time I saw that boy. That was the last day I was a kamishibai man . . ."

ANALYZE THE TEXT

Analyze Illustrations Read the text and look at the illustration. How do the two parts work together to set the mood?

"I was that boy!" a loud voice cried out.

Startled, the kamishibai man looked up and saw that a large crowd had gathered before him.

"We grew up with your stories!" someone else shouted.

"Tell us 'Little One Inch' again!"

"And 'The Bamboo Princess'!"

"'The Peach Boy'!"

He started to say something, and people began to clap their hands. He took a deep bow, and the applause got louder.

A young man with a movie camera struggled up to him. They bowed to each other, and as the old man gave him a candy, a roar went up.

"Look, he has all the same old sweets!"

"Just like the old days!"

And the office clerks and shopkeepers, bankers and waitresses, housewives and deliverymen, all lined up in a big circle around the kamishibai man.

340

It was dark when he got home. Baachan was watching the evening news. The kamishibai man was the featured story.

"I see you had a busy day," she said.

"It was a good day." Jiichan nodded.

"Will you be going out tomorrow?"

"Umm, yes. And the day after."

"Then you need more sweets."

"That would be very nice. Umm, could you make it twice the usual amount?"

"I'll see if I have enough sugar," she said, and shut the television off.

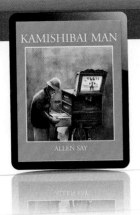

Dig Deeper

How to Analyze the Text

Use these pages to learn about Cause and Effect and Analyzing Illustrations. Then read *Kamishibai Man* again to apply what you learned.

Cause and Effect

Realistic fiction like *Kamishibai Man* tells a story. Often one event in a story makes another event happen. The first event is the **cause.** The event that happens as a result is the **effect.**

You will understand and enjoy a story better if you notice causes and effects. They will help you see why things happen in the story.

Look back at page 324 in *Kamishibai Man*. On this page, you read that Jiichan feels lost in the city. Read to find evidence that shows why he feels this way. What are the causes of his feeling lost?

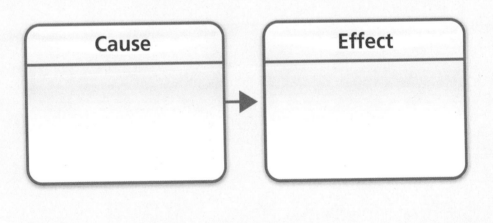

Cause	Effect

RL.3.1 ask and answer questions to demonstrate understanding, referring to the text; **RL.3.5** refer to parts of stories, dramas, and poems/describe how each part builds on earlier sections; **RL.3.7** explain how illustrations contribute to the words

Analyze Illustrations

Illustrations show the events of a story, but they can also do more. An illustration can create a **mood**, or feeling, that helps you understand what is happening in the story. It can show you something about a character or the setting.

Look at the illustration on page 323. You can see the beautiful Japanese countryside where Jiichan lives. The old man is all alone, pedaling his bike. How does the illustration make you feel? What do you learn from it that the words alone do not express?

Your Turn

Review the story with a partner to prepare to talk about this question: *How is a live performance different from other kinds of entertainment?* As you talk, take turns reviewing and explaining key ideas. Include evidence from the text in your discussion.

Classroom Conversation

Continue your discussion of *Kamishibai Man* by explaining your answers to these questions:

1. Why do you think Jiichan decides to go on his rounds after so many years?

2. Why might the people years ago have preferred television to kamishibai?

3. What is the author's message in *Kamishibai Man*?

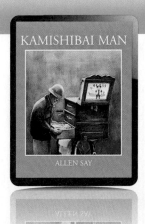

Response In *Kamishibai Man*, Jiichan sees how much the city has changed since he last visited. It now has many cars, tall buildings, and busy people. How do you think these changes make Jiichan feel? How would they make you feel? Write a paragraph telling your thoughts.

Writing Tip

Begin your paragraph by stating your topic. Then state your opinion and reasons why you feel as you do. End your paragraph with a concluding sentence that sums up your ideas.

COMMON CORE **RL.3.1** ask and answer questions to demonstrate understanding, referring to the text; **W.3.1a** introduce the topic, state an opinion, and create an organizational structure; **W.3.1b** provide reasons that support the opinion; **W.3.1d** provide a concluding statement or section; **SL.3.1a** come to discussions prepared/explicitly draw on preparation and other information about the topic; **SL.3.1d** explain own ideas and understanding in light of the discussion

✓ GENRE

Informational text gives factual information about a topic.

✓ TEXT FOCUS

Headings are titles that tell what each section of text is about.

COMMON CORE **RI.3.5** use text features and search tools to locate information; **RI.3.10** read and comprehend informational texts

The True Story of Kamishibai

by Elizabeth Manning

Clacking Sticks

Long ago in Japan, kamishibai men rode around on bicycles with wooden boxes on the back. Each man parked his rickety bike in his own special part of town. At the sound of two wooden sticks clacking together, children came running. They bought the candy the man kept in a drawer in the wooden box. Then they waited.

Kamishibai artist Hikaru Otsuki performs at a park in Tokyo, Japan.

Stories in the Street

The kamishibai man put a picture card in the frame at the top of the box. He began to tell a familiar story. One by one, he slipped the pictures in and out. His movements were smooth, not jerky. In case his memory was blurry, parts of the story were on the back of each picture. The kamishibai storytellers always stopped at an exciting part. The children came back another day to hear what happened next. They greeted the end of the story with applause.

What Happened Next?

In the 1960s, something changed. Children stayed indoors after school, leaving the streets vacant. Paper pictures were no match for stories shown on a new invention called television. The noise of televisions blasted from homes. The sound of two wooden sticks clacking together was now a rude interruption. Were the days of kamishibai over?

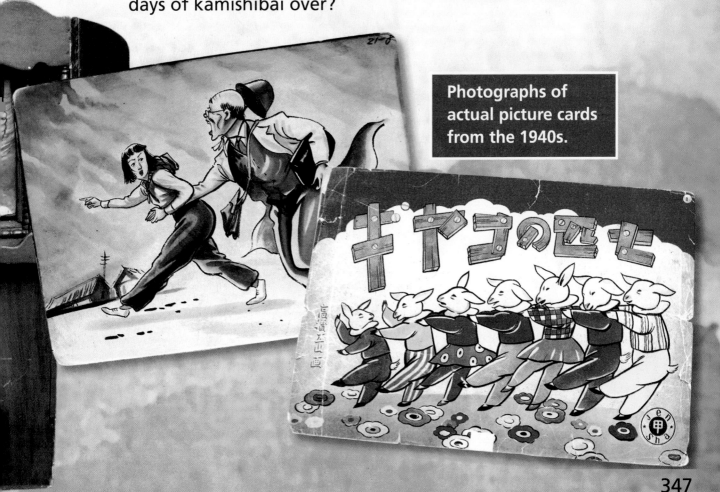

Photographs of actual picture cards from the 1940s.

A New Chapter

Some kamishibai artists found work making other kinds of pictures. They drew for the new Japanese comics, called *manga*. Some of their comics were made into cartoon movies, called *anime*. Today people create and read manga and anime all over the world.

Children can still listen to the old paper-theater stories. Storytellers have brought kamishibai to schools and libraries in Japan and the United States. This paper theater doesn't arrive on the back of a bicycle, but the stories and pictures are still wonderful!

Compare Texts

Compare Information Think about Jiichan in *Kamishibai Man*. How is he like a real kamishibai described in *The True Story of Kamishibai*? How is he different? Discuss your ideas with a partner. Use information from both texts. List similarities and differences that you find.

Tell a Story Choose one of your favorite stories or fairy tales. Draw pictures to illustrate the story. Then tell the story in the kamishibai style to a small group of students in your class.

Apply Character Traits Review *The Harvest Birds* from Lesson 8 with a partner. Then imagine that Jiichan from *Kamishibai Man* could meet Grandpa Chon from *The Harvest Birds*. Do you think they would become friends? Why or why not? Use evidence from the stories to explain your answer.

 RL.3.1 ask and answer questions to demonstrate understanding, referring to the text; **RL.3.2** recount stories and determine the message, lesson or moral; **RI.3.1** ask and answer questions to demonstrate understanding, referring to the text; **RI.3.9** compare and contrast important points and details in texts on the same topic; **SL.3.4** report on a topic or text, tell a story, or recount an experience/speak clearly at an understandable pace

Grammar

Abstract Nouns You already know that a noun names a person, an animal, a place, or a thing. An **abstract noun** is a special kind of noun. It names an idea, a feeling, or a quality. Abstract nouns are things that people cannot see, hear, taste, smell, or touch. All other nouns are concrete nouns.

	bicycle	bravery	food	peace
Can I see?	√		√	
Can I hear?	√			
Can I taste?			√	
Can I smell?			√	
Can I touch?	√		√	
What kind of noun is it?	concrete	abstract	concrete	abstract

Try This! **Work with a partner. Tell whether each underlined noun is abstract or concrete and explain why.**

❶ The storyteller was full of sadness.

❷ He had many happy memories.

❸ His stories brought the children a lot of joy.

Use exact nouns to make your writing clearer and more interesting. Some nouns have similar meanings. When you choose the noun that has the most exact meaning for what you are writing about, your writing will be better.

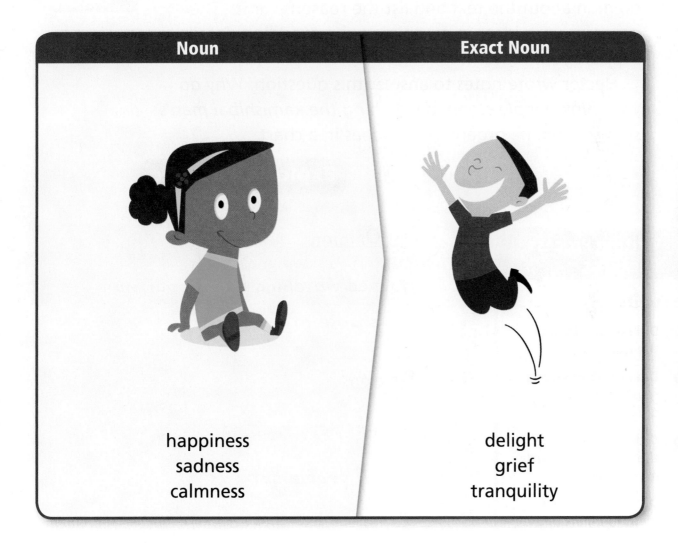

Noun	Exact Noun
happiness sadness calmness	delight grief tranquility

 Connect Grammar to Writing

As you revise your response to literature next week, look closely at the nouns you use. Is there a more exact noun that would make your meaning clearer?

W.3.1a introduce the topic, state an opinion, and create an organizational structure; **W.3.1b** provide reasons that support the opinion; **W.3.5** develop and strengthen writing by planning, revising, and editing

Opinion Writing

Reading-Writing Workshop: Prewrite

✔ **Organization** Good writers think about their ideas before writing a **response to literature.** Write your opinion about the text and list the reasons for it. Then organize your ideas in an opinion chart, adding details to support your reasons.

Hector wrote notes to answer this question: *Why do you think people stopped watching the kamishibai man's show?* Then he organized his ideas in a chart.

Writing Process Checklist

▶ **Prewrite**

☑ Did I understand the question?

☑ Did I think of strong reasons for my opinion?

☑ Did I find details in the story to support my reasons?

☑ Did I organize my ideas in an order that makes sense?

Draft

Revise

Edit

Publish and Share

Exploring a Topic

My Opinion

stopped watching kamishibai man
    because of TV

Reasons

TV was new, exciting

lots of people got TVs

people home watching TV

Opinion Chart

I think people stopped watching the kamishibai man's shows because of television.

Reason:	The people in Jiichan's town were excited by this new invention.
Detail:	Crowds gathered around to look at a television in a shop window.

Reason:	More and more people in the town got their own television sets.
Detail:	Jiichan saw antennas appearing on people's roofs.

Reason:	People watched television instead of the kamishibai man's shows.
Detail:	A girl told him to be quiet.

Reading as a Writer

What other story details could Hector have added in his chart? Where could you add details and examples in your own chart?

When I organized my response to literature, I added details to support my reasons. I will use this structure to organize my draft.

Vocabulary in Context

✓ **TARGET VOCABULARY**

invention
experiment
laboratory
genius
gadget
electric
signal
occasional

Vocabulary Reader

Context Cards

L.3.6 acquire and use conversational, general academic, and domain-specific words and phrases

354

1 invention
The light bulb was an invention that helped people do things at night.

2 experiment
First, an inventor must perform an experiment to test an idea.

3 laboratory
Scientists may test their ideas in a laboratory, using special equipment.

4 genius
Although Einstein acted silly, he was known for his great mind, or genius.

Go Digital

▶ Study each Context Card.

▶ Ask a question that uses one of the Vocabulary words.

5 gadget

A small gadget with many parts, such as a watch, can be hard to repair.

6 electric

The invention of the electric fan helps us to stay cool in hot weather.

7 signal

A red light is a signal to stop. This invention helps to save lives.

8 occasional

A good invention has an occasional problem but should not fail regularly.

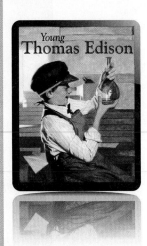

Read and Comprehend

Go Digital

☑ TARGET SKILL

Main Ideas and Details In nonfiction writing such as a biography, the author includes several important ideas about the topic. Each important idea is a **main idea.** Supporting **details** are facts and examples that help explain the main idea. As you read *Young Thomas Edison*, use a chart like this to record details that support a main idea.

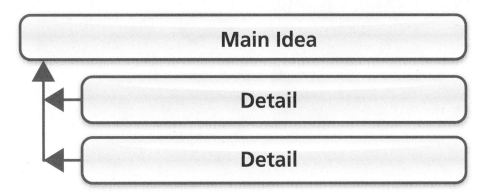

Main Idea
Detail
Detail

☑ TARGET STRATEGY

Summarize As you read *Young Thomas Edison*, you can **summarize,** or retell, the important events in Edison's life.

Inventions

You use inventions every day. Inventions such as bikes and cars move people. Inventions such as telephones and computers help people communicate. Even pencils, crayons, and paper are inventions. Where do inventions come from? They come from people who observe carefully, see a problem, and think of a way to solve it. These people are inventors.

In *Young Thomas Edison*, you'll read about one of the most important inventors of all time. You'll find out that his inventions didn't usually work the first time he tried them. How many times did he try without giving up?

ANCHOR TEXT

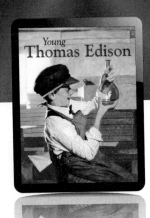

Young **Thomas Edison**

✓ TARGET SKILL

Main Ideas and Details

Think about the most important idea in a section of the text. Look for details that tell you more about the main idea.

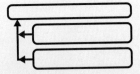

✓ GENRE

A **biography** tells about a person's life. It is written by another person. As you read, look for:

- ▶ information about why the person is important
- ▶ events in time order
- ▶ opinions based on facts

RI.3.2 determine the main idea/recount details and explain how they support the main idea; **RI.3.3** describe the relationship between a series of historical events/scientific ideas/steps in technical procedures; **RI.3.8** describe the connection between sentences and paragraphs in a text

MEET THE AUTHOR AND ILLUSTRATOR

Michael Dooling

When he was researching his book about Thomas Edison, Michael Dooling did a lot of traveling. He went to Edison's birthplace in Ohio and to the train station in Michigan where Edison worked as a boy. He also visited a museum in New Jersey that houses many of Edison's amazing inventions.

Dooling enjoys making history come alive for students. If he ever visited your school, he would most likely show up dressed like Paul Revere.

Young
Thomas Edison

by
Michael
Dooling

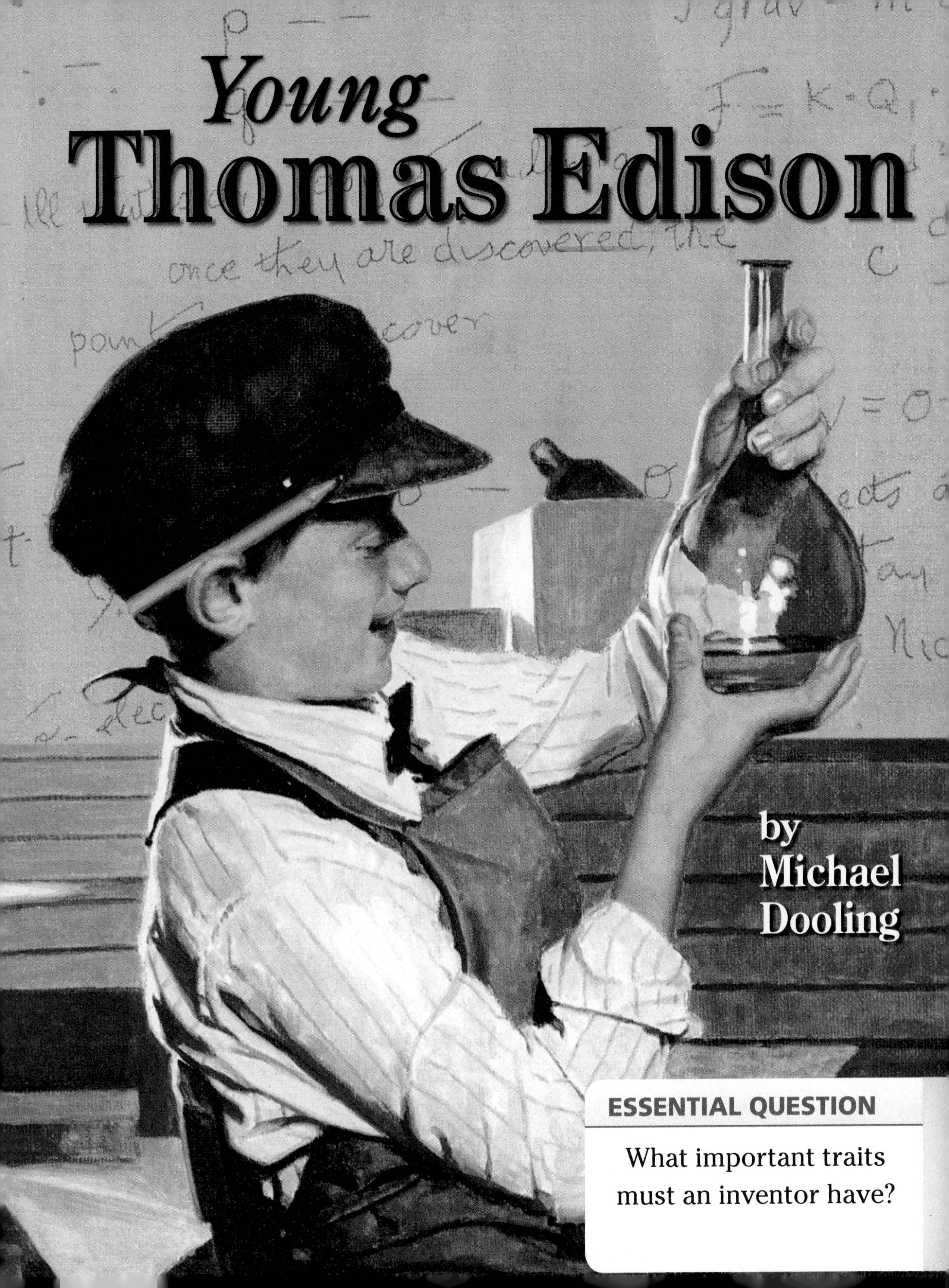

ESSENTIAL QUESTION

What important traits
must an inventor have?

Thomas Alva Edison was born in a little house in Milan, Ohio, on February 11, 1847, to Samuel and Nancy Edison. He was the youngest of seven children.

Thomas, who was called Young Al by his family, lived in an era very different from ours. There was no electric light, no telephone, no radio or CD player; not even a movie theater.

q — — . — $\qquad F = K \cdot Q_1 \cdot Q_2$
$\qquad\qquad\qquad\qquad\qquad\qquad\qquad \overline{d^2}$

truths are easy to understand

 once they are discovered, the $\qquad c \dfrac{dv}{dt}$

point is to discover

 them."

  — Galileo $\qquad\qquad V = 0\, m/s$

3.14159 $\qquad\qquad\qquad\qquad$ bjects at rea

9.6485 × 10⁴ $\qquad\qquad\qquad\qquad$ stay at r

 Ni = Nickel

— electricity

 $\qquad\qquad\qquad\qquad$ P = Phosph

$S = $ $\qquad\qquad\qquad\qquad$ geol

= Copr

Thomas loved to experiment. In 1856, at the age of nine, he turned his family's cellar into a laboratory complete with test tubes, beakers, and whatever chemicals he could buy. It was a mess—bottles were everywhere. Young Al would mix one chemical after another, sometimes following the experiments in his chemistry book—sometimes not. "A little of this and a little of that," he used to mumble.

His mother always encouraged him to ask questions, and he did. What is this? Why does that happen? How does it happen?

ANALYZE THE TEXT

Main Ideas and Details Identify the main idea and supporting details in the first paragraph on this page.

A bout of scarlet fever left Al hard of hearing, which made school difficult. While Al asked many questions at home, he did not ask any at school. Instead he spent his time there daydreaming about his next experiment.

Al's mother, a former teacher, took him out of school after only three months. From then on, she taught him at home. Mrs. Edison made sure he received an excellent education. He read Shakespeare, the Bible, history, and much more. Over the next few years he also studied the great inventors, such as Galileo.

At age twelve Young Al decided to look for a job. He needed money to continue his experiments. So he went into business as a paperboy on the train that went from Port Huron, where the Edisons now lived, to Detroit, Michigan. Every morning from 7 A.M. to 10 A.M. Al sold newspapers.

Then he spent all day at the Detroit library, reading and dreaming about his next experiment. He planned to read every book in the library, starting with the last book on the shelf and working back to the first. At night he took the train home and sold papers again.

Eventually, with the permission of the conductor, Al set up a laboratory in the baggage car of the train. Soon the young scientist was experimenting with everything: chemicals, gadgets, test tubes, beakers, doohickeys, and thingamajigs.

Things were going well until one day when the train made a sudden lurch. Bottles, books, newspapers, candies, and fruits went flying—along with Al. A bottle of phosphorus burst into flames. Al scrambled to put out the flames, but they spread too fast. Soon a very upset conductor rushed in. At the next stop the conductor threw all of Al's things off the train—even him!

Al had never been so disappointed in his life. He went home and set up his laboratory again with the encouragement of his mother. He continued to experiment and tinker with every gadget he could get his hands on. Usually his experiments did not work— but he always kept trying.

Before long Al had another job. He was a "night wire"—a railroad telegraph operator—in Stratford Junction, Canada. There was a lot to learn. For weeks, he soaked up all the information he could about telegraphy.

Al learned Morse code and much more. He worked the 7 P.M. to 7 A.M. shift, often sleeping right in the station. He also set up his laboratory in the back room of the station so that he could experiment in his off-hours. Apart from the occasional explosion, life was grand.

ANALYZE THE TEXT

Sequence of Events What events so far in Al's life have encouraged him to keep experimenting? As you read on, see how the events work together to shape his life.

One of Al's duties as the operator was to send the signal 6 every hour on the hour to show the dispatcher at the next station that he was awake. But the long hours sometimes caught up with him and he would fall asleep, so the scientist in him had an idea. Soon Al had invented a device that hooked the telegraphy key to a clock. When the hour struck, the minute hand of the clock sent the message 6 for him. It was a moment of pure genius, which quickly got him fired when his boss discovered he was sleeping on the job.

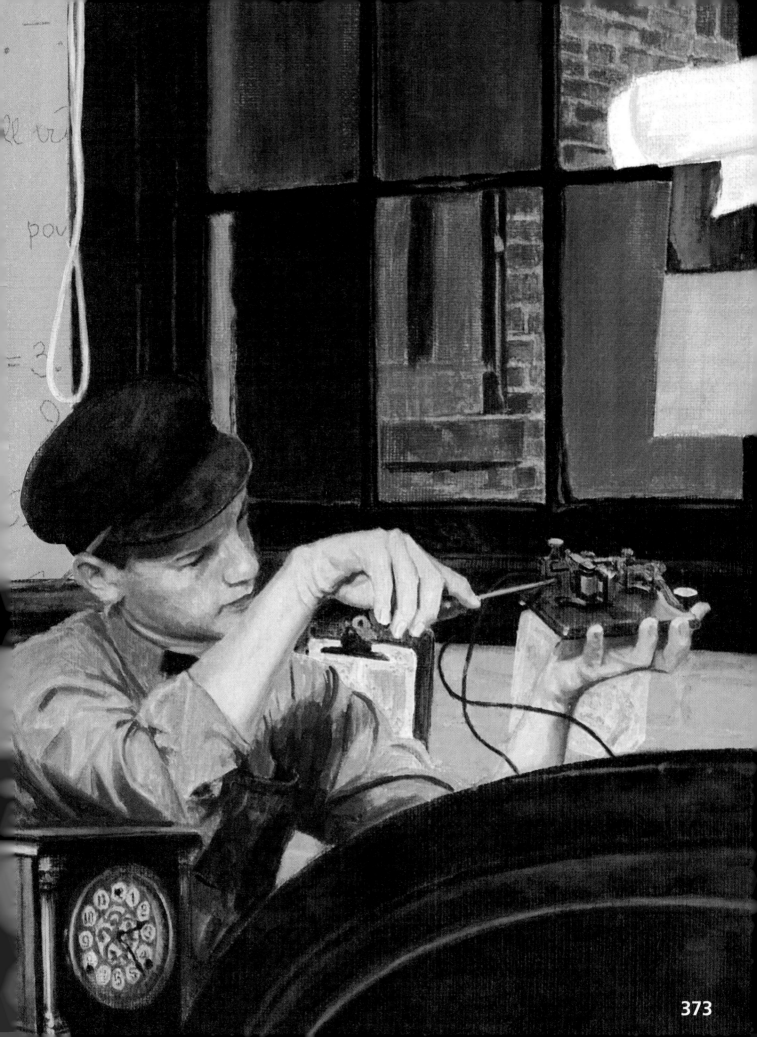

For the next five years, young Edison traveled all over the South and Midwest from one telegraph job to another. He continued to try to find ways to improve the telegraph. At age twenty-one he made his way to Boston, Massachusetts, and started using his first name, Thomas. He decided that he was going to be an inventor, and he set up his latest laboratory. He wanted to learn all he could about electrical forces. His first patented invention was the *Electrical Vote Recorder*. Unfortunately, Congress did not like his invention, and he could not sell it.

Over the years, Thomas's hearing had grown worse. By now, he was nearly deaf. This did not hamper his creative abilities though. In fact, he thought it even helped him to concentrate because he was not distracted by noises. It created solitude where he could tune out the whole world and think.

In 1869 Thomas moved to New York City and then later established his laboratory in Newark, New Jersey. And then bad news came from home. His mother had died. Thomas, at twenty-four, was deeply saddened. For a long time he could not even speak of her. He would miss her letters—her advice and encouragement. He owed everything to his mother.

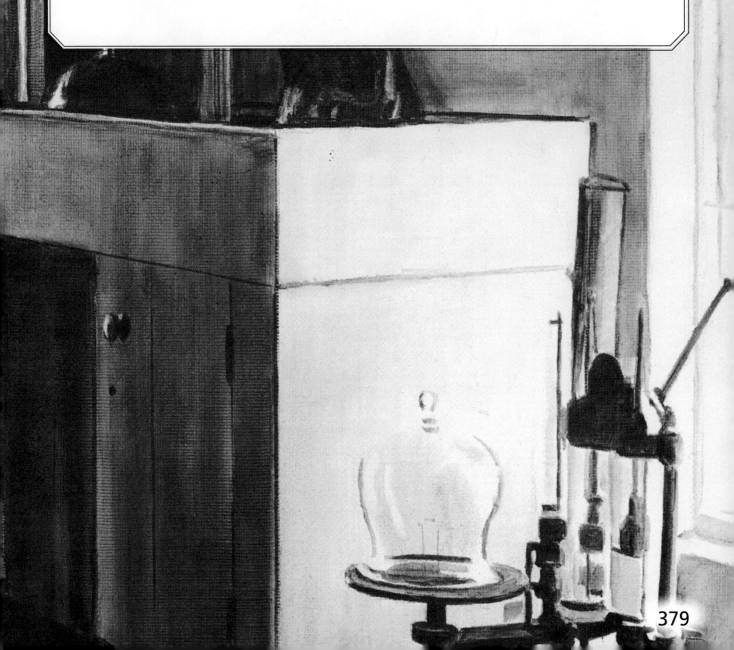

In 1876 Thomas moved his laboratory to Menlo Park, New Jersey. He invented the *carbon transmitter*, which amplified the human voice—making the telephone and microphone possible. He also invented a machine that talked—a *phonograph*. Shortly thereafter, Thomas invented an *electric lightbulb*. He also discovered the principle of sound waves, which made the radio possible. In 1887 he moved his laboratory to West Orange, New Jersey, developing the *motion picture* and much more. At one point he had 250 people working for him and 45 inventions going.

1847-1931

Such strange, incredible inventions were coming out of his laboratory that people started to call Thomas "The Wizard." He would live to be eighty-four years old and patent 1,093 inventions. Thomas would always remember his mother's encouraging words to ask questions. What is this? Why does that happen? How does it happen?

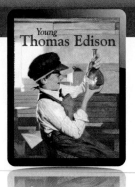

Dig Deeper

How to Analyze the Text

Use these pages to learn about Main Ideas and Details and Sequence of Events. Then read *Young Thomas Edison* again to apply what you learned.

Main Ideas and Details

A biography like *Young Thomas Edison* tells about a person's life. This information leads to what was most important about the person. This is the **main idea** of the biography.

The most important **details** in a biography support, or tell more about, the main idea. They help you understand why the person was important.

Turn to page 364 of *Young Thomas Edison*. Read to find the main idea. Look for details that support the main idea. As you keep reading, keep an eye out for big ideas.

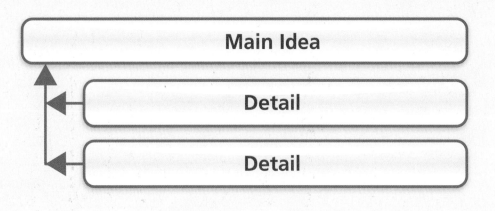

Main Idea
Detail
Detail

COMMON CORE **RI.3.2** determine the main idea/recount details and explain how they support the main idea; **RI.3.3** describe the relationship between a series of historical events/scientific ideas/steps in technical procedures; **RI.3.8** describe the connection between sentences and paragraphs in a text

Sequence of Events

The author of a biography usually tells the events of a person's life in order, or **sequence.** You read about the person as a child, as a young person, and then as a grown-up.

In *Young Thomas Edison*, the author first tells about events in Edison's young life. Then you read how these events led him to become a great inventor. Notice how the author builds the story from one paragraph to the next.

Your Turn

Turn and Talk

Review the selection with a partner to prepare to discuss this question: *What important traits must an inventor have?* In your discussion, think about the main idea you want your partner to understand. Support your ideas with evidence from the selection.

Classroom Conversation

Now talk about these questions with the class.

1. What are some of the ways that Thomas Edison learned about the world around him?

2. How was Edison's education similar to or different from yours?

3. Do you think "The Wizard" was a good nickname for Edison? Why or why not?

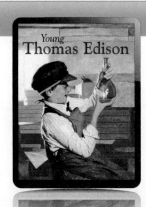

Response Which of Thomas Edison's inventions do you think was the most important? Think about what life would be like without it. Write your opinion about the invention. Include details that describe the invention, and give your reasons for why it was so important.

Writing Tip

Give at least three strong reasons to support your opinion. Use linking phrases such as *for one thing* and *for another*. Save your most important reason for last. End with a strong concluding statement.

COMMON CORE

RI.3.1 ask and answer questions to demonstrate understanding, referring to the text; **RI.3.2** determine the main idea/recount details and explain how they support the main idea; **W.3.1a** introduce the topic, state an opinion, and create an organizational structure; **W.3.1b** provide reasons that support the opinion; **W.3.1c** use linking words and phrases to connect opinion and reasons; **W.3.1d** provide a concluding statement or section; **SL.3.1d** explain own ideas and understanding in light of the discussion

INFORMATIONAL TEXT

 GENRE

Informational text gives factual information about a topic.

 TEXT FOCUS

A **diagram** is a graphic aid that shows how something works. It can be a drawing or a group of pictures.

 RI.3.7 use information gained from illustrations and words to demonstrate understanding; **RI.3.10** read and comprehend informational texts

Moving Pictures

by Andrew Patterson

You can thank the genius Thomas Edison every time you watch a movie. His laboratory conducted one moving picture experiment after another. Workers took just an occasional break. One invention of theirs led to the development of movies. That gadget was the kinetoscope.

Thomas Edison's kinetoscope, invented in the late 1800s.

The Kinetoscope

The kinetoscope was a wooden box with a peephole on top. Inside the box was a strip of film. It had photos of someone moving. Spools pulled the film along quickly. An electric lamp flashed on and off. The lamp lit up each photo so the person peering into the kinetoscope could see it.

The viewer's eye sent a signal to the brain. It told the brain that the figure was moving, so the viewer thought the figure really *was* moving. This special effect, or trick, was a key part of making moving pictures, or movies.

Movie Magic!

By the early 1900s, Hollywood was becoming the world's movie capital. At the same time, westerns were becoming the most popular movies. Westerns often told stories about cowboys, horses, and the wide-open plains. But, in fact, many westerns were filmed in Hollywood studios!

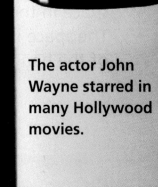

The actor John Wayne starred in many Hollywood movies.

Special Effects

Filmmakers today use special effects, just as Edison did. Some special effects make events seem real. A blue screen is one way to make people look like they are flying!

How Superheroes Fly

1 Filmmakers film an actor hanging in front of a plain blue screen.

2 A film of city skyscrapers becomes the background.

3 Filmmakers make an empty space in the background. The space is the exact shape of the hanging actor.

4 Filmmakers fit the picture of the actor into the empty space to make a movie of a superhero flying above the city.

Compare Texts

TEXT TO TEXT

Compare Inventions Choose an invention from *Young Thomas Edison* that Edison created or made possible. Compare it with the kinetoscope described in *Moving Pictures*. Use information from the texts to discuss the inventions with a partner. Tell what the inventions are used for and how they are alike and different.

TEXT TO SELF

Make a Poster Thomas Edison's inventions changed the way people lived and worked. Many of the inventions are used today. Draw a poster to show how you use Edison's inventions in your life.

TEXT TO WORLD

Connect to Science What do you think Edison would invent today if he were alive? Use text evidence from *Young Thomas Edison* to support your ideas. Talk in a small group. Listen to each other and ask questions to think of new ideas.

COMMON CORE **RI.3.1** ask and answer questions to demonstrate understanding, referring to the text; **RI.3.9** compare and contrast important points and details in texts on the same topic; **SL.3.1a** come to discussions prepared/explicitly draw on preparation and other information about the topic

Grammar

Pronouns and Antecedents A **pronoun** can take the place of one or more nouns in a sentence. **Subject pronouns** take the place of a subject. These are *I, you, he, she, it, we,* and *they*. **Object pronouns** follow action verbs and words such as *to, for, at, of,* and *with*. Object pronouns are *me, you, him, her, it, us,* and *them*.

An **antecedent** is the noun that is being replaced by a pronoun. Always be sure that the pronoun matches its antecedent in number and gender.

Nouns	Pronouns
Ben is an inventor.	He is an inventor.
The lab is in Boston.	It is in Boston.
The workers have many ideas.	They have many ideas.

Antecedent	Pronoun
Ben lives with Aunt Joan	in her apartment.
Luis meets Rob and Ben	at their lab.

Try This! **With a partner, find the pronoun in each sentence. Classify it as a subject pronoun or an object pronoun. Explain your answer. Identify the antecedent when there is one.**

❶ Ruth's mom told her about Thomas Edison.

❷ Do they know the story?

❸ Roy said that he wanted a book to read.

❹ Dad got a library card for him.

Be careful not to repeat a noun too many times in your writing. You can use pronouns in place of nouns to keep your writing from being boring and choppy.

Repeated Nouns	Better Sentences
The inventor had a great idea. The inventor got a patent on the invention. The university gave the inventor an award.	The inventor had a great idea. He got a patent on the invention. The university gave him an award.

 Connect Grammar to Writing

As you revise your response to literature, try to replace repeated nouns with pronouns. Pay attention to antecedents as clues to choosing the correct pronoun.

W.3.1a introduce the topic, state an opinion, and create an organizational structure; **W.3.1b** provide reasons that support the opinion; **W.3.1c** use linking words and phrases to connect opinion and reasons; **W.3.1d** provide a concluding statement or section; **W.3.5** develop and strengthen writing by planning, revising, and editing

Opinion Writing

Reading-Writing Workshop: Revise

✓ **Sentence Fluency** Good writers don't say the same thing twice. Each sentence should say something new. Writers also use linking words, such as *because*, to connect their opinion to reasons that support it. In your **response to literature**, cross out any sentence that repeats what you have already said.

When Hector revised his response to literature, he crossed out sentences that repeated ideas.

Writing Process Checklist

Prewrite

Draft

▶ **Revise**

✓ **Did I state my opinion and support it with reasons?**

✓ **Did I use linking words to connect my opinions and reasons?**

✓ **Did I put my ideas in an order that makes sense?**

✓ **Did I sum up my reasons at the end?**

Edit

Publish and Share

Revised Draft

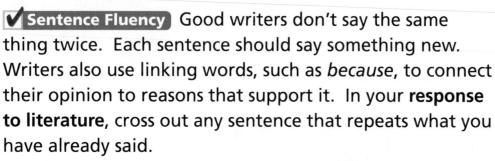

I think people stopped watching the kamishibai man because of television. Television brought many big changes to Jiichan's town. ~~It made things different there.~~

When the kamishibai man first gave shows, television had not been invented. ~~There weren't any TVs.~~ Later, when people saw a TV in a shop, they ~~people~~ gathered around.

392

Television Was the Reason

by Hector Suarez

I think people stopped watching the kamishibai man because of television. Television brought many big changes to Jiichan's town.

When the kamishibai man first gave shows, television had not been invented. Later, when people saw a TV in a shop, they gathered around. They left Jiichan's show to go stare at the television screen. They were excited by the moving pictures.

Over time, more and more people in the kamishibai man's town bought televisions for their homes. For this reason, children did not play outside as much anymore. They did not even see the kamishibai man and so could not stop to listen to his stories. The televisions brought so many changes that most people were no longer interested in the kamishibai man.

Reading as a Writer

Why is Hector's paper better without the two sentences that he crossed out? Cross out ideas in your paper that are repeated.

I made sure each sentence states a new idea. I also used pronouns to avoid repeating nouns.

Read the article "What Makes Bees So Busy?" As you read, stop and answer each question using text evidence.

What Makes Bees So Busy?

Have you ever seen a honeybee fly back and forth? You might think the bee is flying around just for fun. Actually, the bee is hard at work.

Bees spend a lot of time searching for food. They buzz from flower to flower, searching for nectar and pollen. Nectar is a sweet liquid inside the flower. Bees suck it up with their long tongues. The nectar is stored in a special sac called a honey stomach.

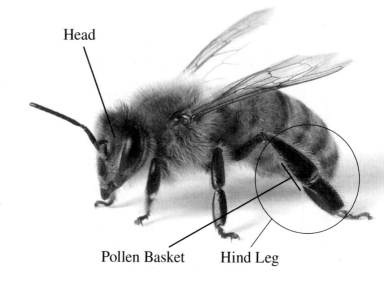

Head

Pollen Basket   Hind Leg

Pollen is a powder made by plants. Bees gather the pollen with their hind legs. The pollen collects on an area of the hind legs called the pollen basket.

1 How does the picture help you better understand the article?

In one trip, a bee may visit as many as 50 or even 100 flowers. Then it carries the nectar and pollen home. Each bee can carry over half its own weight.

COMMON CORE

RI.3.2 determine the main idea/recount details and explain how they support the main idea; **RI.3.3** describe the relationship between a series of historical events/scientific ideas/steps in technical procedures; **RI.3.7** use information gained from illustrations and words to demonstrate understanding; **RI.3.8** describe the connection between sentences and paragraphs in a text

Honeybees live in homes called hives. Thousands of honeybees live and work in each hive. The three kinds of bees that live in the hive are the queen bee, worker bees, and drones. The queen and the worker bees are female. The drones are male bees.

The queen is a very important bee. Only one queen bee lives in a hive at a time. Her body is longer than the bodies of the other bees. She is the mother of all the other bees that live in the hive. The queen bee lays all the eggs for her hive. One queen bee can lay more than a thousand eggs in a day. Young bees will hatch from these eggs and grow into adults.

---

2 What is the main idea of this paragraph? Explain how details in the paragraph support the main idea.

Worker bees do all the other jobs in the hive. They build structures called honeycombs. Their bodies produce a special kind of wax for this purpose. The honeycomb has many small sections called cells. Each cell has six sides. Food is stored in some cells of the honeycomb. The queen lays eggs in other cells. That is where the young bees grow.

The worker bees keep the hive clean. They attack bees from other hives who try to take their honey. They also attack animals, such as bears. Even people who try to take the honey can get stung by worker bees.

The workers take care of the queen and protect her. They even feed her because she cannot feed herself. They fly away from the hive to look for pollen and nectar. When they return, they use the pollen to make a special food for the young bees. They also make nectar into honey for the adult bees to eat.

Honeybees communicate with one another. Some worker bees act as scouts. They look for food for the hive. When they find it, they fly back to the hive. They do a special kind of dance to tell the other bees where the food is. The dance also tells how far away the food is. The faster the scout dances, the closer the food is to the hive.

 What steps do the scouts follow? Use time-order words in your response.

Bees are not the only fans of honey. People eat honey, too. Some people keep bees and collect honey to sell. These people are called beekeepers. Often, beekeepers keep their bees in what are called standard hives. The standard hives have sections called supers. The supers can be pulled in and out like drawers.

Beekeepers wear special clothes to protect themselves from bee stings. They cover their faces with wire screen. They tie the ends of their pants and sleeves. They make slow movements so they don't upset the bees.

Bees do another important job. When they land on a plant, pollen clings to their fuzzy bodies. Then bees fly to other plants, bringing bits of pollen with them. This helps certain plants make new plants.

 What are the cause and the effect that are explained in the paragraph?

Bees are interesting and hardworking insects. The phrase "busy as a bee" certainly makes sense!

Unit 3

contribute
athletes
improve
power
process
flexible
fraction
compete

Vocabulary Reader   Context Cards

COMMON CORE **L.3.6** acquire and use conversational, general academic, and domain-specific words and phrases

Vocabulary in Context

1 **contribute**

All members of a team contribute to the team's success by doing their job.

2 **athletes**

Athletes train hard to be the best that they can be at their sport.

3 **improve**

Coaching helps tennis players improve, or get better.

4 **power**

This player uses all his power, or strength, to hit the ball out of the park.

Go Digital

▶ Study each Context Card.

▶ Place the Vocabulary words in alphabetical order.

5 process

Workers follow many steps during the process of making a bicycle.

6 flexible

To move her leg up so high, the gymnast must keep her body flexible.

7 fraction

The player slides onto the base. He is safe by just a fraction of an inch!

8 compete

The two players compete against each other to win the game.

Read and Comprehend

 Go Digital

☑ TARGET SKILL

Sequence of Events In a process, one step follows another. Each step is important, and the **sequence,** or order, of the steps is just as important. As you read *Technology Wins the Game*, use a chart like this to show how the sequence of steps that have been used to invent new sports technology are related.

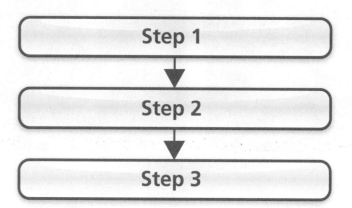

Step 1

↓

Step 2

↓

Step 3

☑ TARGET STRATEGY

Question As you read *Technology Wins the Game*, keep track of how the sequence of events on your chart answers questions you may have. Also, ask yourself new questions as you read on. Use text evidence to answer your questions.

 RI.3.3 describe the relationship between a series of historical events/scientific ideas/steps in technical procedures; **RI.3.8** describe the connection between sentences and paragraphs in a text

Inventions

If you have ever seen a photograph of a football player from long ago, you probably thought his uniform looked very odd. Sports equipment has changed over the years. Inventors known as sports engineers have used new knowledge about the human body, along with new materials, to design better and safer equipment.

In *Technology Wins the Game*, you'll read about some of these important advances in sports technology. You'll also discover the process that engineers use to help athletes move more quickly and play more safely.

 TARGET SKILL

Sequence of Events
Look for the order of steps in a process as you read.

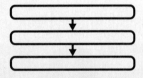

 GENRE

Informational text gives facts and other information about a topic. As you read, look for:

▶ headings that begin sections of text with related information

▶ photographs and captions

▶ graphics, such as diagrams, that help explain the topic

 COMMON CORE **RI.3.3** describe the relationship between a series of historical events/scientific ideas/steps in technical procedures; **RI.3.8** describe the connection between sentences and paragraphs in a text; **RI.3.10** read and comprehend informational texts

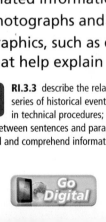

TECHNOLOGY WINS THE GAME

by Mark Andrews

ESSENTIAL QUESTION

How do inventions help athletes?

Changing the Game

Let's take a look at tennis. This is a sport where sports engineers have made several changes.

What a Racket!

Tennis rackets have changed a lot. When the sport began, tennis rackets were made out of wood. Then in the 1960s, a metal racket was developed. Metal rackets were stronger and lighter than wood. Today, rackets are made out of different materials mixed together. These rackets are very light and provide more power than the old ones. The ball moves faster than ever.

Today's rackets also have a larger head, or string area, than before. This makes it easier for the tennis player to reach more balls. A player can also control the ball better and make it move in different ways.

More Bounce to the Ball

Tennis balls have come a long way, too. The first tennis balls were made of leather or cloth stuffed with wool or horsehair. These balls did not bounce very high. In the 1870s, rubber was first used to make tennis balls. These balls bounced better, but the cloth that covered the ball would fall off.

Today, tennis balls are still made of rubber. First, two matching "half-shell" pieces of rubber are joined together. This makes the hollow, round shape of the ball. Second, two pieces of felt are wrapped around the ball. Third, a rubber seam is added to keep the felt cover together. Finally, the balls are put in a can that is under pressure. This helps keep them bouncy. The whole process ensures that each tennis ball bounces exactly the same way. Where the ball bounces is up to the player!

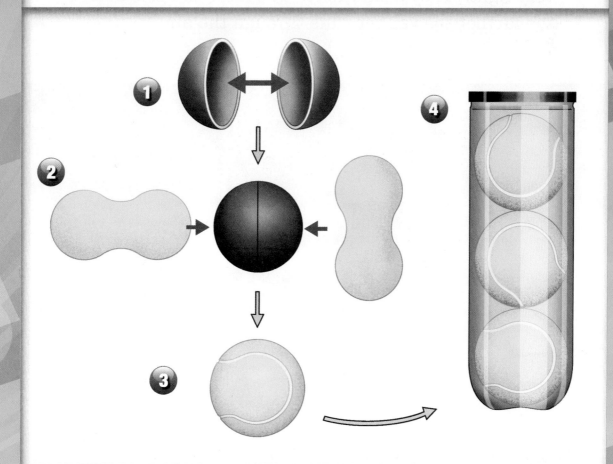

● Higher and Faster

Sports engineers help athletes perform in just about every sport. Track and field athletes run, jump, and throw. Sports engineers help these athletes run faster, jump higher, and throw farther. They design new and better track and field equipment, surfaces, and clothing.

Jump Higher

Have you ever watched a pole vaulter at the Olympics? A good pole vaulter must have speed, strength, and the right pole. The pole must be flexible and strong enough to bend and lift the vaulter over the bar. Poles used to be made of wood. These were very stiff and heavy. Later, poles were made of more flexible bamboo. Then engineers designed poles made of aluminum. Today, poles are made of fiberglass and are very light. They bend easily. The more the pole bends, the farther the vaulter sails through the air.

Run Faster

What makes a runner fast? Athletic ability and good training are most important. Engineers have designed new track surfaces and clothing to help.

Track runners used to run on grass fields. When it rained, the tracks would become soggy and slippery. Now, most runners run on "all-weather" tracks. These are man-made surfaces with a top coating of rubber chips. The rubber chips make the runners' shoes bounce off the track better. This increases speed.

New kinds of clothing also help runners speed up. Many track stars don't wear shirts and shorts like they used to. They wear lightweight body suits that fit tightly. When they run in these suits, the wind does not slow them down. Every fraction of a second counts!

A New Kind of Racing

The Boston Marathon is the oldest and most famous marathon race in the world. Each year thousands of athletes run the 26.2-mile course through the hilly streets of Boston and neighboring towns.

In 1975, Bob Hall finished the marathon in a different way. He wheeled his way to the finish line. Bob Hall was the first official wheelchair athlete to complete the Boston Marathon. He finished the race in less than 3 hours, faster than most runners.

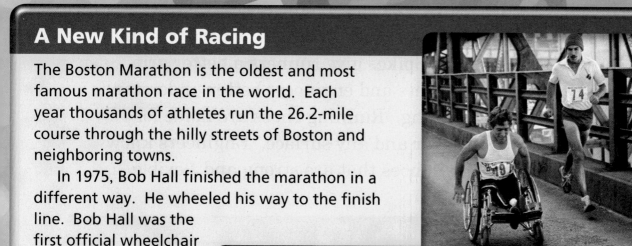

▲ Bob Hall used a simple wheelchair in the Boston Marathon.

Today, wheelchair athletes compete with high-tech wheelchairs. ▶

In *These* Shoes?

Sport engineers have also designed shoes to make athletes faster and to give them more support. Athletes need different kinds of shoes for different sports. If you want to win, you need to wear the right shoes!

A History of Running Shoes

In ancient times, runners ran barefoot. As time went on, athletes began to run in sandals. Soon, the sandal wearers were winning most of the races. The running shoe was born.

The next big change came in the 1830s in England. The first running shoe with a rubber sole was introduced. Rubber soles were light and comfortable. They also easily gripped the ground.

Spikes were added to running shoes as early as 1852. In the 1920s, a German named Adi Dassler improved the design and sold the first modern running shoes with spikes. Spikes give runners a better grip.

Today, shoemakers and engineers better understand the science of running. Running shoes are made for every style of runner and any surface. Engineers know that runners need shoes that are strong and flexible.

Changes in Running Shoes

5th century B.C.
ancient Greece: bare feet and sandals

1830s
shoes with rubber soles for a better grip

1850s
first use of spikes for running shoes

1920s
modern spiked running shoes

1972
extra cushioning in heels and soles

Extra Bounce

Long jumpers need shoes that give the athletes extra bounce. The soles must be firm but able to bend. These shoes have metal spikes in the front of the shoe only. This helps the jumper grip the ground and spring from the toes right before the jump.

Quick Movement

Soccer shoes have plastic or metal cleats, or rounded spikes, on the bottom. Cleats keep soccer players from slipping in the dirt, grass, and mud. Soccer players need to change direction quickly. Without cleats, soccer would be a slower, sloppier game!

ANALYZE THE TEXT

Text and Graphic Features
If you wanted to quickly get information about how running shoes have changed over time, where would you look on pages 410–411?

● Play Safely

Athletes also need special equipment and clothing to protect them from injury. Sports can be dangerous, and professional athletes often take risks.

Football Helmets

Over 100 years ago, football players did not wear helmets. Ouch! Then in the 1900s, players began to wear leather helmets. These early helmets did not provide much comfort or protection. Changes were needed. First, more padding was added. Second, a face mask was added to protect the nose and teeth. Also, the top of the helmet was made more round. This allowed a blow to slide off the helmet rather than strike head-on. Next, in 1939, the first plastic helmet was invented.

Today's football helmets are made of a special plastic that is light and strong. The helmet design protects players from head injuries. Some football helmets are being tested with tiny computer chips inside them. If a player hits his head, the chip sends a message to a computer. Scientists hope that these chips could tell coaches when a player needs medical help.

Other Safety Features

Some ski clothes are made to help skiers in trouble. Sometimes back-country skiers get lost or are injured miles away from anyone. Sports engineers developed special sensors for their clothing. The sensors send information about a skier's location. A rescue team receives the information, which helps the team find skiers who have fallen or are buried under the snow.

Brightly colored jackets and vests, called reflective wear, make bicyclists easier to see in the dark.

🔵 Just for Fun

The next time you play your favorite sport, think about some of the equipment you use. Think about the kind of surface on which you are standing, running, or jumping. Notice how your sports shoes look or feel and help you perform. Now that you have read about sports engineering, you can think about how technology has helped to improve your sport. Technology not only makes our lives easier and better, it also makes our lives a lot more fun!

Dig Deeper

How to Analyze the Text

Use these pages to learn about Sequence of Events and Text and Graphic Features. Then read *Technology Wins the Game* again to apply what you learned.

Sequence of Events

The informational text *Technology Wins the Game* explains how engineers use technology to improve sports equipment such as tennis balls. The engineers follow steps in a process. These steps are connected by their order, or **sequence.** The text also gives a sequence of events to tell when these improvements were made.

Look back at page 407 in *Technology Wins the Game*. The text explains the steps it takes to make a tennis ball. You can use a chart like the one below to record steps in a process or a sequence of events.

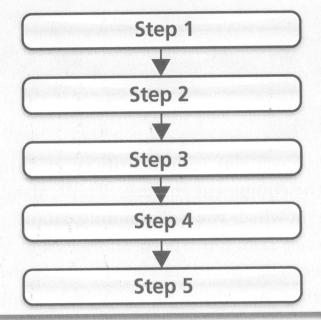

Step 1

Step 2

Step 3

Step 4

Step 5

COMMON CORE

RI.3.3 describe the relationship between a series of historical events/scientific ideas/steps in technical procedures; **RI.3.5** use text features and search tools to locate information; **RI.3.7** use information gained from illustrations and words to demonstrate understanding; **RI.3.8** describe the connection between sentences and paragraphs in a text

Text and Graphic Features

Informational text often uses special text features and graphic features along with the main text to help explain a topic and to make it easier for readers to locate information. One kind of text feature is called a **sidebar.** It is an outlined box that includes an example or information about a subtopic. A sidebar may also include a photo or other picture. A graphic feature is a visual aid. It can be a **chart,** a **diagram,** or a **timeline.** Look back at page 407 to find a diagram. It shows the steps in making a tennis ball and makes the text easier to understand.

Your Turn

RETURN TO THE ESSENTIAL QUESTION

 Turn and Talk Review the selection with a partner to prepare to discuss this question: *How do inventions help athletes?* Use text evidence to support your ideas. Take turns reviewing and explaining your opinion.

Classroom Conversation

Continue your discussion of *Technology Wins the Game* by explaining your answers to these questions:

1. Why is making a model an important step in the process of inventing new sports technology?

2. How did all the changes in tennis equipment affect the game itself?

3. What skills and knowledge do you think a sports engineer needs?

Response Think about your favorite sport. Identify something about the sport that could be improved. It could be a piece of equipment, part of the playing field, or something else. Write a paragraph using facts, definitions, and details to explain the problem and offer a possible solution.

 Writing Tip

Be specific about what the problem is and how you would solve it. If possible, include a drawing that illustrates the problem and one that shows the solution.

COMMON CORE **RI.3.1** ask and answer questions to demonstrate understanding, referring to the text; **RI.3.3** describe the relationship between a series of historical events/scientific ideas/steps in technical procedures; **RI.3.8** describe the connection between sentences and paragraphs in a text; **W.3.2a** introduce a topic and group related information/include illustrations; **W.3.2b** develop the topic with facts, definitions, and details; **W.3.10** write routinely over extended time frames or short time frames; **SL.3.1a** come to discussions prepared/explicitly draw on preparation and other information about the topic

INFORMATIONAL TEXT

Science for Sports Fans

by Alice Cary

Think about science the next time you are rooting for your favorite team. Science is at work every time an athlete hits a home run or slam-dunks a basketball.

How high professional basketball players jump depends on how much force, or power, they use to push off the court. They jump higher when they push harder. As a result, they fly through the air longer. Scientists say that a player who jumps four feet to slam-dunk hangs in the air for one full second.

RI.3.3 describe the relationship between a series of historical events/scientific ideas/steps in technical procedures; **RI.3.8** describe the connection between sentences and paragraphs in a text

WHERE IS THE SWEET SPOT?

Do you want to win a baseball championship? You can send the ball flying if you hit it with the bat's *sweet spot*. To find it, get a wooden baseball bat and a hammer. Then follow these steps.

1 Hold the bat between your thumb and index finger, just below the knob.

2 Have a friend use the hammer to tap the bat, starting at the bottom and moving up inch by inch.

3 The entire bat should vibrate with each tap, but you won't feel a thing when your friend taps the sweet spot.

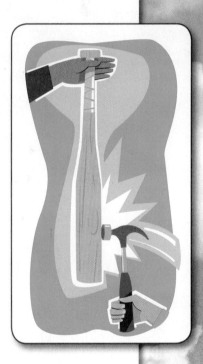

▶ What's Happening?

The bat hardly vibrates when you hit the ball at the sweet spot. Instead, more energy goes into the baseball, sending it farther.

Mastering the *Ollie*

Every skateboard competitor knows how to do an *ollie*. This trick allows skaters to jump over things. When airborne, the board seems glued to their feet.

This trick isn't magic. It's science. A skater pushes down with one foot on the back of the board when he or she jumps. This force raises the front of the board.

Next, the skater pushes the front of the board down. As the skateboard levels, the skater seems to fly through the air without losing contact with the board.

Compare Texts

TEXT TO TEXT

Compare Sports Science Compare and contrast the key ideas about sports-related science presented in *Technology Wins the Game* and *Science for Sports Fans*. How are the ideas alike? How are they different? Use text evidence to support your responses.

TEXT TO SELF

Choose a Sport Think about the sports described in *Technology Wins the Game*. If you could choose just one of those sports, which would you most like to try? Tell why, using details from the text to support your opinion.

TEXT TO WORLD

Compare Processes Think about the process that Thomas Edison used to create his inventions in *Young Thomas Edison* from Lesson 10. How is his process the same as the one sports engineers use in *Technology Wins the Game*? How is it different? Use text evidence to write two paragraphs that compare these processes.

Go Digital

COMMON CORE **RI.3.3** describe the relationship between a series of historical events/scientific ideas/steps in technical procedures; **RI.3.9** compare and contrast important points and details in texts on the same topic; **W.3.10** write routinely over extended time frames or short time frames

Grammar

More Plural Nouns If a noun ends with a consonant and *y*, change *y* to *i*, and add *-es*.

Singular: Marta picked a berry.

Plural: Marta picked berries.

Most nouns can be made plural by adding *-s* or *-es*. These are **regular plural nouns.** Sometimes the spelling of a noun changes in a special way to make it a plural. These are **irregular plural nouns.**

Singular	Plural
woman	women
child	children
mouse	mice
tooth	teeth
foot	feet

Try This! **Change each singular noun to a plural noun. Write your answer.**

❶ city

❷ foot

❸ child

❹ body

❺ tooth

❻ man

Good writers pay attention to the spellings of plural nouns. Your writing will be clearer if you spell plural nouns correctly. Remember that not every noun is made plural by adding *-s* or *-es*.

Singular	Plural
We stopped in one city on our basketball trip.	We stopped in three cities on our basketball trip.

Singular: The player stood on one foot to take her foul shot.

Plural: The player stood on two feet to take her foul shot.

 ## Connect Grammar to Writing

As you edit your cause-and-effect paragraph, check that you have spelled all plural nouns correctly.

Informative Writing

✔ **Word Choice** A good **cause-and-effect paragraph** begins by stating the topic. Next, the writer may explain what causes an event, or the writer may explain the effect. Linking words and phrases are used to connect ideas. Definitions are given for special words. A concluding statement sums up the information.

Jessica wrote a first draft of a cause-and-effect paragraph about soccer shoes. Then she revised her draft. She added a definition, a new cause and an effect, and a linking word.

Writing Traits Checklist

✔ **Ideas**
Did I include a definition?

✔ **Organization**
Did I begin with a clear topic sentence?

✔ **Word Choice**
Did I use linking words to connect causes and effects?

✔ **Voice**
Did I let my feelings come through?

✔ **Sentence Fluency**
Do my sentences flow smoothly?

✔ **Conventions**
Did I edit my work for correct grammar and punctuation?

Revised Draft

However,
^The bottoms of soccer shoes are
The soles have rounded spikes called cleats. The
different. ^Cleats cover the whole bottom
of the shoe. They grip the ground slightly
so soccer players can change direction
without slipping. ^Engineers have designed
soccer shoes so well, ^Soccer is an exciting
game to play and watch.

If the soles were flat, then soccer players' feet could slide out from underneath them! Because

Special Shoes for a Special Sport

by Jessica Olsen

Every athlete needs special shoes, and soccer players are no exception. Soccer players have to move quickly in every direction—left, right, forward, and backward. So they need shoes that will allow them to do this. The tops of soccer shoes look like many other sports shoes. They are ankle high and tie with laces. However, the bottoms of soccer shoes are different. The soles have rounded spikes called cleats. The cleats cover the whole bottom of the shoe. They grip the ground slightly so soccer players can change direction without slipping. If the soles were flat, then soccer players' feet could slide out from underneath them! Because engineers have designed soccer shoes so well, soccer is an exciting game to play and watch.

Reading as a Writer

Jessica added an idea, a definition, and a linking word to help make her paragraph stronger. What can you add to improve your cause-and-effect paragraph?

I added another cause and effect to help explain why cleats are important. I also defined *cleats* and added the linking word *because*.

Vocabulary in Context

risky
grunted
profit
crops
plucked
scowled
tugged
hollered

Vocabulary Reader   Context Cards

COMMON CORE **L.3.6** acquire and use conversational, general academic, and domain-specific words and phrases

426

---

1 risky

Picking fruit from a tall tree can be a risky job. Don't fall!

2 grunted

Instead of squealing, the piglet grunted when it was picked up.

3 profit

To make a profit, sell your products for more than it costs to make them.

4 crops

Wheat is just one of the crops grown on this farm.

Go Digital

▶ Study each Context Card.

▶ Make up a new context sentence that uses two Vocabulary words.

5 plucked

The girl plucked, or picked, a flower to give to her mother.

6 scowled

The children scowled at the idea of gardening in their good clothes.

7 tugged

The puppy tugged on the toy, trying to pull it from the boy's hands.

8 hollered

The children hollered loudly. They yelled, "Come play with us!"

Read and Comprehend

 Go Digital

☑ TARGET SKILL

Theme As you read *Tops and Bottoms*, notice what the characters do and what happens as a result. What message about life can you learn from the story? That message is the **theme**. Use an organizer like this one to keep track of important details about the plot and characters. This text evidence will help you identify the theme.

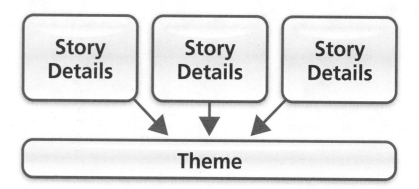

| Story Details | Story Details | Story Details |

Theme

☑ TARGET STRATEGY

Visualize Pay attention to words that describe characters, setting, and story events. They will help you **visualize,** or picture, what you read.

Agriculture

The business of agriculture includes growing, harvesting, and selling crops. Vegetables are common crops. All over the world, people grow thousands of different kinds of vegetables.

Some vegetables, like lettuce, are leafy. You eat the part of the plant that grows above the ground. Other vegetables, like carrots, are roots. You eat the part that grows under the ground. There are even fruit vegetables, such as tomatoes and cucumbers.

In *Tops and Bottoms*, you'll find out why knowing about vegetables is a smart way to do business.

ANCHOR TEXT

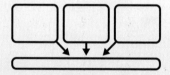

✓ TARGET SKILL

Theme Note important details in the story. Think about what these details mean and the message the story gives about life.

✓ GENRE

A **trickster tale** is an imaginative story in which one character tricks another. As you read, look for:

▸ animals that act like people

▸ humorous events

▸ a lesson, or moral, about life

COMMON CORE **RL.3.2** recount stories and determine the message, lesson, or moral; **RL.3.6** distinguish own point of view from the narrator or characters' point of view; **RL.3.10** read and comprehend literature

430

MEET THE AUTHOR AND ILLUSTRATOR

Janet Stevens

As a child, Janet Stevens loved to draw! She wasn't very good at drawing, but she kept practicing anyway. By the time she had finished high school, Janet Stevens decided that she would study art in college. She eventually started to illustrate children's books.

Janet Stevens is also a writer. She wrote and illustrated *Tops and Bottoms* on her own. She never imagined she would be a writer, as she found reading difficult when she was at school.

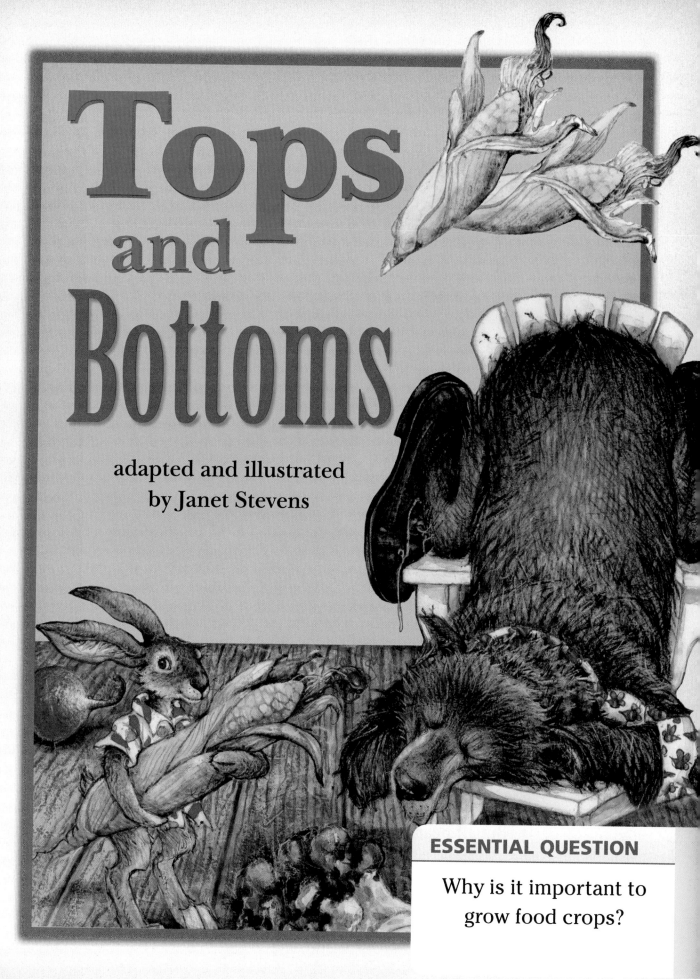

Tops
and
Bottoms

adapted and illustrated
by Janet Stevens

ESSENTIAL QUESTION

Why is it important to
grow food crops?

Once upon a time there lived a very lazy
bear who had lots of money and lots of land.
His father had been a hard worker and a smart
business bear, and he had given all of his
wealth to his son.

But all Bear wanted to do was sleep.

Not far down the road lived a hare. Although Hare was clever, he sometimes got into trouble. He had once owned land, too, but now he had nothing. He had lost a risky bet with a tortoise and had sold all of his land to Bear to pay off the debt.

Hare and his family were in very bad shape.

"The children are so hungry, Father Hare! We must think of something!" Mrs. Hare cried one day. So Hare and Mrs. Hare put their heads together and cooked up a plan.

The next day Hare hopped down the road to Bear's house. Bear, of course, was asleep.

"Hello, Bear, wake up! It's your neighbor, Hare, and I have an idea!"

Bear opened one eye and grunted.

"We can be business partners!" Hare said. "All we need is this field right here in front of your house. I'll do the hard work of planting and harvesting, and we can split the profit right down the middle. Yes, sir, Bear, we're in this together. I'll work and you sleep."

"Huh?" said Bear.

"So, what will it be, Bear?" asked Hare. "The top half or the bottom half? It's up to you—tops or bottoms?"

"Uh, let's see," Bear said with a yawn. "I'll take the top half, Hare. Right—tops."

Hare smiled. "It's a done deal, Bear."

So bear went back to sleep, and Hare and his family went to work. Hare planted, Mrs. Hare watered, and everyone weeded.

Bear slept as the crops grew.

When it was time for the harvest, Hare
called out, "Wake up, Bear! You get the
tops and I get the bottoms."

Hare and his family dug up the carrots, the radishes, and the beets. Hare plucked off all the tops, tossed them into a pile for Bear, and put the bottoms aside for himself.

Bear stared at his pile. "But, Hare, all the best parts are in your half!"

"You chose the tops, Bear," Hare said.

"Now, Hare, you've tricked me. You plant this field again—and this season I want the bottoms!"

Hare agreed. "It's a done deal, Bear."

ANALYZE THE TEXT

Point of View From Bear's point of view, is Rabbit giving him a good deal? What is your point of view?

So bear went back to sleep, and Hare and his family
went to work. They planted, watered, and weeded.

Bear slept as the crops grew.

When it was time for the harvest, Hare called out, "Wake up, Bear! You get the bottoms and I get the tops."

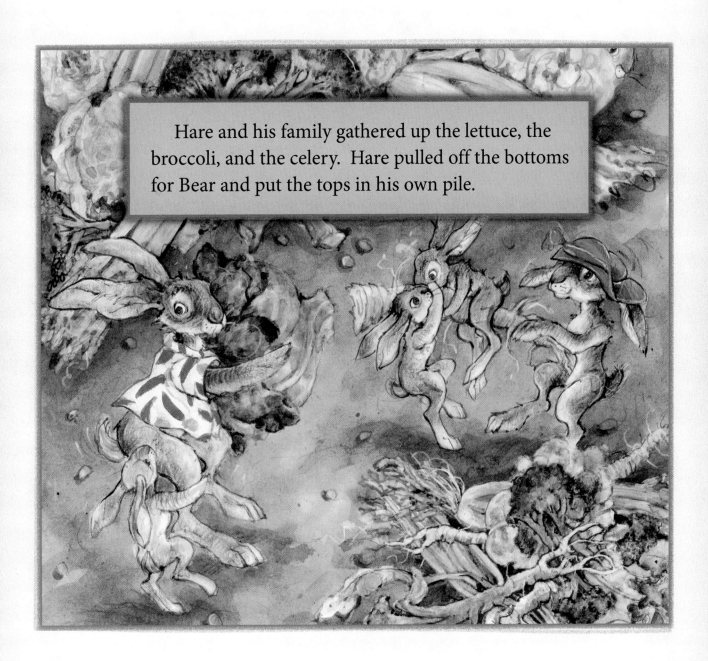

Hare and his family gathered up the lettuce, the broccoli, and the celery. Hare pulled off the bottoms for Bear and put the tops in his own pile.

Bear looked at his pile and scowled. "Hare, you have cheated me again."

"But, Bear," Hare said, "you wanted the bottoms this time."

Bear growled. "You plant this field again, Hare. You've tricked me twice, and you owe me one season of both tops and bottoms!"

"You're right, poor old Bear," sighed Hare. "It's only fair that you get both tops and bottoms this time. It's a done deal, Bear."

So Bear went back to sleep, and Hare and his family went to work. They planted, watered, and weeded, then watered and weeded some more.

Bear slept as the crops grew.

When it was time for the harvest, Hare called out, "Wake up, Bear! This time you get the tops and the bottoms!"

There in front of Bear's house lay a high field of corn. Hare and his family yanked up every cornstalk. Hare tugged off the roots at the bottom and the tassels at the top and put them in a pile for Bear. Then he carefully collected the ears of corn in the middle and placed them in his own pile.

448

Bear rubbed his eyes and watched.
"See, Bear? You get the tops and the bottoms. I get the middles. Yes, sir, Bear. It's a done deal!"

By now Bear was wide awake. "That's it, Hare!" he hollered. "From now on I'll plant my own crops and take the tops, bottoms, and middles!"

Hare and his family scooped up the corn and hopped down the road toward home.

Bear never again slept through a season of planting and harvesting. Hare bought back his land with the profit from the crops, and he and Mrs. Hare opened a vegetable stand.

And although Hare and Bear learned to live happily as neighbors, they never became business partners again!

ANALYZE THE TEXT

Theme What is the theme, or message, of the story?

Dig Deeper

How to Analyze the Text

Use these pages to learn about Theme and Point of View. Then read *Tops and Bottoms* again to apply what you learned.

Theme

A story like *Tops and Bottoms* has an important message for the reader. This message is the **theme.** A theme is a lesson about life. It is not stated directly, but can be figured out by how the characters act and what happens to them. Pay attention to these details.

Look at page 432 in *Tops and Bottoms*. What do you learn about Bear from the text evidence and the picture? Using this information and details that you read later in the story will help you figure out the theme of the story.

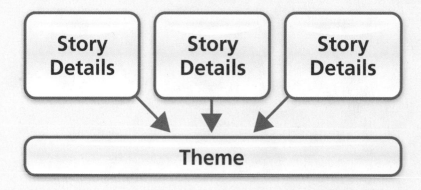

RL.3.2 recount stories and determine the message, lesson, or moral; **RL.3.6** distinguish own point of view from the narrator or characters' point of view

Point of View

Authors choose a **point of view** for their stories. The point of view is the author's message for the reader. This message is delivered through the actions, thoughts, words, and feelings of the story's narrator or characters. Authors may use the point of view to focus their readers' attention on an important idea, opinion, or feeling from the story.

Readers usually have their own point of view about what happens in a story. In *Tops and Bottoms*, Bear says that Hare tricked him. Hare says that Bear chose what he wanted. As a reader, you should decide if you agree with one character or if you have a completely different opinion about what happened.

Your Turn

Turn and Talk Review the story with a partner to prepare to discuss this question: *Why is it important to grow food crops?* As you discuss, take turns speaking. Explain your own ideas as they relate to what your partner has said.

Classroom Conversation

Continue your discussion of *Tops and Bottoms* by using text evidence to explain your answers to these questions:

1. What type of character is Bear? What type of character is Hare?

2. How does the author let you know that Hare intends to trick Bear?

3. Do you think Bear deserves to be tricked? Why or why not?

Response In *Tops and Bottoms*, Hare tricks Bear. Do you agree with what Hare does? Write a paragraph explaining what you think. Use evidence from the text to support your opinion.

Writing Tip

State your opinion clearly. Then give reasons to support it. Use parts of the text to explain your reasons. Finally, add a concluding statement that summarizes your ideas.

COMMON CORE **RL.3.1** ask and answer questions to demonstrate understanding, referring to the text; **RL.3.3** describe characters and explain how their actions contribute to the sequence of events; **W.3.1a** introduce the topic, state an opinion, and create an organizational structure; **W.3.1b** provide reasons that support the opinion; **W.3.1d** provide a concluding statement or section; **W.3.10** write routinely over extended time frames or short time frames; **SL.3.1d** explain own ideas and understanding in light of the discussion

Goodness Grows in
Gardens

Goodness Grows in
Gardens

by Tina Brigham

Community gardens come in many shapes and sizes. They are found in big cities, suburbs, and small country towns. These gardens are tended by people of all ages. Some gardeners grow beautiful flowers, but many choose to grow food. There are good reasons for having community gardens.

Good for You

You know that fruits and vegetables are good for you. You can buy these foods in grocery stores, so why take the trouble to grow them yourself? Instead of sitting inside while other people grow the food you eat, you can enjoy being outdoors. Growing a garden is a lot of work, so you get lots of exercise. Many people say they are more excited about eating food that they have grown themselves.

Good for Communities

There are thousands of community gardens in the United States. They can be found in cities like Boston, Massachusetts, and small towns like Winter Garden, Florida. Wherever they are, community gardens help people make new friends and grow good food to eat. Gardens improve communities by turning empty or overgrown plots of land into something useful and attractive. Children and adults work together and learn from one another. Volunteer gardeners provide food for those in need.

Good for Our Country

In the spring of 2009, a community garden sprang up at the White House. The White House is the official home of the President. Soon after Barack Obama and his family moved into the White House, Mrs. Obama decided to plant a garden. Everyone would share the garden, and that meant sharing the work that went with it. Even the President would have to help.

White House gardeners prepared the land, and elementary students from Washington, D.C., helped Mrs. Obama to plant seeds. They planted carrots, potatoes, strawberries, tomatoes, and other foods. The White House Kitchen Garden has fed the President and his family, special guests, and also homeless families in Washington, D.C. Our nation's Kitchen Garden has set a good example for others to follow.

Mrs. Obama believes it is important to get children involved in growing fresh fruits and vegetables.

Compare Texts

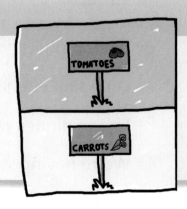

Go Digital

COMMON CORE   **RL.3.2** recount stories and determine the message, lesson, or moral; **RI.3.9** compare and contrast important points and details in texts on the same topic

Grammar

Writing Quotations Use **quotation marks** (" ") to show the exact words a person says. Quotation marks are put at the beginning and end of the words a person says. The quotation within the marks starts with a capital letter. It ends with a period inside the quotation marks.

When the tag, such as *Dad said,* comes before the quotation, use a comma before the quotation mark.

> Dad said, "Please pass the potatoes."

When the tag comes after the quotation mark, use a comma instead of a period at the end of the quotation.

> "Please pass the potatoes," Dad said.

 **Copy and write each sentence correctly by adding quotation marks and commas or periods.**

1. Lana said I'm hungry

2. I hope dinner will be ready soon Josh said

3. We're having stew Dad said

4. Lana replied A good stew has lots of vegetables

462

Questions and exclamations can be quoted, too. The question mark or the exclamation point goes inside the quotation marks.

"Would you like some potatoes?" Mom asked.

Mom asked, "Would you like some potatoes?"

"These potatoes are hot!" exclaimed Josh.

Josh exclaimed, "These potatoes are hot!"

 Connect Grammar to Writing

As you edit your compare-and-contrast paragraph, be sure to use quotation marks if you are using someone's exact words. Check that you correctly use other punctuation with quotation marks.

W.3.2a introduce a topic and group related information/include illustrations; **W.3.2b** develop the topic with facts, definitions, and details; **W.3.2c** use linking words and phrases to connect ideas within categories of information; **W.3.2d** provide a concluding statement or section; **W.3.8** recall information from experiences or gather information from print and digital sources/take brief notes and sort evidence; **W.3.10** write routinely over extended time frames or short time frames

Informative Writing

✔ **Word Choice**   A good **compare-and-contrast paragraph** begins with a topic sentence that tells which two things are being compared and contrasted. Next, the writer may tell how the things are similar. Then the writer may explain how they are different. The paragraph ends with a concluding statement.

    Ben wrote a first draft of a compare-and-contrast paragraph about his favorite foods. Then he revised his draft. He added details to make his writing stronger. He also added words to connect his ideas.

Writing Traits Checklist

✔ **Ideas**
Did I state my topic clearly?

✔ **Organization**
Did I tell how the two things are alike and different?

✔ **Word Choice**
Did I use linking words for comparing and contrasting?

✔ **Voice**
Did I let readers know my opinions?

✔ **Sentence Fluency**
Did I write complete sentences?

✔ **Conventions**
Did I use punctuation marks correctly?

Revised Draft

Yet in other ways,

∧The two foods are alike. My

               vegetable
family grows both in our ∧

garden. Both are good for you.
 My dad says, "Corn and carrots have a
lot of nutrients."
∧Nutrients help your body grow and stay

healthy. Finally, both taste great.

Corn and Carrots—Yum!

by Ben Alvarez

Two of my favorite foods are corn and carrots. In some ways, they are very different. It's not just that corn is yellow and carrots are orange. Corn grows above the ground, but carrots grow underground. Also, you have to cook corn, but you can eat carrots cooked or raw. Yet in other ways, the two foods are alike. My family grows both in our vegetable garden. Both are good for you. My dad says, "Corn and carrots have a lot of nutrients." Nutrients help your body grow and stay healthy. Finally, both taste great. Raw carrots have a crunch that makes them fun to eat, and the thought of eating sweet corn makes my mouth water!

Reading as a Writer

Which details did Ben add to make his writing stronger? What details can you add to your own paragraph?

In my final paper, I added details and linking words.

Yonder Mountain
A CHEROKEE LEGEND

THE TRAIL OF TEARS

✓ TARGET VOCABULARY

examined
peak
fondly
steep
rugged
mist
pausing
pleaded

Vocabulary Reader

The Daily Life of the Cherokee

Context Cards

COMMON CORE **L.3.6** acquire and use conversational, general academic, and domain-specific words and phrases

Vocabulary in Context

1 examined

The hiker examined the tree and saw claw marks left by bears.

2 peak

This goat lives near the peak, or top, of a mountain. It likes high, rocky cliffs.

3 fondly

Wolf mothers treat their pups fondly. They are always kind and gentle.

4 steep

This mountain is steep. It reaches straight up into the sky!

Go Digital

▶ Study each Context Card.

▶ Make up a new context sentence that uses two Vocabulary words.

5 rugged

Riders on rugged trails go slowly to avoid bumps, rocks, and holes.

6 mist

Most animals enjoy a gentle mist but look for shelter in pouring rain.

7 pausing

The buffalo in this stream is pausing, or stopping briefly, to drink.

8 pleaded

This hungry eaglet pleaded with, or begged, its mother for food.

Read and Comprehend

Go Digital

☑ TARGET SKILL

Compare and Contrast When you **compare** characters in a story, you look for details that tell how they are alike. When you **contrast** characters, you look for details that tell how they are different.

As you read *Yonder Mountain*, pay attention to how the three young men in the story deal with the challenge they face. Use a chart like this one to record text evidence about these three characters and their experiences.

Character 1	Character 2	Character 3

☑ TARGET STRATEGY

Analyze/Evaluate When you think about what you read, you **analyze** the information. This helps you **evaluate** the characters, or form an opinion about what they are like.

American Indian History

The Cherokee are Native Americans whose ancestors lived in the mountains and valleys of the southeastern United States. Each village was ruled by a chief. Like many cultures, the Cherokee have legends. These stories are from long ago and tell of important deeds.

In a Cherokee legend called *Yonder Mountain*, you will read about an old chief who tests three young men to decide which one of them will replace him as leader of their people.

ANCHOR TEXT

Yonder Mountain
A CHEROKEE LEGEND

As told by Robert H. Bushyhead
Written by Kay Thorpe Bannon
Illustrated by Kristina Rodanas

✓ TARGET SKILL

Compare and Contrast
Tell how characters are alike and different.

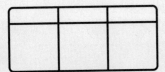

✓ GENRE

A **legend** is an old story that people have told for many years. The events in the story may or may not be true. As you read, look for:

▶ a character who does an important deed
▶ a setting that is long ago

COMMON CORE **RL.3.2** recount stories and determine the message, lesson, or moral; **RL.3.3** describe characters and explain how their actions contribute to the sequence of events; **RL.3.10** read and comprehend literature

 Go Digital

MEET THE AUTHOR
Robert H. Bushyhead

Yonder Mountain is a story that was passed down in the Bushyhead family. Robert Bushyhead grew up speaking the Cherokee language, a language so beautiful that he once compared it to the sound of "a waterfall flowing." He worked to record the language so future generations could enjoy its beauty as much as he does.

MEET THE ILLUSTRATOR
Kristina Rodanas

Kristina Rodanas uses watercolors, pastels, and colored pencils to create her illustrations. After reading one of the books that Rodanas illustrated, a student once wrote her a letter, saying, "I can still see the pictures in my mind long after I closed the book."

Yonder Mountain
A Cherokee Legend

by Robert H. Bushyhead
illustrated by Kristina Rodanas

ESSENTIAL QUESTION

Why are stories from different cultures important?

Chief Sky has grown too old to lead his people, and he's looking for someone to replace him. What is he looking for in a new chief? Find out by reading this Cherokee legend.

Once in the land of the Cherokee people, there lived a beloved chief called Sky. Chief Sky had seen many summers and winters. He had led his people through long seasons of peace. He had seen their warriors go through great battles with enemies. But now his step was slow, and his hand trembled on the bow. He could no longer spot brother deer among the trees. He was no longer able to lead his people.

One day in the season of falling leaves, the chief called three young men to him and said, "One of you will take my place and become chief and lead our people. But first, I must put you to the test."

Chief Sky turned slowly, looking into the distance. "Do you see yonder mountain?"

The three young men followed the gaze of their chief and saw a great mountain rising out of the mist in the distance. "Yes," they answered. "We see the mountain."

Chief Sky pointed toward the highest peak. "I want you to go to the mountaintop. Bring back to me what you find there."

The first young man called Black Bear quickly started up the side of the mountain. After the sun reached the middle of the day, Black Bear came to a wide place in the trail where he stopped to rest. He leaned his head upon a rock, and his eyes grew heavy. Just as his eyes were closing, he caught sight of a thousand lights twinkling in the sun. Black Bear sat up straight and saw stones of great beauty lining each side of the trail. They sparkled and glowed in the sunlight. Black Bear examined a stone, carefully turning it over and over in his hand and watching the sun dance on each surface. "If my people had these stones, they would never be hungry again," he said. "We could trade them for food and our lives would be better."

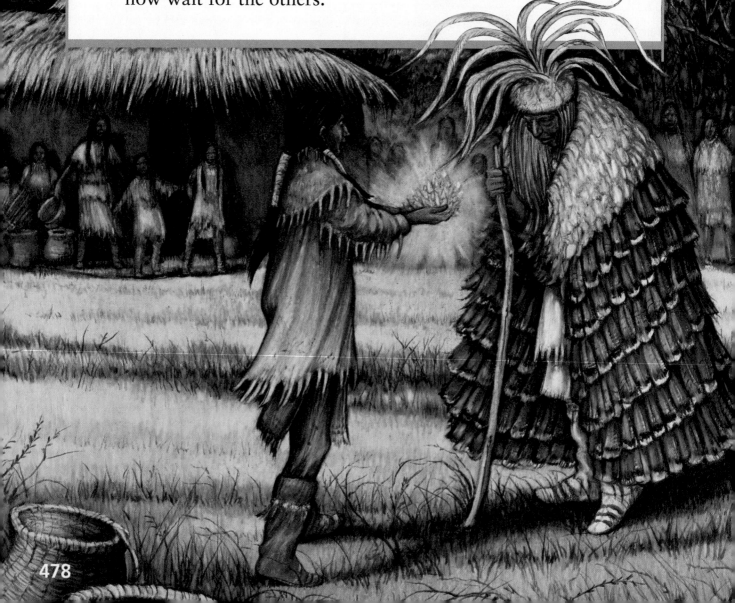

Black Bear gathered many sparkling stones and ran down the mountain and back to his village. The people saw him coming and lined the path as he entered the village. The children pointed to the sparkling stones and said, "See the pretty stones Black Bear has found." Black Bear handed the stones to Chief Sky and said, "My chief, look what I have found—beautiful stones! We can trade them for food and will never go hungry. We will be safe through many winters."

The chief smiled fondly upon the young man and said, "You have done well, my son. You have done well. Let us now wait for the others."

The second young man called Gray Wolf climbed the mountain and went past the place of the sparkling stones. He climbed higher and higher. The trail became steep and rugged. Finally, he came to an open place where he rested beside the trail. He picked an herb, looking closely at its pointed leaves and long roots. "These are the healing plants of our medicine man," he said. "If my people have these herbs and roots, they will no longer be sick and suffer. We could be healed with these plants." Gray Wolf gathered one of each of the plants and hurried down the mountain.

The people saw him coming and lined the pathway. The children waved and the elders said, "See all the herbs Gray Wolf has found. We will never be sick again!"

Gray Wolf ran to his chief and spread the plants before him. "Look, my chief, what I have found. We no longer need to suffer. I have found all kinds of herbs, and we can be healed."

The old chief smiled fondly on Gray Wolf and said, "You have done well, my son. You have done well. Now let us wait for Soaring Eagle, our last young man."

They waited. Days went by and Soaring Eagle did not return. Still the village waited. After six days, the people began to murmur. "Something must have happened to Soaring Eagle. Why wait any longer?" But Chief Sky said to his people, "We will wait one day longer." And so they waited.

On the seventh day, as the sun cast its long shadow over the village, the people saw Soaring Eagle coming. He stumbled with bleeding feet. His clothes were ripped and torn. He held nothing in his hands.

The people were quiet as Soaring Eagle fell at the feet of his chief. Soaring Eagle spoke softly to Chief Sky. "I went to the top of the mountain, my chief. But I bring back nothing in my hands. I passed a place where there were sparkling stones, but I remembered you said go to the top of the mountain. I passed a place where all sorts of herbs grew, but I remembered your words. The path was rough. There were great cliffs and sharp rocks. I have nothing in my hands to show you, but I bring back a story from the top of the mountain."

ANALYZE THE TEXT

Compare and Contrast How are the journeys of the three young men the same? How are they different? Compare and contrast how each man's actions affect the story's events.

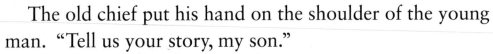

The old chief put his hand on the shoulder of the young man. "Tell us your story, my son."

Soaring Eagle began. "As I stood on yonder mountain and looked across the valley and beyond the farthest mountain, I saw a smoke signal. It was a signal calling for help. The signal said 'We are dying,' and then 'Come and help us.'"

Soaring Eagle rose to his feet. "Chief Sky," he pleaded. "We need to go to them quickly. They are in trouble."

Chief Sky stood straight before his people and the three young men. Pausing for a time, he lifted his eyes to the mountains and watched the mist settle on the peaks. He then turned to his people and spoke. "We need a leader who has climbed to the top of the mountain. We need one who has seen beyond the mountain to other people who are in need."

The people watched as Chief Sky carefully began to remove his robe. He turned to face Soaring Eagle. "You, my son, shall wear the chief's robe," the beloved old leader declared. Chief Sky placed the robe over the torn clothing of the chosen young man. "You shall be our next chief, Soaring Eagle. You will lead our people and help those in need. Yes, you will be our chief and help us climb yonder mountain."

ANALYZE THE TEXT

Story Message What message does the author want readers to understand?

Dig Deeper

How to Analyze the Text

Use these pages to learn about Comparing and Contrasting and Story Message. Then read *Yonder Mountain* again to apply what you learned.

Compare and Contrast

The legend *Yonder Mountain* tells the story of Chief Sky and three young men. The characters' actions contribute to the story's sequence of events. These characters and their experiences can be compared and contrasted.

When you **compare**, you describe how two or more things are alike. When you **contrast**, you describe how they are different.

Look back at pages 474 and 475 of *Yonder Mountain*. In this part of the story, you find out what Chief Sky wants the three young men to do. As you read, look for text evidence about what each man finds on his journey. Notice what is the same and what is different about how each character affects the story plot.

Character 1	Character 2	Character 3

RL.3.2 recount stories and determine the message, lesson, or moral; **RL.3.3** describe characters and explain how their actions contribute to the sequence of events

488

Story Message

A story like this legend is told over and over again for many years because it has an important **message**. The message is a lesson about life. It is not stated in the story. Instead, the characters and events help show what the lesson is. Readers can look at what happens and why it happens to learn the story's message.

Your Turn

Turn and Talk Review the story with a partner to prepare to discuss this question: *Why are stories from different cultures important?* As you talk, use evidence from *Yonder Mountain* to explain the key ideas in your discussion.

Classroom Conversation

Continue your discussion of *Yonder Mountain.* Use text evidence to explain your answers to these questions:

1. Why does Chief Sky feel he must choose someone else to be chief? Do you agree with him? Why or why not?

2. How do the Cherokee feel about helping people? How can you tell?

3. If you were Chief Sky, which young man would you choose to be chief? Why?

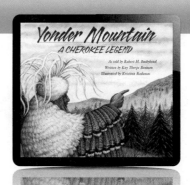

Response What makes a person a great leader? Write a paragraph about this topic. Describe the qualities that Chief Sky thinks a leader should have. Then explain the qualities you think are important in a leader. Give reasons for your ideas. End with a concluding statement.

Writing Tip

Organize the ideas in your paragraph. First, state the leadership qualities Chief Sky thinks are important. Then compare or contrast them with the qualities you think are important.

COMMON CORE **RL.3.1** ask and answer questions to demonstrate understanding, referring to the text; **RL.3.3** describe characters and explain how their actions contribute to the sequence of events; **W.3.1a** introduce the topic, state an opinion, and create an organizational structure; **W.3.1b** provide reasons that support the opinion; **W.3.1d** provide a concluding statement or section; **W.3.4** produce writing in which development and organization are appropriate to task and purpose

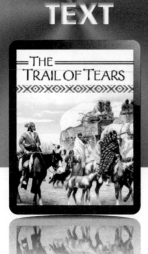

THE TRAIL OF TEARS

by Samuel Winters

The Cherokee Homeland

In 1830, the Cherokee lived in the southeast part of the United States. White settlers wanted Cherokee land. They wanted it to farm. They wanted to look for gold on it. Why? People had found gold in Georgia. Most of the gold was on Cherokee land.

Most Cherokee did not want to move west. The U.S. army watched them closely as they marched to make sure no Cherokee escaped.

Loss of Land

The U.S. government passed a law in 1830. It was the Indian Removal Act. The law let the President give land to Native Americans. The land was west of the Mississippi. In return, Native Americans would give up their land in the east. Then white settlers could have it.

In 1835, a small group of Cherokee signed a treaty. They sold their land to the U.S. government. They would move west. Most Cherokee did not want to give up their land, but the U.S. government said the treaty meant that all Cherokee had to move.

The Hard Journey

In 1838, the U.S. Army forced about sixteen thousand Cherokee from their homes. They left the farms they had tended fondly. They moved to what is now Oklahoma. Some went by boat. Most of them marched.

Parts of the trail were steep and rugged. Women carried their babies over each mountain peak. The weak and very young rode. Mist swirled around them. Rain and snow lashed at them. The Cherokee marched on, pausing only briefly for rest. Many people became ill. They had little food. Thousands died. The Cherokee pleaded with the soldiers to stop long enough to allow them to bury those who had died.

A survivor told what the sad journey was like. "Children cry and many men cry . . . . Many days pass and people die . . . ." The Cherokee reached Oklahoma in the winter. They called the hard journey *The Trail Where They Cried*.

The U.S. government created the *Trail of Tears National Historic Trail* in 1987 to honor the Cherokee. It stretches for 2,200 miles across nine states.

The Trail of Tears

This map shows the route the Cherokee traveled in 1838. What made the journey so difficult?

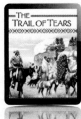

Compare Texts

Compare Experiences How were the journeys of the Cherokee men in *Yonder Mountain* similar to the journey of the Cherokee described in *The Trail of Tears*? How were they different? With a partner, compare and contrast the reasons each group had for traveling. Discuss the challenges they faced.

Write About Legends *Yonder Mountain* is a legend that teaches a lesson and also teaches about the Cherokee people. Think about a time when you learned a lesson. Write about it as a story so that it teaches the reader about you and about what you learned.

An Important Lesson About Helping Others

Connect to Social Studies Identify three historical details about the Cherokee people. Use *Yonder Mountain, The Trail of Tears,* and your own research to find the information. Make a list to show the information, and display it for the class.

Go Digital

COMMON CORE **RI.3.9** compare and contrast important points and details in texts on the same topic; **W.3.8** recall information from experiences or gather information from print and digital sources/take brief notes and sort evidence; **SL.3.1a** come to discussions prepared/explicitly draw on preparation and other information about the topic

L.3.1.a explain the function of nouns, pronouns, verbs, adjectives, and adverbs; **L.3.1d** form and use regular and irregular verbs; **L.3.1f** ensure subject-verb and pronoun-antecedent agreement

Grammar

Subject-Verb Agreement Verbs in the present tense have two forms. When the **subject** is singular, add -s or -es to the **verb**. When the subject is plural, do not add -s or -es to the verb.

Singular	Plural
The boy climbs a mountain.	The boys climb a mountain.
The group waits below.	The groups wait below.
One scout returns.	The scouts return.
He watches the boys.	They watch the boys.

Try This! **Work with a partner. Read each sentence aloud. Choose the correct verb for each sentence. What function, or job, does the verb have in each sentence?**

❶ The scouts (start, starts) their hike.

❷ A hill (rise, rises) sharply.

❸ They (struggle, struggles) over the rocks.

❹ The hot sun (shine, shines) down on them.

❺ David (get, gets) to the top first.

In your writing, pay attention to the endings of the verbs you use. The correct form to use depends on what the subject of the sentence is. Always check the spelling of each verb ending.

Singular Subject	Plural Subject
The <u>hiker</u> climbs the mountain.	The <u>hikers</u> climb the mountain.

Singular Subject: The <u>man</u> watches an eagle.
The <u>eagle</u> carries a fish in its talons.
Plural Subject: The <u>men</u> watch an eagle.
<u>Eagles</u> carry fish in their talons.

 Connect Grammar to Writing

As you edit your informative paragraph, look for incorrect spellings of verbs in the present tense. Be sure the verb form agrees with the subject.

COMMON CORE **W.3.2a** introduce a topic and group related information/include illustrations; **W.3.2b** develop the topic with facts, definitions, and details; **W.3.2d** provide a concluding statement or section; **W.3.8** recall information from experiences or gather information from print and digital sources/take brief notes and sort evidence

Informative Writing

✔ **Organization** Informative writing explains or gives information about a topic. A good **informative paragraph** begins by clearly stating the topic. Using experience or information gathered from a source, the writer then presents facts, examples, and other details. The writer also defines, or explains, special words for readers. The writer ends with a statement that sums up the information.

Chloe wrote a first draft of her informative paragraph about legends. Then she revised her draft. She added a detail to make her writing stronger. She also added a statement at the end.

Writing Traits Checklist

✔ **Ideas**
Did I include facts and examples?

✔ **Organization**
Did I group related information?

✔ **Word Choice**
Did I define special words?

✔ **Voice**
Did I show what the reader should know?

✔ **Sentence Fluency**
Did I write complete sentences?

✔ **Conventions**
Did I edit my work for spelling, grammar, and punctuation?

Revised Draft

Legends often have heroes.
∧In <u>Yonder Mountain</u>, one young man climbs to the top of a mountain and comes back to say he saw a smoke signal for help. He becomes the new chief. <u>Yonder Mountain</u> shows us the Cherokee thought helping other people was important. ∧So, legends are not just interesting stories. They show us what is important to the people who tell them.

498

Legends

by Chloe Williams

Some people think legends are the same as fairytales, but they are not. A legend is an old story that a group of people have told for many years. Some parts of the story might really have happened. The Cherokee legend in <u>Yonder Mountain</u> has been told in Robert Bushyhead's family for a long time. Legends often have heroes. In <u>Yonder Mountain</u>, one young man climbs to the top of a mountain and comes back to say he saw a smoke signal for help. He becomes the new chief. <u>Yonder Mountain</u> shows us that the Cherokee thought helping other people was important. So, legends are not just interesting stories. They show us what is important to the people who tell them.

Reading as a Writer

Chloe added an important detail and an ending statement to help make her paragraph stronger. What can you add to improve your informative paragraph?

In my final paper, I added another important detail about legends. I also added a concluding statement that sums up what legends are.

Aero and Officer Mike
POLICE PARTNERS

Kids and Critters

☑ **TARGET VOCABULARY**

lying
loyal
partners
shift
quiver
patrol
ability
snap

Vocabulary Reader

Context Cards

Dog Helpers

COMMON CORE **L.3.6** acquire and use conversational, general academic, and domain-specific words and phrases

Vocabulary in Context

1 lying
This dog is lying down. It is stretched out on the floor.

2 loyal
Dogs are usually loyal pets. They stick by their human friends.

3 partners
Many police officers have partners they work with daily.

4 shift
A shift is a period of working time. A shift may be during the day or at night.

Go Digital

► Study each Context Card.

► Discuss one picture. Use a different Vocabulary word from the one on the card.

5 **quiver**

A dog has a strong sense of smell. Its nose may quiver, or twitch, when it sniffs.

6 **patrol**

When police officers patrol, they watch over an area to make sure it is safe.

7 **ability**

An ability is a special skill. Dogs have the ability to run fast.

8 **snap**

Never pet a strange dog without asking permission. It might snap at you.

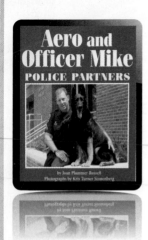

Read and Comprehend

Go Digital

☑ TARGET SKILL

Author's Purpose As you read *Aero and Officer Mike*, think about the **author's purpose** for writing. Is it to inform, to persuade, or to entertain readers? Look for text evidence about the topic and think about how the author presents her ideas. Use a graphic organizer like this one to list clues from the text that help you identify the author's purpose.

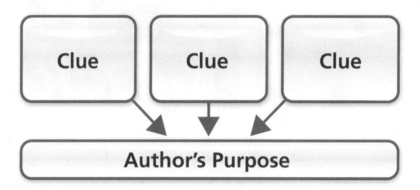

☑ TARGET STRATEGY

Summarize As you read *Aero and Officer Mike*, pay close attention to main ideas and events. Then retell these ideas in your own words to **summarize** the text.

RI.3.1 ask and answer questions to demonstrate understanding, referring to the text; **RI.3.2** determine the main idea/recount details and explain how they support the main idea

COMMON CORE

502

People and Animals

Dogs and humans have always had a special relationship. In fact, dogs were probably the first real pets that humans had. People in ancient times realized that dogs could help and protect them. They also learned that dogs often had strong affection for people.

Dogs truly are good partners. They have an incredible sense of smell, they are fast, and they are loyal. When they are well trained, dogs are also determined to do what their humans want them to do. They will not give up. In *Aero and Officer Mike,* you'll see what incredible things a dog can do.

ANCHOR TEXT

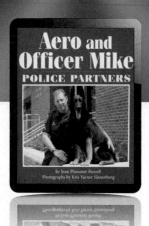

To prepare to write this book, Joan Plummer Russell rode along with Officer Mike and Aero twice a month for two years. She took notes and some photographs as part of her research, and she recorded many conversations. Some of her recordings are filled with Aero's barking!

✅ TARGET SKILL

Author's Purpose Use information in the text to figure out why the author wrote the selection. How does she feel about the topic?

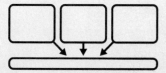

✅ GENRE

Informational text gives facts and information about a topic. As you read, look for:

► headings that tell about the content of the sections

► photographs

► clues that tell how the author feels about the topic

RI.3.1 ask and answer questions to demonstrate understanding, referring to the text; **RI.3.6** distinguish own point of view from that of the author; **RI.3.10** read and comprehend informational texts

AERO AND OFFICER MIKE

POLICE PARTNERS

by
Joan Plummer Russell

photographs by
Kris Turner Sinnenberg

ESSENTIAL QUESTION

What are some benefits
of dogs interacting
with people?

It is very early in the morning. Everyone in the house is still asleep. A large black-and-tan German shepherd is lying on the floor by Officer Mike's bed. The alarm rings. Officer Mike reaches down to pet his dog, Aero.

Aero is a police dog, also known as a K-9 officer. When Officer Mike puts on his uniform with a silver badge on his chest, Aero jumps up, ready to have his wide black leather collar with a police badge on it slipped over his head. He knows this will be a work day.

WORK AND PLAY

Officer Mike and Aero are partners. They work together. They practice together. They play together.

Aero, with his powerful nose, can do many things Officer Mike cannot. He can sniff and find lost children. He can sniff and find lost things.

Police dogs are very strong and well trained. They have to be ready to go anywhere they are needed. They can be very fierce when they are helping to catch criminals. They can run faster than any human being. But when police dogs are not working, they are gentle pets that like to have their tummies scratched.

Aero's most important jobs are to help and to protect his partner, Officer Mike. Together, Aero and Officer Mike patrol in all kinds of weather. Some weeks they patrol from early morning until dinnertime. Some weeks they sleep in the daytime and work all night.

ON DUTY

Aero is always eager to jump into the back of the police car. Officer Mike's car is different from other police cars. There is no back seat. The floor is flat and covered with carpet for Aero to lie on. There is a water bowl built into the floor and a small fan keeps Aero cool in the summer. Screens cover the windows so no one can reach in and pet him.

When Aero is on duty, he's not allowed to play. Officer Mike sits in the driver's seat, but Aero will not let anyone else sit in the front until Officer Mike tells Aero it is OK.

Aero knows that one of his jobs is to protect the police car. When Officer Mike leaves the car, he either opens the front window for Aero to jump through or uses a remote control to open the back door when he needs Aero's help.

TIME FOR A BREAK

When Aero and Officer Mike have been in the police car for a few hours, Aero will need to take a break. Aero pushes his head against his partner's head to let him know. Officer Mike parks the cruiser as soon as he can and says to Aero, "Go be a dog!" Aero knows he'll also have time to explore a little and maybe chase a tennis ball while they are stopped.

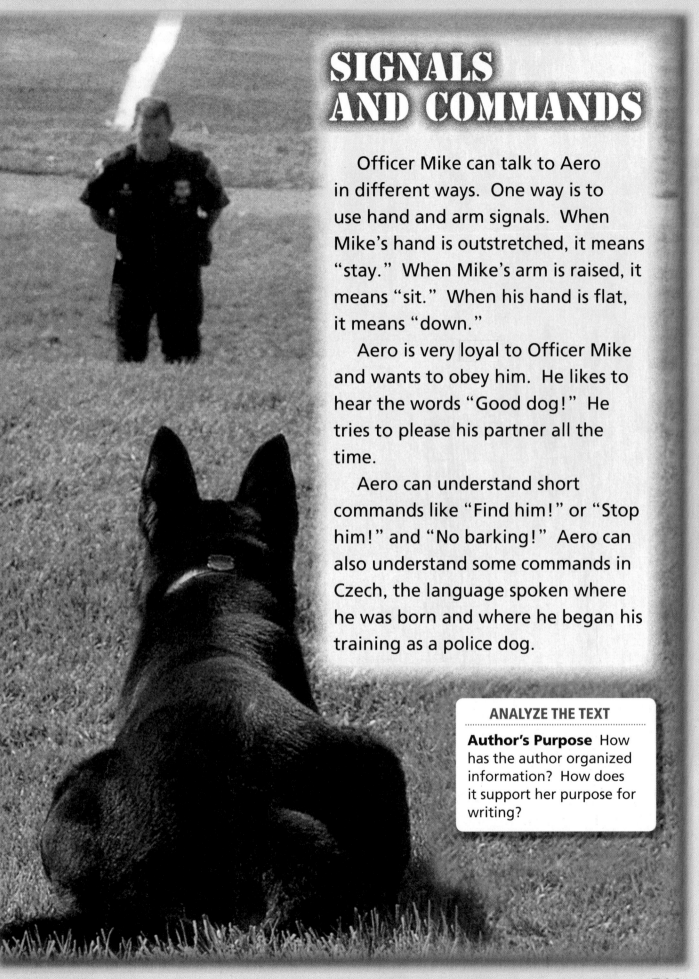

SIGNALS AND COMMANDS

Officer Mike can talk to Aero in different ways. One way is to use hand and arm signals. When Mike's hand is outstretched, it means "stay." When Mike's arm is raised, it means "sit." When his hand is flat, it means "down."

Aero is very loyal to Officer Mike and wants to obey him. He likes to hear the words "Good dog!" He tries to please his partner all the time.

Aero can understand short commands like "Find him!" or "Stop him!" and "No barking!" Aero can also understand some commands in Czech, the language spoken where he was born and where he began his training as a police dog.

ANALYZE THE TEXT

Author's Purpose How has the author organized information? How does it support her purpose for writing?

K-9 TRAINING

Aero's training never ends. Several times a month Aero and Officer Mike train with other officers and their K-9 partners. One exercise the police dogs do is to run through an obstacle course. The dogs practice getting over, under, around, and through difficult spots.

Aero had to learn how to walk up and down very steep, open stairs. He also had to learn to walk over a large, open grating, the kind you often see on city streets. At first he spread his paws to help keep his balance. His legs began to quiver, and he whined a frightened cry. He had to practice over and over. Officer Mike kept saying, "Good boy, you can do it." Aero was brave and trusted his partner, but he still does not like open gratings or steep stairs.

AERO'S SENSE OF SMELL

K-9s have very powerful noses—hundreds of times more powerful than human noses. That's why one of Aero's most helpful talents on the police force is his ability to find things by smell.

When children play hide-and-seek, they may think they are well hidden. Their dog can find them right away. The same is true when a child is lost or wanders away from home. Aero can find the child by using his sense of smell. Each person has a scent that is different from everyone else's scent. Even twins do not smell the same. A person's unique smell comes from the food he or she eats, the soap and shampoo he or she uses, the clothes he or she wears, and the place he or she lives.

AT THE VET'S

Aero goes to Dr. Morse, a veterinarian, for regular checkups. Aero must lie still on a table while the doctor examines him. Once Aero had a small infection on his neck. Dr. Morse gave him some medicine so he would get better. Because a police dog works so hard and has such an important job, he needs to be healthy. At the end of the checkup, Dr. Morse lifts Aero to the floor, pets him, and says, "Good dog."

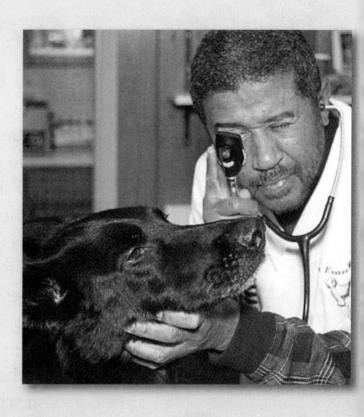

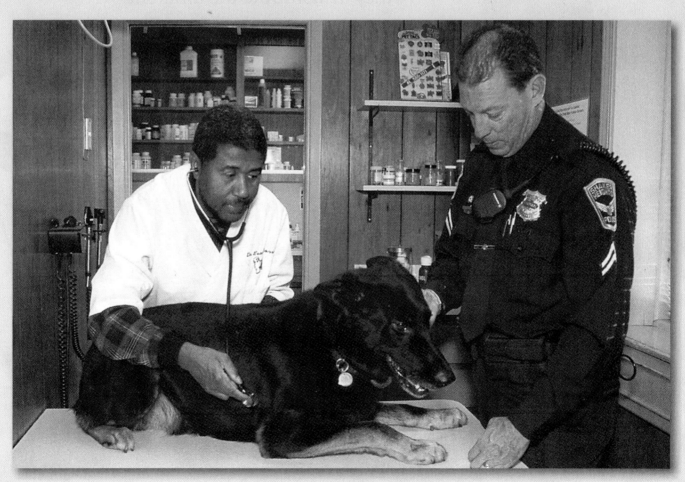

515

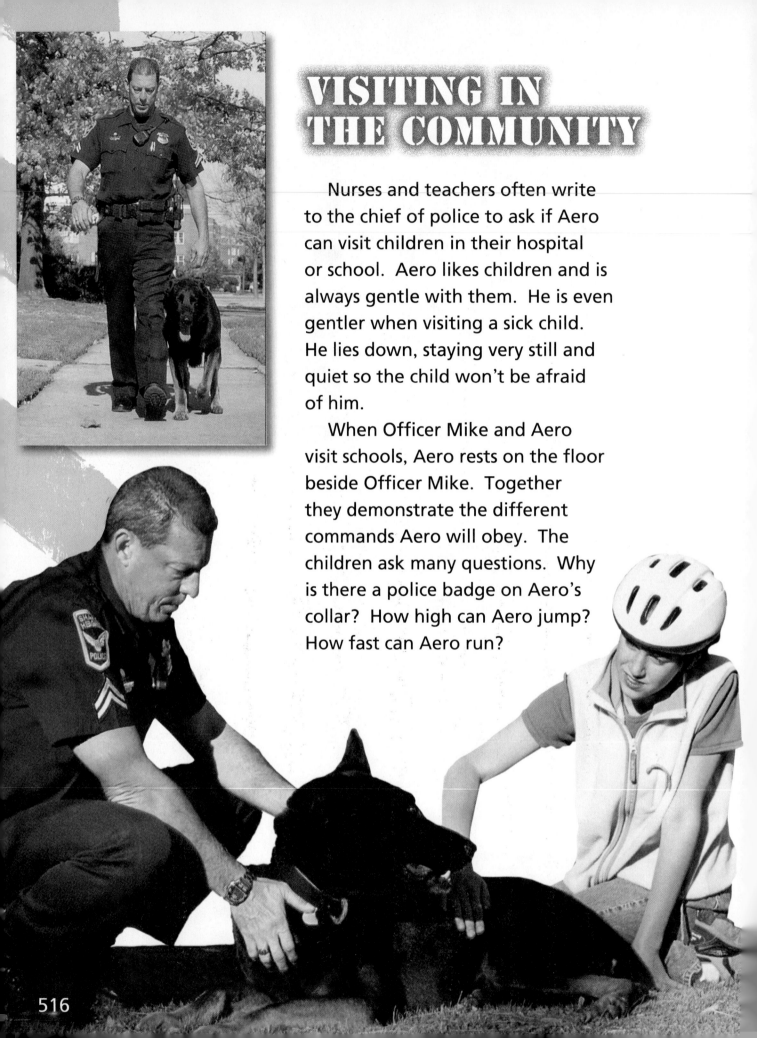

VISITING IN THE COMMUNITY

Nurses and teachers often write to the chief of police to ask if Aero can visit children in their hospital or school. Aero likes children and is always gentle with them. He is even gentler when visiting a sick child. He lies down, staying very still and quiet so the child won't be afraid of him.

When Officer Mike and Aero visit schools, Aero rests on the floor beside Officer Mike. Together they demonstrate the different commands Aero will obey. The children ask many questions. Why is there a police badge on Aero's collar? How high can Aero jump? How fast can Aero run?

Officer Mike carefully answers the questions. Aero's badge shows everyone that he is a working police dog. He can jump over an eight-foot wall when he is chasing a criminal. He can run very fast, about forty miles an hour. Even the fastest person can only run about twenty-four miles an hour.

PETTING AERO

Children often want to pet Aero. Officer Mike tells them the rules. Never try to pet a strange dog until you ask permission from the owner. Never come up behind Aero. He might get frightened and snap at you. Never ever hug a K-9 around the neck. Walk up to a police dog slowly from the front so he can see you. Let him sniff your hand. Pet his head and ears gently. Talk to him softly.

BACK AT THE STATION

At the end of a twelve-hour work shift, there is always a final job to be done at the police station. After talking with his friends on the force, Officer Mike sits down and writes a report for the police chief about the whole day or night. Aero lies down by Officer Mike's chair.

FELLOW OFFICERS

After the report is written, Officer Mike and Aero go home together. When Officer Mike goes to bed, Aero will plop down on the floor near the bed. He lays his head on his paws, and with a sigh goes to sleep near his best friend. Neither of them knows what surprises tomorrow's patrol will bring, but they are well prepared. They both love being police officers.

ANALYZE THE TEXT

Point of View What is the author's point of view about K-9 officers? Do you share her point of view? Why or why not?

Dig Deeper

How to Analyze the Text

Use these pages to learn about Author's Purpose and Point of View. Then read *Aero and Officer Mike* again to apply what you learned.

Author's Purpose

The **author's purpose** is the reason an author has for writing. Authors who write to inform give facts and details about a subject. They might use photos or illustrations to help readers understand the subject.

The author's purpose is not usually stated directly. Readers have to figure out the purpose by looking for evidence in the text. As you read, ask yourself what the author wants you to understand from reading. Then list the clues that help you determine the author's purpose.

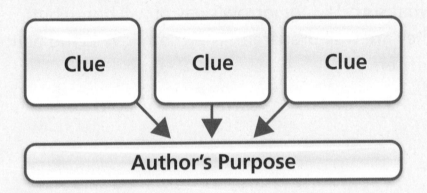

RI.3.1 ask and answer questions to demonstrate understanding, referring to the text; **RI.3.6** distinguish own point of view from that of the author

Point of View

Authors usually have a **point of view** about their subject. A point of view is how the author "sees," or thinks and feels about, a subject. Look at the words the author uses. This can help you identify the point of view.

Review the second paragraph on page 507. The author says that Aero has a "powerful nose" and "can do many things Officer Mike cannot." These words show that the author's point of view in this section is that Aero has valuable skills. You may have a point of view that is different from the author's, or it may be the same.

Your Turn

 Turn and Talk Review the selection with a partner to prepare to discuss this question: *What are some benefits of dogs interacting with people?* Talk about your response using text evidence and your own experiences. Use terms such as *in my opinion.*

Classroom Conversation

Continue your discussion of *Aero and Officer Mike* by explaining your answers to these questions:

1. What benefits do you think both Officer Mike and Aero get from their relationship?

2. Why do you think trust between a police officer and a police dog is so important?

3. How would you describe Aero to a friend who hasn't read the selection?

WRITE ABOUT READING

Response Officer Mike and Aero work hard together and make a good team. What other animals could help police officers do their job? How do you think these other animals could help their human partners? Write a paragraph to explain your ideas.

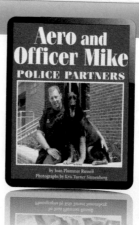

Writing Tip

Introduce your topic and then support it with text evidence such as facts, definitions, and details from the selection. Use linking words and phrases to connect your ideas. End with a strong conclusion.

INFORMATIONAL TEXT

✓ GENRE

Informational text gives factual information about a topic.

✓ TEXT FOCUS

Headings help readers locate information. They tell what each section of text is about.

RI.3.5 use text features and search tools to locate information; **RI.3.10** read and comprehend informational texts

Go Digital

Kids and Critters
A NATURE NEWSLETTER

What Is 4-H?

4-H is a program for boys and girls ages eight to eighteen. In a 4-H club, you'll make new friends and find new interests. You might care for animals, work with partners to plant a community garden, or patrol a park to pick up litter. You'll learn the 4-H motto, "To Make the Best Better."

All fifty states have 4-H programs. Look for a club near you.

Get the Rabbit Habit

4-H boys and girls in Bell County, Texas, have the rabbit habit. Each year they show their rabbits at 4-H fairs.

You don't need any special skill or ability to care for a rabbit. Just give your pet plenty of love, food, and water, and a clean, cozy place to live. Your rabbit will quiver its nose with delight!

This is how to pose a rabbit for a judge.

A City Nature Walk

There's so much to see on a city nature walk. Your 4-H leader can supervise the walk. Be attentive to what you see. You may spot a bird's nest, some squirrels, or even a coyote!

A NATURE NEWSLETTER

Use What You Learn!

In 4-H, you use what you learn to help your community. Maybe you can use what you learn about animals to work a shift in a local animal shelter.

Shelter animals can't spend all day lying in their cages. They need exercise and attention. By walking dogs or cuddling cats, a loyal volunteer can make a big difference. With your help, an animal that used to be shy can become a friendly tail-wagger!

Summer Fair

August 10, at 1:00 P.M.
Juniper Park

Do not miss this exciting summer event!

- Groom your pet.
- Pick your biggest tomato.
- Choose something you've made.
- Show off your hard work!

Blue ribbons in these groups:

Animals

Vegetables

Handicrafts

Compare Texts

Compare Relationships Think about the people and the animals in *Aero and Officer Mike* and *Kids and Critters*. Talk with a partner about how Aero and the animals in a 4-H program are similar. Then talk about how they are different. Which of the animals would make good pets? Explain your reasons.

Write a Letter Imagine that you would like to be a police officer who works with a K-9 like Aero. Write a letter to 4-H asking if you may join. Use text evidence from both selections to explain how 4-H will help prepare you for this job.

Connect to Social Studies With a small group, find out different ways animals work to help people. Use reference books or the Internet, or interview someone. Make a poster that shows the animals and their jobs.

 RI.3.1 ask and answer questions to demonstrate understanding, referring to the text; **RI.3.9** compare and contrast important points and details in texts on the same topic; **W.3.7** conduct short research projects that build knowledge about a topic

Grammar

Pronoun–Verb Agreement You know that a **pronoun** can be the **subject** of a sentence. Remember that **verbs** in the present have two forms. The correct form of the verb to use depends on the subject pronoun. The pronoun and the verb should agree.

Subject	Present-Tense Verb
he, she, it He places the collar on the dog. It fits the dog perfectly.	Add -*s* or -*es*
I, you, we, they I like the collar. They wear their collars proudly.	Do not add -*s* or -*es*

Try This! **Work with a partner. Read each sentence aloud. Decide which verb form completes each sentence.**

1 They (train, trains) police dogs.

2 She (watch, watches) them learn.

3 We (like, likes) our police officers.

4 They (keep, keeps) us safe.

Be careful not to repeat a noun too many times. When two sentences have the same noun as the subject, you can put the sentences together. Change one noun to a pronoun. Then join the two subjects and use the word *and* between them.

Short, Choppy Sentences

Mack barks at birds.

Mack chases them.

Longer, Smoother Sentence

Mack barks at birds, and he chases them.

 Connect Grammar to Writing

As you revise your explanatory essay next week, look for short, choppy sentences that repeat a noun. Replace one of the repeated nouns with a pronoun and combine the sentences. Check that the verb and pronoun agree.

W.3.2a introduce a topic and group related information/include illustrations; **W.3.2b** develop the topic with facts, definitions, and details; **W.3.5** develop and strengthen writing by planning, revising, and editing; **W.3.8** recall information from experiences or gather information from print and digital sources/take brief notes and sort evidence

Informative Writing

Reading-Writing Workshop: Prewrite

An **explanatory essay** gives ideas and details, along with facts, to clearly explain a topic to readers.

The first step is to decide what you want to write about. This is your **topic**. The topic should not be too general. It is easier to give good information about a smaller idea. Then take notes about the main ideas and details you want to include. Next, organize the main ideas and details in an outline.

Jill wants to write about how dogs help people. Her topic is too big, so she works to make it more focused.

Writing Process Checklist

▶ **Prewrite**

- ☑ Is my topic the right size?
- ☑ Is there one idea I can focus on to make my topic smaller?
- ☑ Did I make notes on facts and details I found on my topic?
- ☑ Did I organize my notes in an outline?

Draft

Revise

Edit

Publish and Share

Exploring a Topic

Dogs that help people
K-9s, rescue workers, service dogs, farming

⬇

Service dogs
guide dogs, hearing dogs, mobility dogs, therapy dogs

⬇

Mobility dogs
for people who have trouble walking

An Amazing Helper
by Jill F. Baugh

I. Service dogs

    A. What are service dogs?

    B. A guide dog is a service dog.

II. Mobility dogs

    A. What are mobility dogs?

    B. What they can do

III. Mobility dogs and people

    A. What training do they need?

    B. How they are matched with people

IV. Conclusion

Reading as a Writer

How can you narrow your topic and organize your ideas for your explanatory essay?

At first, I had too many kinds of working dogs that help people. Then I focused on service dogs. I then chose one kind of service dog.

☑ **TARGET VOCABULARY**

festive
ingredients
degrees
recommended
anxiously
cross
remarked
tense

Vocabulary   Context
Reader   Cards

 L.3.6 acquire and use conversational, general academic, and domain-specific words and phrases

Vocabulary in Context

1 festive
Everybody felt happy and merry at the festive birthday dinner.

2 ingredients
The ingredients in this salad include tomatoes, lettuce, and cucumbers.

3 degrees
This snack was baked in a hot oven. It was set to 350 degrees.

4 recommended
It is recommended that pizza cool before you eat it. That is good advice.

▶ Study each Context Card.

▶ Use two Vocabulary words to tell about an experience you had.

5 **anxiously**

This boy **anxiously** measured the sugar. He was afraid of making a mistake.

6 **cross**

Children often feel **cross**, or angry, when asked to eat food they dislike.

7 **remarked**

The guest **remarked**, or said, that the meal was delicious.

8 **tense**

Relax when you frost a cake. If you're **tense**, your hand will shake and ruin it.

Read and Comprehend

☑ TARGET SKILL

Understanding Characters As you read *The Extra-good Sunday*, notice the characters' thoughts, actions, and words. These are clues to the **characters' traits,** or what the characters are like, and their **motivations,** or reasons for their actions. Use a graphic organizer like this one to help you list details about a character. You can then use the text evidence to describe his or her traits, motivations, and feelings.

Traits	Motivations	Feelings

☑ TARGET STRATEGY

Infer/Predict Use what you know about the characters to think more about, or **infer,** why they think, speak, and act as they do. Use text evidence to **predict,** or figure out, what the characters might do next.

Cooking

To make a good and healthful meal, cooks need to know many things. For example, they need to store, prepare, and cook different foods so they are safe to eat as well as tasty. Good cooks also know how to safely operate cooking tools and equipment such as stoves, ovens, mixers, knives, and graters. All this makes preparing and cooking good meals hard work. In *The Extra-good Sunday*, two sisters learn just how challenging it can be to prepare a good meal.

ANCHOR TEXT

Ramona Quimby, Age 8
Beverly Cleary

✅ TARGET SKILL

Understanding Characters
Describe the characters in the story, and tell why they act as they do.

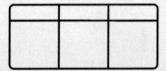

✅ GENRE

Humorous fiction is a
funny, imaginative story. As you read, look for:

▶ story events that are meant to be funny

▶ characters that act in amusing ways

▶ a plot with a beginning, a middle, and an ending

COMMON CORE **RL.3.3** describe characters and explain how their actions contribute to the sequence of events; **L.3.3b** recognize and observe differences between conventions of spoken and written standard English

Meet the Author

Beverly Cleary

One day, while working on one of her first stories about Klickitat Street, Beverly Cleary couldn't come up with a name for the bothersome younger sister. "At the moment when I needed a name," says Cleary, "a neighbor called out 'Ramona!' to another neighbor, and so I just named her Ramona."

Meet the Illustrator

Sam Valentino

Sam Valentino is an illustrator and a dad. His three kids are learning how to cook, so the scenes Sam drew for "The Extra-good Sunday" are very familiar!

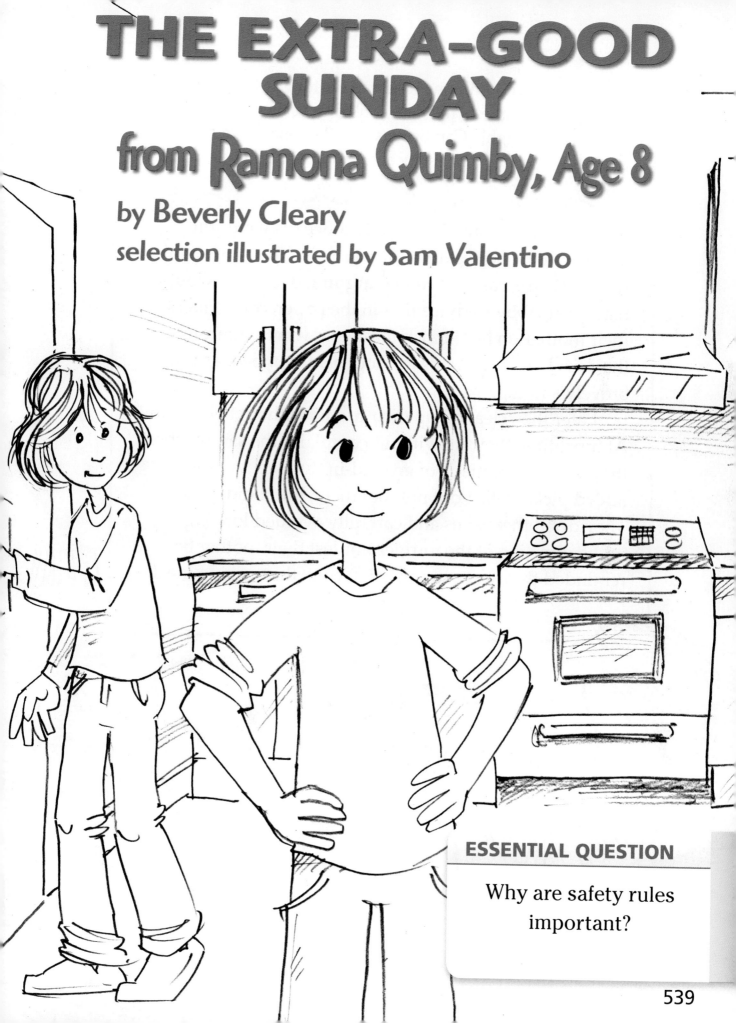

THE EXTRA-GOOD SUNDAY

from Ramona Quimby, Age 8

by Beverly Cleary

selection illustrated by Sam Valentino

ESSENTIAL QUESTION

Why are safety rules important?

After Beezus and Ramona refuse to eat tongue for dinner, Mr. Quimby suggests the girls cook dinner themselves the very next night. Can Beezus and Ramona make their parents forget this request by acting on their best behavior?

Sunday morning Ramona and Beezus were still resolved to be perfect until dinnertime. They got up without being called, avoided arguing over who should read Dear Abby's advice first in the paper, complimented their mother on her French toast, and went off through the drizzly rain to Sunday school neat, combed, and bravely smiling.

Later they cleaned up their rooms without being told. At lunchtime they ate without complaint the sandwiches they knew were made of ground-up tongue. A little added pickle relish did not fool them, but it did help. They dried the dishes and carefully avoided looking in the direction of the refrigerator lest their mother be reminded they were supposed to cook the evening meal.

Mr. and Mrs. Quimby were good-humored. In fact, everyone was so unnaturally pleasant that Ramona almost wished someone would say something cross. By early afternoon the question was still hanging in the air. Would the girls really have to prepare dinner?

Why doesn't somebody say something? Ramona thought, weary of being so good.

"Well, back to the old foot," said Mr. Quimby, as he once more settled himself on the couch with the drawing pad and pencil and pulled off his shoe and sock.

The rain finally stopped. Ramona watched for dry spots to appear on the sidewalk and thought of her roller skates in the closet. She looked into Beezus's room and found her sister reading. The day dragged on.

When dry spots on the concrete in front of the
Quimbys' house widened until moisture remained only
in the cracks of the sidewalk, Ramona pulled her skates
out of her closet. To her father, who was holding
a drawing of his foot at arm's length to study it, she said,
"Well, I guess I'll go out and skate."

"Aren't you forgetting something?" he asked.

"What?" asked Ramona, knowing very well what.

"Dinner," he said.

The question that had hung in the air all day was
answered. The matter was settled.

"We're stuck," Ramona told Beezus. "Now we can stop being so good."

The sisters went into the kitchen, shut the door, and opened the refrigerator.

"A package of chicken thighs," said Beezus with a groan. "And a package of frozen peas. And yogurt, one carton of plain and one of banana. There must have been a special on yogurt." She closed the refrigerator and reached for a cookbook.

"I could make place cards," said Ramona, as Beezus frantically flipped pages.

"We can't eat place cards," said Beezus. "Besides, corn bread is your job because you brought it up." Both girls spoke in whispers. There was no need to let their parents, their mean old parents, know what was going on in the kitchen.

In her mother's recipe file, Ramona found the card for corn bread written in Mr. Quimby's grandmother's shaky handwriting, which Ramona found difficult to read.

"I can't find a recipe for chicken thighs," said Beezus, "just whole chicken. All I know is that Mother bakes thighs in the flat glass dish with some kind of sauce."

"Mushroom soup mixed with something and with some kind of little specks stirred in." Ramona remembered that much from watching her mother.

Beezus opened the cupboard of canned goods. "But there isn't any mushroom soup," she said. "What are we going to do?"

"Mix up something wet," suggested Ramona. "It would serve them right if it tasted awful."

"Why don't we make something awful?" asked Beezus. "So they will know how we feel when we have to eat tongue."

"What tastes really awful?" Ramona was eager to go along with the suggestion, united with her sister against their enemy—for the moment, their parents.

Beezus, always practical, changed her mind. "It wouldn't work. We have to eat it too, and they're so mean we'll probably have to do the dishes besides. Anyway, I guess you might say our honor is at stake, because they think we can't cook a good meal."

Ramona was ready with another solution. "Throw everything in one dish."

Beezus opened the package of chicken thighs and stared at them with distaste. "I can't stand touching raw meat," she said, as she picked up a thigh between two forks.

"Do we have to eat the skin?" asked Ramona. "All those yucky little bumps."

Beezus found a pair of kitchen tongs. She tried holding down a thigh with a fork and pulling off the skin with the tongs.

"Here, let me hold it," said Ramona, who was not squeamish about touching such things as worms or raw meat. She took a firm hold on the thigh while Beezus grasped the skin with the tongs. Both pulled, and the skin peeled away. They played tug-of-war with each thigh, leaving a sad-looking heap of skins on the counter and a layer of chicken thighs in the glass dish.

"Can't you remember what little specks Mother uses?" asked Beezus. Ramona could not. The girls studied the spice shelf, unscrewed jar lids and sniffed. Nutmeg? No. Cloves? Terrible. Cinnamon? Uh-uh. Chili powder? Well. . . . Yes, that must be it. Ramona remembered that the specks were red. Beezus stirred half a teaspoon of the dark red powder into the yogurt, which she poured over the chicken. She slid the dish into the oven set at 350 degrees, the temperature for chicken recommended by the cookbook.

ANALYZE THE TEXT

Formal and Informal Language Which parts of the story sound informal? Why do other words or phrases sound more formal?

From the living room came the sound of their parents' conversation, sometimes serious and sometimes highlighted by laughter. While we're slaving out here, thought Ramona, as she climbed up on the counter to reach a box of cornmeal. After she climbed down, she discovered she had to climb up again for baking powder and soda. She finally knelt on the counter to save time and asked Beezus to bring her an egg.

"It's a good thing Mother can't see you up there," remarked Beezus, as she handed Ramona an egg.

"How else am I supposed to reach things?" Ramona successfully broke the egg and tossed the shell onto the counter. "Now I need buttermilk."

Beezus broke the news. There was no buttermilk in the refrigerator. "What'll I do?" whispered Ramona in a panic.

"Here. Use this." Beezus thrust the carton of banana yogurt at her sister. "Yogurt is sort of sour, so it might work."

The kitchen door opened a crack. "What's going on in there?" inquired Mr. Quimby.

Beezus hurled herself against the door. "You stay out!" she ordered. "Dinner is going to be a—surprise!"

For a moment Ramona thought Beezus had been going to say a mess. She stirred egg and yogurt together, measured flour, spilling some on the floor, and then discovered she was short of cornmeal. More panic.

"My cooking teacher says you should always check to see if you have all the ingredients before you start to cook," said Beezus.

"Oh, shut up." Ramona reached for a package of hot breakfast cereal, because its grains were about the same size as cornmeal. She scattered only a little on the floor.

ANALYZE THE TEXT

Understanding Characters Does Beezus answer truthfully when Mr. Quimby asks what's going on? Why is Beezus so determined to keep him out of the kitchen?

Something was needed to sop up the sauce with the little red specks when the chicken was served. Rice! The spilled cereal gritted underneath Beezus's feet as she measured rice and boiled water according to the directions on the package. When the rice was cooking, she slipped into the dining room to set the table and then remembered they had forgotten salad. Salad! Carrot sticks were quickest. Beezus began to scrape carrots into the sink.

"Yipe!" yelped Ramona from the counter. "The rice!" The lid of the pan was chittering. Beezus snatched a larger pan from the cupboard and transferred the rice.

"Do you girls need any help?" Mrs. Quimby called from the living room.

"No!" answered her daughters.

Another calamity. The corn bread should bake at 400 degrees, a higher temperature than that needed for the chicken. What was Ramona to do?

"Stick it in the oven anyway." Beezus's face was flushed.

In went the corn bread beside the chicken.

"Dessert!" whispered Beezus. All she could find was a can of boring pear halves. Back to the cookbook. "Heat with a little butter and serve with jelly in each half," she read. Jelly. Half a jar of apricot jam would have to do. The pears and butter went into the saucepan. Never mind the syrup spilled on the floor.

"Beezus!" Ramona held up the package of peas.

Beezus groaned. Out came the partially cooked chicken while she stirred the thawing peas into the yogurt and shoved the dish back into the oven.

The rice! They had forgotten the rice, which was only beginning to stick to the pan. Quick! Take it off the burner. How did their mother manage to get everything cooked at the right time? Put the carrot sticks on a dish. Pour the milk. "Candles!" Beezus whispered. "Dinner might look better if we have candles."

Ramona found two candle holders and two partly melted candles of uneven length. Beezus struck the match to light them, because although Ramona was brave about touching raw meat, she was skittish about lighting matches.

Was the chicken done? The girls anxiously examined their main dish, bubbling and brown around the edges. Beezus stabbed a thigh with a fork, and when it did not bleed, she decided it must be done. A toothpick pricked into the corn bread came out clean. The corn bread was done—flat, but done.

Grit, grit, grit sounded the girls' feet. It was amazing how a tiny bit of spilled cereal could make the entire kitchen floor gritty. At last their dinner was served, the dining-room light turned off, dinner announced, and the cooks, tense with anxiety that was hidden by candlelight, fell into their chairs as their parents seated themselves. Was this dinner going to be edible?

"Candles!" exclaimed Mrs. Quimby. "What a festive meal!"

"Let's taste it before we decide," said Mr. Quimby with his most wicked grin.

The girls watched anxiously as their father took his first bite of chicken. He chewed thoughtfully and said with more surprise than necessary, "Why this is good!"

"It really is," agreed Mrs. Quimby, and took a bit of corn bread. "Very good, Ramona," she said.

Mr. Quimby tasted the corn bread. "Just like Grandmother used to make," he pronounced.

The girls exchanged suppressed smiles. They could not taste the banana yogurt, and by candlelight no one could tell that the corn bread was a little pale. The chicken, Ramona decided, was not as good as her parents thought—or pretended to think—but she could eat it without gagging.

Everyone relaxed, and Mrs. Quimby said chili powder was more interesting than paprika and asked which recipe they used for the chicken.

Ramona answered, "Our own," as she exchanged another look with Beezus. Paprika! Those little specks in the sauce should have been paprika.

"We wanted to be creative," said Beezus.

Conversation was more comfortable than it had been the previous evening. Mr. Quimby said he was finally satisfied with his drawing, which looked like a real foot. Beezus said her cooking class was studying the food groups everyone should eat every day. Ramona said there was this boy at school who called her Egghead. Mr. Quimby explained that Egghead was slang for a very smart person.

The meal was a success. If the chicken did not taste as good as the girls had hoped and the corn bread did not rise like their mother's, both were edible. Beezus and Ramona were silently grateful to their parents for enjoying—or pretending to enjoy—their cooking. The whole family cheered up.

When they had finished their pears with apricot jam, Ramona gave her mother a shy smile. Mrs. Quimby smiled back and patted Ramona's hand. Ramona felt much lighter.

"You cooks have worked so hard," said Mr. Quimby, "that I'm going to wash the dishes. I'll even finish clearing the table."

"I'll help," volunteered Mrs. Quimby.

The girls exchanged another secret smile as they excused themselves and skipped off to their rooms before their parents discovered the pile of chicken skins and the broken eggshell on the counter, the carrot scrapings in the sink, and the cereal, flour, and pear syrup on the floor.

Dig Deeper

How to Analyze the Text

Use these pages to learn about Understanding Characters and Formal and Informal Language. Then read *The Extra-good Sunday* again to apply what you learned.

Understanding Characters

In fiction stories like *The Extra-good Sunday*, **characters** can seem like real people. They have **traits,** or qualities, such as kindness that show what kind of people they are. Their **motivations,** or reasons for their actions, are like those that real people have. The characters also have **feelings** such as happiness. Readers can identify these traits, motivations, and feelings through a character's actions, words, and thoughts, and use them to describe the character.

Look at page 545 in *The Extra-good Sunday*. Beezus suggests that she and Ramona make an awful dinner. Their motivation is that they feel upset with their parents. The author says that Beezus is practical. How does this trait affect the girls' decision?

Traits	Motivations	Feelings

RL.3.3 describe characters and explain how their actions contribute to the sequence of events; **L.3.3b** recognize and observe differences between conventions of spoken and written standard English

Formal and Informal Language

Written language and spoken language often sound different. Written language can be **formal.** Writers decide what they want to say and then carefully choose their words to create sentences. Spoken language is usually more relaxed, or **informal.** People are not as careful when they speak, especially when talking to friends.

Think of examples of formal and informal language in *The Extra-good Sunday*. Which does the author use when she tells what the characters do? Which does she use when she shows what the characters say?

Your Turn

 Review the story with a partner to prepare to discuss this question: *Why are safety rules important?* During your discussion, take turns speaking, listening carefully, and asking each other questions. Use text evidence to support your ideas, and add to what your partner has said.

 **Classroom Conversation**

Continue your discussion of *The Extra-good Sunday* by explaining your answers to these questions:

1. What safety rules do you think Ramona and Beezus might not have followed in *The Extra-good Sunday*?

2. How do you think Mr. and Mrs. Quimby will react when they see the kitchen after dinner?

3. Would you eat a meal cooked by Ramona and Beezus?

Response Mr. and Mrs. Quimby make Beezus and Ramona cook because they complained about what they had to eat. Do you think that was a good idea? Write a paragraph that states your opinion. Give reasons for your opinion, using text evidence and what you see in the pictures.

Writing Tip

State your opinion at the beginning of your response. Provide reasons for your opinion and examples from the story to support it. Finish your paragraph with a strong concluding statement.

COMMON CORE **W.3.1a** introduce the topic, state an opinion, and create an organizational structure; **W.3.1b** provide reasons that support the opinion; **W.3.1d** provide a concluding statement or section; **W.3.10** write routinely over extended time frames or short time frames; **SL.3.1a** come to discussions prepared/explicitly draw on preparation and other information about the topic; **SL.3.1d** explain own ideas and understanding in light of the discussion

INFORMATIONAL TEXT

Imagine a Recipe

GENRE

Informational text gives facts and information about a topic. It can include directions for making something.

TEXT FOCUS

The **steps in a procedure** are written in time order. This helps readers understand how a process works.

COMMON CORE

RI.3.3 describe the relationship between a series of historical events/scientific ideas/steps in technical procedures

Imagine a Recipe

by Cameron Hart

Being a chef is a lot like being an artist. A chef's materials are the foods in a kitchen. To be a chef, you need to express yourself in many different ways. Chefs combine flavors that taste delicious. They present food that smells good and that looks good, too.

Sometimes, chefs use their imaginations to make up a recipe for a new dish. At other times, they start with a recipe that has been around for ages. Then they change a few ingredients or cook it in a different way.

You can be a chef in your own kitchen. Follow the steps in the recipe below to make flan. Flan is a popular dessert in many Spanish-speaking countries, including Puerto Rico. The traditional flavor is caramel. There are also different flavors, such as orange or vanilla. Use your imagination to add flavor and make this recipe your own.

PUERTO RICAN FLAN

Ingredients:

1 c. sugar

4 eggs

1 (14 oz.) can condensed milk

1 3/4 c. water

1/4 tsp. salt

1 tsp. vanilla or other flavoring

1. Ask an adult to heat the oven to 350 degrees.

2. Have an adult help you slowly melt the sugar until it is the color of caramel. Swirl the melted sugar onto the sides of a pie dish. Then set the dish on a wire rack.

3. Mix the other ingredients in a bowl. Pour the mixture through a strainer to make it smooth. Then pour it into the dish.

4. Pour warm water into a large baking pan until it is about one inch deep. Set the pie dish in the warm water. Have an adult help you put the whole thing in the oven. Bake for one hour.

5. Have an adult help you take the pie dish out of the oven. Let it cool and then put it in the refrigerator. When the flan is cold, carefully turn the flan onto a plate and serve in slices.

Compare Texts

TEXT TO TEXT

Compare Recipes Think about how Beezus and Ramona created recipes. Compare and contrast their methods to the chef's in *Imagine a Recipe*. Use text evidence to list three ways the methods are the same and three ways they are different. Explain your ideas to a partner.

TEXT TO SELF

Perform a Skit Perform a short skit that shows what happened when you made something in the kitchen. Tell how you put ingredients together and how the food turned out.

TEXT TO WORLD

Use Digital Sources Use the Internet to find a recipe for a food from another country. Copy the ingredients and directions. Print out a picture to put with your recipe. Put your recipe in a class cookbook.

COMMON CORE **RI.3.3** describe the relationship between a series of historical events/scientific ideas/steps in technical procedures; **RI.3.9** compare and contrast important points and details in texts on the same topic; **W.3.8** recall information from experiences or gather information from print and digital sources/take brief notes and sort evidence

Grammar

Verb Tenses A verb's tense shows when action takes place. **Present tense** shows action happening now. Present tense verbs that tell about *he, she,* or *it* often end with *-s*. For verbs that end in *y*, change the *y* to an *i* and add *-es*.

Past tense shows action that has happened. Past tense verbs often end with *-ed*. For verbs that end with *e*, drop the *e* and add *-ed*. For verbs that end in *y*, change the *y* to an *i* and add *-ed*. For verbs that end with a vowel and one consonant, double the consonant before adding *-ed*.

Future tense shows action that will happen. The word *will* before a verb shows future tense.

Present Tense	Past Tense	Future Tense
drop	dropped	will drop
study	studied	will study
smile	smiled	will smile

 **Work with a partner. Choose the correct verb tense for each sentence.**

① The rabbits (escape, escaped) from the cage. (past tense)

② Our plane (flies, will fly) at noon. (future tense)

③ He (carries, carried) a heavy backpack. (present tense)

An incorrect verb tense can confuse your readers. Think about an action that you want to write about. Then decide when it should happen. Check that you have used the correct tense to show present, past, or future action.

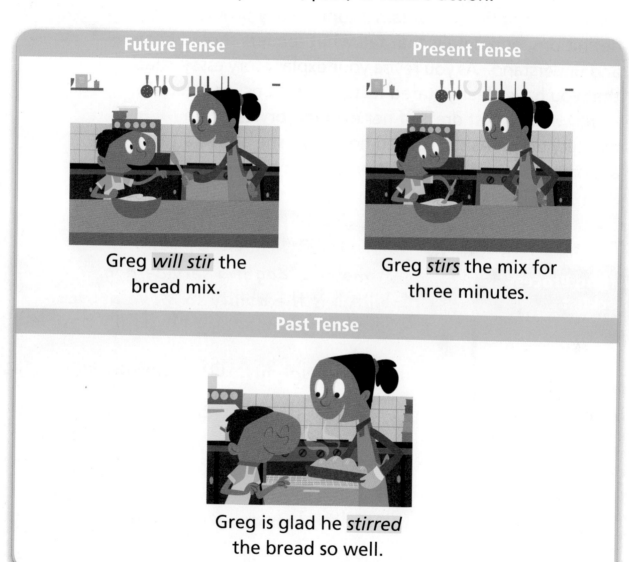

Future Tense

Greg *will stir* the bread mix.

Present Tense

Greg *stirs* the mix for three minutes.

Past Tense

Greg is glad he *stirred* the bread so well.

 Connect Grammar to Writing

As you revise your explanatory essay, look closely at the verbs you use. Correct any errors you notice. Using verb tenses correctly is an important part of good writing.

W.3.2a introduce a topic and group related information/include illustration; **W.3.2b** develop the topic with facts, definitions, and details; **W.3.2d** provide a concluding statement or section; **W.3.5** develop and strengthen writing by planning, revising, and editing

Informative Writing

Reading-Writing Workshop: **Revise**

✔️ **Ideas** In an **explanatory essay**, good writers focus on giving information to explain a topic. They provide facts, definitions, and details that tell what readers should know and understand. As you revise your explanatory essay, check that you have clearly stated facts, definitions, and details.

Jill wrote a first draft of her explanatory essay on mobility dogs. As she revised her draft, she added a fact and strengthened her definition of a mobility dog.

Writing Process Checklist

Prewrite

Draft

▶ **Revise**

✔ Did I develop my topic with facts, definitions, and details?

✔ Did I use linking words to connect my ideas?

✔ Did I provide a closing statement?

Edit

Publish and Share

Revised Draft

A mobility dog is a service dog. "Mobility" is the ability to move around. ∧Some people who are physically disabled are in wheelchairs. Others cannot do things like change clothes or pick things up. Mobility dogs help.

Mobility dogs are well trained. They
open doors,
can ∧turn lights off and on, push elevator buttons, and more.

568

An Amazing Helper
by Jill F. Baugh

Have you ever seen a guide dog help a person cross a street? A guide dog is the best-known kind of service dog. A guide dog helps a person who has vision loss. Other service dogs do different things to help people.

A mobility dog is a service dog. "Mobility" is the ability to move around. Some people who are physically disabled are in wheelchairs. Others cannot do things like change clothes or pick things up. Mobility dogs help.

Mobility dogs are well trained. They can open doors, turn lights off and on, push elevator buttons, and more. They also can help people walk without falling and help them get in and out of a wheelchair.

Each mobility dog is paired with a person who is disabled. The dog is trained to do what that person needs. That means the skills of each dog are different.

Mobility dogs are not pets, but people love them as if they were.

Reading as a Writer

In her final copy, Jill added facts and details, and she strengthened a definition. What could you do to your essay to develop your topic?

In my final paper, I added facts and details. I strengthened definitions. I added linking words to connect my ideas.

Read the articles "Kids Invent!" and "Television History." As you read, stop and answer each question using text evidence.

Science*Kids*

Volume 7, Issue 6

Kids Invent!
by Roberto Gutierrez

Matthew had a problem that many other people have. Sometimes soup or other foods would drip down his chin while he was eating. He used to wipe his mouth on his sleeve, but his parents did not like that. They said it did not show good manners. Besides, it got his sleeve dirty.

So Matthew invented, or came up with an idea for, a new kind of shirt. It held a paper napkin on one sleeve. That solved Matthew's problem. After he ate a meal, he just threw away the napkin.

This may seem like a silly example, but many inventors get ideas in the same way Matthew did. They see problems that need to be solved. They come up with ideas to solve the problems or to make something better.

> ❶ What is the author's point of view about the example he used? Tell whether you agree or disagree and why.

COMMON CORE

RI.3.1 ask and answer questions to demonstrate understanding, referring to the text; **RI.3.5** use text features and search tools to locate information; **RI.3.6** distinguish own point of view from that of the author; **RI.3.9** compare and contrast important points and details in texts on the same topic

The gym teacher at Jessica's school taught the students some great jump-rope games. Different games needed ropes of different sizes. So the kids had to change ropes when they changed games. Jessica decided to invent a new kind of jump rope that could be made into different lengths. She thought it could also be worn as a belt.

Jessica's first jump-rope belt did not work, but she did not give up. She just made some changes. First, she made a model of her belt for a doll. The model worked, so then Jessica made a full-size belt for herself. Inventors almost always have to try several times before they have success.

Be an Inventor

1. Make a list of problems.

2. List possible solutions.

3. Choose an idea you could turn into an invention.

4. Draw and label a picture to show how your invention will work.

5. Build a model.

6. Test the model and make changes.

 Where in this article can you find information about how to become an inventor? Tell why the information is in this form.

Larry is another inventor who made something better. When Larry watered the trees in his yard, he saw that a lot of water was wasted. So Larry invented a new kind of sprinkler. Shaped like a circle, the sprinkler has holes on the top and on the bottom. It fits around the base of a tree. Because water comes out of both the top and the bottom, more water soaks into the ground and reaches the tree roots. Thousands of people have bought Larry's sprinkler.

Television History

Did you know that one hundred years ago, television had not been invented yet? Today there are few homes without at least one TV. Take a guess about how TV was invented.

Did you guess that television was invented by a boy who first thought of the idea when he was only fourteen years old? The boy, Philo T. Farnsworth, made a drawing of the idea for his science teacher. His drawing did not show what you see when you look at a TV. It showed how pictures could be sent by electricity through the air to people's homes. Nobody had ever succeeded in figuring out how to do that before.

> **3** Why was Philo's drawing important? Use evidence from the article in your response.

When Philo was twenty years old, he built a glass tube that glowed with light. A year later, on September 7, 1927, he sent the first television picture over the air. He went on to create television as we know it today.

Philo T. Farnsworth received many honors over the years. He is in the National Inventors Hall of Fame. The United States government put his picture on a postage stamp. A statue of Farnsworth stands in Washington, D.C. The words on the statue say, "Philo Taylor Farnsworth: Inventor of Television."

> **4** How are important points and details in the two articles alike, and how are they different?

Glossary

This glossary contains meanings and pronunciations for some of the words in this book. The Full Pronunciation Key shows how to pronounce each consonant and vowel in a special spelling. At the bottom of the glossary pages is a shortened form of the full key.

Full Pronunciation Key

Consonant Sounds

b	**b**i**b**, ca**bb**age	kw	**ch**oir, **qu**ick	t	**t**igh**t**, stopp**ed**
ch	**ch**ur**ch**, sti**tch**	l	**l**id, need**l**e, ta**ll**	th	ba**th**, **th**in
d	**d**ee**d**, mail**ed**, pu**dd**le	m	a**m**, **m**an, du**mb**	*th*	ba**the**, **this**
f	**f**ast, **f**i**f**e, o**ff**, **ph**rase, rou**gh**	n	**n**o, sudde**n**	v	ca**v**e, val**v**e, **v**ine
		ng	thi**ng**, i**nk**	w	**w**ith, **w**olf
g	**g**a**g**, **g**et, fin**g**er	p	**p**o**p**, ha**pp**y	y	**y**es, **y**olk, on**i**on
h	**h**at, **wh**o	r	**r**oar, **rh**yme	z	ro**s**e, si**z**e, **x**ylophone, **z**ebra
hw	**wh**ich, **wh**ere	s	mi**ss**, **s**au**c**e, **sc**ene, **s**ee	zh	gara**g**e, plea**s**ure, vi**s**ion
j	**j**u**dg**e, **g**em	sh	di**sh**, **sh**ip, **s**ugar, ti**ss**ue		
k	**c**at, **k**i**ck**, s**ch**ool				

Vowel Sounds

ă	p**a**t, l**au**gh	ŏ	h**o**rrible, p**o**t	ŭ	c**u**t, fl**oo**d, r**ou**gh, s**o**me
ā	**a**pe, **ai**d, p**ay**	ō	g**o**, r**ow**, t**oe**, th**ough**	û	c**i**rcle, f**u**r, h**ear**d, t**er**m, t**ur**n, **ur**ge, w**or**d
â	**ai**r, c**a**re, w**ea**r	ô	**a**ll, c**augh**t, f**or**, p**aw**		
ä	f**a**ther, k**o**ala, y**a**rd	oi	b**oy**, n**oi**se, **oi**l		
ě	p**e**t, ple**a**sure, **a**ny	ou	c**ow**, **ou**t	yo͞o	c**u**re
ē	b**e**, b**ee**, **ea**sy, pian**o**	o͝o	f**u**ll, b**oo**k, w**o**lf	yo͞o	**a**b**u**se, **u**se
ĭ	**i**f, p**i**t, b**u**sy	o͞o	b**oo**t, r**u**de, fr**ui**t, fl**ew**	ə	**a**go, sil**e**nt, penc**i**l, lem**o**n, circ**u**s
ī	r**i**de, b**y**, p**ie**, h**igh**				
î	d**ea**r, d**ee**r, f**ie**rce, m**e**re				

Stress Marks

Primary Stress ´: bi·ol·o·gy [bī **ŏl**′ ə jē]
Secondary Stress ´: bi·o·log·i·cal [bī′ ə **lŏj**′ ĭ kəl]

A

a·bil·i·ty (ə **bĭl´** ə tē´)
noun The quality of being
able to do something: *Most
cats have the **ability** to land on
their feet.*

ad·vice (ăd **vīs´**) *noun* An
idea or suggestion about how
to solve a problem: *Josh gave
me **advice** about writing well.*

af·ford (ə **fôrd´**) *verb* To be
able to pay for or spare: *We
can't **afford** a new car.*

an·nounce (ə **nŏuns´**) *verb*
To officially make known: *The
mayor **announced** the date of
the parade.*

anx·ious·ly (**ăngk´** shəs lē)
adverb Nervously or fearfully:
*I waited **anxiously** for the bus
on my first day of school.*

ap·plause (ə **plôz´**) *noun*
Enjoyment or approval shown
especially by clapping hands:
*The audience gave the actors a
long round of **applause.***

a·shamed (ə **shāmd´**)
adjective Feeling shame or
guilt: *The team was **ashamed**
of its poor performance at the
soccer game.*

ath·lete (**ăth´** lēt´) *noun* A
person who is trained in or
is good at physical exercises,
games, or sports: *Athletes
train hard to do well in their
sport.*

athlete
The word
athlete comes
from the Greek
word *athlon,*
meaning "prize."

B

bal·ance (**băl´** əns) *verb* To
put in a steady or stable
condition: *That girl is
balancing a ball on her head.*

blast (blăst) *verb* To give off
a loud noise: *The sound of a
siren **blasted** through the air.*

block (blŏk) *noun* A part of
a street marked off by the two
nearest cross streets: *Everyone
who lives on our **block** is
coming to the party.*

blur·ry (**blûr´** ē) *adjective*
Dim or hard to see:
*Everything looks **blurry** if I'm
not wearing my glasses.*

bor·der (**bôr´** dər) *noun* Outer
parts or edges: *White lines
mark the field's **borders.***

bor·row (**bŏr´** ō) *verb* To get
something from someone else
and plan to return or replace
it later: *You can **borrow** my
notebook for an hour.*

C

cer·tain·ly (**sûr´** tn lē) *adverb*
Surely; without a doubt: *I will
certainly be there by noon.*

cling (klĭng) *verb* To stick or
hold tight to: *Dirt will **cling** to
a wet rug.*

ă rat / ā **pay** / â c**are** / ä f**ather** / ĕ **pet** / ē **be** / ĭ **pit** / ī **pie** / î **fie**rce / ŏ p**ot** /
ō **go** / ô **paw, for** / oi **oil** / ŏŏ b**ook**

com·pete (kəm **pēt´**) *verb* To take part in a race or contest against another person: *Ava will **compete** in the school spelling bee.*

con·tact (**kŏn´** tăkt´) *verb* To get in touch with: *Every parent was **contacted** and invited to the meeting.*

con·tri·b·ute (kən **trĭb´** yo͞ot) *verb* To give your part towards a group effort: *The students each **contribute** their talents to the group project.*

con·vince (kən **vĭns´**) *verb* To persuade to do or to believe: *Have you **convinced** your sister to go on the trip?*

crew (kro͞o) *noun* A group of people who work together: *It took a large **crew** to build this skyscraper.*

crop (krŏp) *noun* A farm product grown to be harvested, often for food: *The tomato and melon **crops** grew well this summer.*

cross (krôs) *adjective* In a bad mood; grumpy; grouchy: *Mom calls me an old grump when I am feeling **cross**.*

cus·tom·er (**kŭs´** tə mər) *noun* A person who buys goods or services: *Many **customers** were shocked to learn the store was closing.*

D

de·gree (dĭ **grē´**) *noun* One of the units into which a measuring instrument, such as a thermometer, is divided: *Water boils at a temperature of 212 **degrees**.*

de·tail (**dē´** tāl) *noun* A small piece of information: *John noticed an unusual **detail** about the new doors.*

dis·ap·pear (dĭs´ ə **pîr´**) *verb* To pass out of sight; vanish: *My dog **disappears** when it is time for her bath.*

doze (dōz) *verb* To sleep lightly: *Grandpa **dozes** on the sofa while we watch football.*

E

earn (ûrn) *verb* To gain by working or by supplying service: *I **earn** money each week by doing chores.*

echo (**ĕk´** ō) *noun* The repetition of a sound, sent back by sound waves: *We heard **echoes** when we yelled in the empty room.*

e·lec·tric (ĭ **lĕk´** trĭk) *adjective* Of, relating to, or produced by electricity: *An **electric** current runs through the wiring of a house.*

disappear
Disappear contains the prefix *dis-*, which means "not" or "opposite of." The prefix *un-* also means "not" or "opposite of," as in *unkind*.

electric

---

o͞o b**oo**t / ou **out** / ŭ c**u**t / û f**u**r / hw **wh**ich / th **th**in / *th* **th**is / zh vi**si**on / ə **a**go, sil**e**nt, penc**i**l, lem**o**n, circ**u**s

ex•am•ine (ĭg zăm´ ĭn) *verb* To look at carefully: *We **examined** the plant cells under a microscope.*

ex•cite•ment (ĭk sīt´ mənt) *noun* The state of being excited: *As the game went on, the **excitement** grew.*

ex•per•i•ment (ĭk spĕr´ ə mənt´) *noun* A test to find out or prove something: *Let's try an **experiment** to see if our idea works.*

F

fa•mil•iar (fə mĭl´ yər) *adjective* Well known, as from repeated experience: *I heard the **familiar** voice of the announcer.*

fan (făn) *noun* A person with a keen interest in or admiration for someone or something: *My friends are basketball **fans**.*

fes•tive (fĕs´ tĭv) *adjective* Merry; joyous: *We were in a **festive** mood at the parade.*

fig•ure (fĭg´ yər) *verb* To work out by thinking: *The guide will **figure** out a way to cross the mountains.*

fine (fīn) *adjective* Excellent; of high quality: *This shop sells only **fine** foods.*

flex•i•ble (flĕk´ sə bəl´) *adjective* Easily bent; bendable: *For running, choose shoes with **flexible** soles.*

fog•gy (fô´ gē) *adjective* Full of, having, or covered by fog: *Lighthouses are a big help to ships on **foggy** nights.*

fond•ly (fŏnd´ lē) *adverb* Lovingly or tenderly: *Mom always looks at me **fondly**.*

frac•tion (frăk´ shən´) *noun* Part of a whole unit: *Learning new things takes a large **fraction** of the school day.*

G

gadg•et (găj´ ĭt) *noun* A small mechanical device: *A can opener is a **gadget**.*

gen•ius (jēn´ yəs) *noun* Extraordinary intellectual power, especially seen in creative ability: *Her winning idea for the science fair project was pure **genius**!*

grunt (grŭnt) *verb* To make a short, deep sound with one's voice: *Max **grunted** as he tried to lift the heavy log.*

guilt•y (gĭl´ tē) *adjective* Having committed a crime or bad deed: *The jury found them **guilty** of stealing.*

ă rat / ā pay / â care / ä father / ĕ pet / ē be / ĭ pit / ī pie / î fierce / ŏ pot /
ō go / ô paw, for / oi oil / o͞o book

H

har·vest (**här´** vĭst) *noun*
Crops that are gathered or
ready to be gathered: *We pick
the corn* **harvest** *each summer.*

hol·ler (**hŏl´** lûr) *verb* To
shout, yell: *"Come back here!"
my brother* **hollered.**

hon·est (**ŏn´** ĭst)
adjective Not lying, stealing,
or cheating: *I admire people
who are* **honest,** *and I don't
like liars.*

I

il·lus·trate (**ĭl´** ə strāt´)
verb To add photographs,
drawings, diagrams, or maps
that explain or decorate books
or magazines: *Let's* **illustrate**
*the book about their journey
with a map of their travels.*

i·mag·ine (ĭ **măj´** ĭn) *verb* To
form a mental picture or idea
of: *Can you* **imagine** *a blue
horse with a yellow mane?*

im·prove (ĭm **prōōv´**) *verb*
To get better: *The more you
practice, the more quickly your
skills will* **improve.**

in·gre·di·ent (ĭn **grē´** dē ənt)
noun One of the parts
that make up a mixture or
combination: *Flour is one of
the* **ingredients** *of bread.*

in·ven·tion (ĭn **vĕn´** shən)
noun An original device,
system, or process: *The
washing machine was a useful*
invention.

J

jerk·y (**jûr´** kē) *adjective*
Marked by sudden, sharp
motions: *We had a* **jerky** *ride
over the rough road.*

ju·ry (**jōōr´** ē) *noun* A group
of citizens chosen to listen to
the facts and proof on cases
presented in a court of law:
The **jury** *listened carefully
as the lawyers summed up
their cases.*

L

lab·o·ra·to·ry (**lăb´** rə tôr´ ē)
noun A room or building
holding special equipment for
doing scientific tests, research,
and experiments: *You'll find
some test tubes and droppers
in the science* **laboratory.**

league (lēg) *noun* A group
of sports teams that compete
mainly among themselves:
All the teams in our baseball
league *are here in the city.*

lie (lī) *verb* To take or be in a
flat or resting position: *He is*
lying *on the couch and resting.*

loy·al (**loi´** əl) *adjective*
Faithful: *She is a* **loyal** *friend
who always helps me.*

jerky
The word *jerky*
can also be a
noun. *Jerky* is
meat cut into
strips and dried or
cured. The noun
jerky comes from
the Spanish word
charqui, which in
turn came from
the Quechua word
ch'arki.

ōō **boo**t / ou **ou**t / ŭ **c**u**t** / û **f**u**r** / hw **wh**ich / th **th**in / *th* **th**is / zh vi**s**ion /
ə **a**go, sil**e**nt, penc**i**l, lem**o**n, circ**u**s

M

mist (mĭst) *noun* A mass of tiny drops of water in the air: *Fog is a kind of* **mist.**

mur•mur (**mûr´** mər) *noun* A low, continuous sound: *I could hear a* **murmur** *of voices from the next room.*

O

oc•ca•sion•al (ə **kā´** zhə nəl) *adjective* Happening or encountered from time to time: *Except for an* **occasional** *cold, I have been well this winter.*

P

part•ner (**pärt´** nər) *noun* One of two or more people working or playing together: *As tennis* **partners,** *Leah and Josh hit the ball to each other.*

patch (păch) *noun* A small area: *Only one* **patch** *of snow is left on the ground.*

pa•trol (pə **trōl´**) *verb* To move about an area to watch or guard: *We will* **patrol** *the halls to make sure they are empty.*

pause (pôz) *verb* To stop briefly: *The players are* **pausing** *because one team has called a time-out.*

peak (pēk) *noun* The top of a mountain: *We can see for miles from the mountain* **peak.**

plead (plēd) *verb* To make an urgent request; appeal: *The boy* **pleaded** *for candy, but his mother said no.*

pluck (plŭk) *verb* To remove by pulling quickly: *Lucas* **plucked** *the weeds from his flower garden.*

point (point) *verb* To call attention to something with the finger: *The librarian* **pointed** *to the sign that said "Quiet."*

pol•ish (**pŏl´** ĭsh) *verb* To make smooth and shiny, especially by rubbing: *We* **polish** *the floor weekly.*

pow•er (**pou´** ər) *noun* The force, strength, or ability to do something: *It took all my* **power** *to lift the heavy couch.*

prin•ci•pal (**prĭn´** sə pəl) *noun* The head of a school: *Our* **principal** *read the new rules to each class.*

point

ă rat / ā **pay** / â **care** / ä **father** / ĕ **pet** / ē be / ĭ **pit** / ī **pie** / î **fierce** / ŏ **pot** / ō **go** / ô **paw, for** / oi **oil** / o͝o b**oo**k

proc•ess (**prŏ´** sĕs´) *noun* A series of steps needed to do something: *I am teaching my little brother the* **process** *of tying shoe laces.*

prof•it (**prŏ´** fĭt) *noun* The money made from selling something: *Tanesha made a* **profit** *from selling cupcakes.*

pro•nounce (prə **nouns´**) *verb* To say clearly, correctly, or in a given manner: *I'm afraid I* **pronounced** *your last name incorrectly.*

proud (proud) *adjective* Feeling pleased and satisfied over something owned, made, or done: *You should be* **proud** *of how well you can sing.*

Q

quiv•er (**kwĭv´** ər) *verb* To shake with a slight vibrating motion: *My voice may* **quiver** *if I get nervous.*

R

raise (rāz) *verb* To gather together; collect: *We're trying to* **raise** *money for a new animal shelter.*

rec•om•mend (rĕk´ ə **mĕnd´**) *verb* To advise: *My dentist* **recommended** *that I floss every day.*

re•mark (rĭ **märk´**) *verb* To say or write casually: *They* **remarked** *about the weather.*

re•search (rĭ **sûrch´**) *noun* Careful study of a subject or problem: *Medical* **research** *has saved many lives.*

rick•et•y (**rĭk´** ĭ tē) *adjective* Likely to fall apart or break: *Don't sit in that* **rickety** *old chair.*

risk•y (**rĭs´** kē) *adjective* Having a chance of danger: *It is* **risky** *to skateboard without a helmet.*

rude (ro͞od) *adjective* Not considerate of others; impolite: *It is* **rude** *to break into someone else's conversation.*

rug•ged (**rŭg´** ĭd) *adjective* Having a rough surface or jagged outline: *We flew over the* **rugged** *mountains.*

S

score (skôr) *verb* To gain a point or points in a game, contest, or test: *Did you really* **score** *ten points in the game?*

scowl (skoul) *verb* To wrinkle the forehead in anger: *Liam* **scowled** *when he saw that the ball park was closed.*

scrib•ble (**skrĭb´** əl) *noun* Careless writing or drawing: *Don't hand in homework that has sloppy* **scribbles** *on it.*

rugged

---

o͞o b**oo**t / ou **ou**t / ŭ c**u**t / û f**u**r / hw **wh**ich / th **th**in / *th* **th**is / zh vi**si**on / ə **a**go, sil**e**nt, penc**i**l, lem**o**n, circ**u**s

sep•ar•ate (sĕp´ ə rāt´) *verb* Divide into parts or sections: *We can* **separate** *these apples into four piles.*

ser•i•ous (sîr´ ē əs) *adjective* Not joking or fooling: *I'm* **serious** *when I tell you I want to be an astronaut.*

shift (shĭft) *noun* A period of working time: *Dad works the late* **shift** *at the hospital.*

sig•nal (sĭg´ nəl) *noun* A sign, gesture, or device that gives a command, a warning, or other information: *The traffic* **signal** *was not working properly.*

sketch (skĕch) *noun* A rough drawing or outline: *An artist might do many* **sketches** *before making a final drawing.*

slam (slăm) *verb* To strike with force; crash: *One of the cars* **slammed** *into the wall of the racetrack.*

slither (slĭth´ ûr) *verb* To move in a slippery way: *This gooey paste* **slithers** *through our fingers!*

snap (snăp) *verb* To bite, seize, or grasp with a snatching motion: *A wild animal may* **snap** *at you if you touch it.*

snuggle (snŭg´ gəl) *verb* To curl up closely, cuddle: *The mother cat* **snuggles** *with her kittens.*

soar (sôr) *verb* To rise or fly high in the air: *My kite* **soared** *into the sky when the wind picked up.*

spread (sprĕd) *verb* To open out wide or wider: *The children are* **spreading** *the blanket on the ground.*

squeak (skwēk) *noun* A short, high sound like that made by a mouse: *The door made a* **squeak** *when I closed it.*

stand (stănd) *noun* The place taken by a witness in court: *An expert witness was called to the* **stand** *during the trial.*

stands (stăndz) *noun* The bleachers at a playing field or stadium: *Wild cheers arose from fans in the playing field's* **stands**.

steep (stēp) *adjective* Rising or falling sharply: *We climbed a* **steep** *hill.*

stretch (strĕch) *verb* To extend: *After sitting for a long time, I get up and* **stretch** *my arms and legs.*

stroll (strōl) *verb* To walk in a slow, relaxed way: *I ran to school but* **strolled** *home.*

style (stīl) *noun* A way of dressing or acting: *Our teacher has a special* **style** *that makes learning fun.*

ă **r**at / ā **p**ay / â **c**are / ä **f**ather / ĕ **p**et / ē **b**e / ĭ **p**it / ī **p**ie / î **fi**erce / ŏ **p**ot / ō **g**o / ô **p**aw, **for** / oi **oil** / o͝o **b**ook

swoop (swo͞op) *verb* To drop suddenly, especially when flying: *The eagle* **swoops** *down to grab a fish from the lake.*

twitch (twĭch) *verb* To make a sudden, jumpy movement: *Have you ever seen a rabbit's nose* **twitch** *as it sniffs the air?*

T

tense (tĕns) *adjective* Anxious or nervous: *Taking a deep breath can help you relax when you're feeling* **tense.**

tex·ture (tĕks´ chər) *noun* The look or feel of a surface: *Both silk and velvet have soft, smooth* **textures.**

tide (tīd) *noun* The regular rising and falling of the surface level of the oceans, caused by the pull of the moon and the sun: *Each high* **tide** *carries new seashells to the shore.*

tool (to͞ol) *noun* A device, such as a hammer or an ax, that is specially made or shaped to help a person do work: *Dad's electric screwdriver is one of his favorite* **tools.**

trac·ing (trās´ ĭng) *adjective* Used to copy, or trace, lines: *Try using* **tracing** *paper to copy something exactly.*

tri·al (trī´ əl) *noun* The studying and deciding of a case in a court of law: *The judge called the* **trial** *to order.*

tug (tŭg) *verb* To pull at with force: *The gardener* **tugged** *at the roots of the dead shrub.*

V

va·cant (vā´ kənt) *adjective* Not occupied or rented: *The house was* **vacant** *for a year.*

W

wor·ried (wûr´ ēd) *adjective* Uneasy; anxious: *I am* **worried** *about my sick dog.*

tide

---

o͞o **boo**t / ou **ou**t / ŭ **cut** / û **fur** / hw **wh**ich / th **th**in / *th* **th**is / zh vi**s**ion / ə **a**go, sil**e**nt, penc**i**l, lem**o**n, circ**u**s

Acknowledgments

Main Literature Selections

Aero and Officer Mike: Police Partners by Joan Plummer Russell, photographs by Kris Turner Sinnenberg. (Caroline House, an imprint of Boyds Mills Press, Inc. 2001) Text © 2001 by Joan Plummer Russell. Photographs © 2001 by Kris Turner Sinnenberg. Reprinted by permission of Boyds Mills Press, Inc.

"A Bat Is Born" from *The Bat-Poet* by Randall Jarrell. Text copyright © 1964 by Randall Jarrell. Reprinted by permission of The Estate of Randall Jarrell.

"The Ball Game Is Over" from *Good Sports: Rhymes About Running, Jumping, Throwing, and More* by Jack Prelutsky and Chris Rasehka. Copyright © 2007 Jack Prelutsky. Reprinted by permission of Alfred A. Knopf, an imprint of Random House Children's Books, a division of Random House, Inc.

Excerpt from *Bat Loves the Night* by Nicola Davies, illustrated by Sarah Fox-Davies. Text copyright © 2001 by Nicola Davies. Illustrations copyright © 2001 by Sarah Fox-Davies. Reprinted by permission of Candlewick Press.

Destiny's Gift by Natasha Anastasia Tarpley, illustrated by Adjoa J. Burrowes. Text copyright © 2004 by Natasha Anastasia Tarpley. Illustrations copyright © 2004 by Adjoa J. Burrowes. Reprinted by permission of Lee & Low Books Inc., New York, NY 10016.

"The Extra-good Sunday" from *Ramona Quimby, Age 8* by Beverly Cleary. Copyright © 1981 by Beverly Cleary. All rights reserved. Reprinted by permission of HarperCollins Children's Books, a division of HarperCollins Publishers.

A Fine, Fine School by Sharon Creech, illustrated by Harry Bliss. Text copyright © 2001 by Sharon Creech. Illustrations copyright © 2001 by Harry Bliss. All rights reserved. Reprinted by permission of Johanna Cotler Books, an imprint of HarperCollins Publishers.

The Harvest Birds/Los pájaros del la cosecha by Blanca López de Mariscal. English translation copyright © 1995 by Children's Book Press. Reprinted by permission of Children's Book Press, San Francisco, CA, www.childrensbookpress.org

"Homer" from *A Pocketful of Poems* by Nikki Grimes. Copyright © 2001 by Nikki Grimes. Reprinted by permission of Houghton Mifflin Harcourt Publishing Company.

Kamishibai Man written and illustrated by Allen Say. Copyright © 2005 by Allen Say. All rights reserved. Reprinted by permission of Houghton Mifflin Harcourt Publishing Company.

Pop's Bridge by Eve Bunting, illustrated by C.F. Payne. Text copyright © 2006 by Eve Bunting. Illustrations copyright © 2006 by C. F. Payne. Reprinted by permission of Houghton Mifflin Harcourt Publishing Company.

Roberto Clemente, Pride of the Pittsburgh Pirates by Jonah Winter, illustrated by Raúl Colón. Text copyright © 2005 by Jonah Winter. Illustrations copyright © 2005 by Raúl Colón. Reprinted by permission of Atheneum Books for Young Readers, an imprint of Simon & Schuster Children's Publishing Division. All rights reserved.

Treasure by Uri Shulevitz. Copyright © 1978. Reprinted by permission of Farrar, Straus and Giroux.

al of Cardigan Jones written and illustrated by Egan. Copyright © 2004 by Tim Egan. All rights Reprinted by permission of Houghton Mifflin Publishing Company.

Tops and Bottoms by Janet Stevens. Copyright © 1995 by Janet Stevens. Reprinted by permission of Houghton Mifflin Harcourt Publishing Company.

What Do Illustrators Do? written and illustrated by Eileen Christelow. Text and illustrations copyright © 1999 by Eileen Christelow. All rights reserved. Reprinted by permission of Houghton Mifflin Harcourt Publishing Company.

Yonder Mountain: A Cherokee Legend as told by Robert H. Bushyhead, written by Kay Thorpe Bannon, illustrated by Kristina Rodanas. Copyright © 2002 by Kay Thorpe Bannon. Illustrations copyright © 2002 by Kristina Rodanas. All rights reserved. Reprinted by permission of Marshall Cavendish Corporation.

Young Thomas Edison written and illustrated by Michael Dooling. Copyright © 2005 by Michael Dooling. All rights reserved. Adapted by permission of Holiday House, New York.

Credits